Vivas as Critic

Vivas as Critic

Essays in Poetics and Criticism

edited by

Hugh Mercer Curtler

ॐ

The Whitston Publishing Company
Troy, New York
1982

ACKNOWLEDGEMENTS

I wish to thank the following publishers for permission to reprint copyrighted material:

1. *The Iowa Reviw* for "Reality In Literature."

2. Florida Atlantic University for "In The Presence of Art" published here as "Intercourse With Art."

3. The University of Tulsa Monograph Series for "Literary Criticism and Aesthetics" which first appeared in *The Philosopher-Critic* (ed.) R. Scholes.

4. Intercollegiate Studies Institute for "Dostoevsky, Philosopher or Novelist?"

5. Northwestern University Press for the appendix to *D. H. Lawrence: The Failure and Triumph of Art*, entitled "The Constituitive Symbol." (© 1960 Northwestern University Press, Evanston, Illinois.)

6. The University of Iowa for "Atrabilious Thoughts on a Theory of Tragedy" from *Papers In Dramatic Theory and Criticism* (ed.) David M. Knauf.

7. *The Sewanee Review* for "Mr. Leavis on D. H. Lawrence."

8. *The Southern Review* for "Dostoevsky: 'Poet' In Spite of Himself;" and "Tragedy and the Broader Consciousness."

Hugh Mercer Curtler

CONTENTS

INTRODUCTION

The purpose of the present collection of essays is to bring together in one volume some of the best of Eliseo Vivas' published work in Poetics and Criticism. This applies especially to the work he has done recently and the work that has not, for the most part, appeared in previous collections. Given that Vivas is a major American critic and that his last book of essays on this topic appeared in 1963, this collection seems especially timely.

In selecting the essays collected here, with Professor Vivas' help, I sought to accomplish a number of goals. First, I wanted to give the reader a sense of some of the important work Vivas has done in aesthetics—work that is available elsewhere. Second, I wanted to show how his theory of criticism rests comfortably on the foundation of his aesthetics and how they both inform his practical criticism. Finally, I wanted to bring together Vivas' essays on what he calls "unmitigated" tragedy, essays which, like his critical essays themselves, demonstrate the truth of Robert Heilman's comment that Vivas brings with him to criticism "an acute sense of text. . .and [its] implications." Indeed, in the end, it is Vivas' close reading of literature coupled with his concern for critical theory as a way of informing and directing criticism and thereby deepening our appreciation for literature that sets him apart from the majority of his fellows.

Some of the essays collected here have appeared in other collections of essays. Several were written early in Vivas' career. Together, however, they evidence the scope and quality of the man's thinking about literature and criticism in a way that none of his other books does—with the possible exception of *Creation and Discovery,* to which I would consider the present volume a companion piece. I hope that despite the repetition inevitable in a volume of this sort the reader will find a sense of coherence among these essays. Toward that end, I should like to explain the thread of thought I followed through Vivas' varied, compendious writings to put together these particular selections. In doing this, I shall also elaborate somewhat on certain salient points of Vivas' philosophy of art and thereby prepare the reader for the material that follows.

The initial part of this collection, entitled "Poetics," contains a variety of essays that deal with "poetry" and its place in culture. This has always been one of Vivas' favorite themes and his first essay "Poetry and Culture" lays the groundwork nicely for much of what follows. It appears here for the first time, in English, and includes a number of responses to criticisms that have been directed at Vivas' position over the years. Specifically, the essay shows us that Vivas sees poetry as one of man's four symbolic activities, propaedeutic to all other activities and differing from them in being primarily imaginative while the rest are primarily reflective. Vivas characterizes poetry as an "intransitive" mental activity to distinguish it from cognition, religion, and moral activity—all of which are "transitive." Vivas developed this neo-Kantian doctrine after following Earnst Cassirer part way to his own conclusions about man's symbolic activities and the constitutive nature of the human mind, the view that the human mind constitutes the world in the process of coming to know it.

Because mankind has art he can discover his world through the schemata he finds in the work of the poets. Without poetry, and art generally, we would presumably live in a world greatly diminished in its richness and texture. What this means is that art does not yield knowledge (in any straightforward sense of that term) but it makes knowledge possible as the *conditio sine qua non* of all reflective, discursive thinking. Of all Vivas' doctrines, this has caused his critics the greatest difficulties, so we might well sort out the elements of this basic point of view so there can be no further misunderstanding.

The aesthetic "mode" of human interaction with the world "out there" is active and imaginative: intransitive in the sense that in this mode, to the extent to which such is possible, one is in direct contact with the world in "rapt, intransitive attention."

Literature, or poetry as Vivas prefers to call it because it is *primarily* art, ought to be viewed intransitively. This is a normative claim and does not pretend to be a description of the way people in fact read literature. To the extent to which one properly regards the poem intransitively one is preoccupied with the work's "residential" aspect. Once the aesthetic moment passes (and it will, invariably, if it ever arises in the first place) we then consider the poem "non-residentially" as a source of reflection, or "food for thought." Thus, literature provides a deepening of our sensibilities and a new way of "knowing" *after* we read it as poetry and begin to consider it thoughtfully. These points are made carefully and at some length in the remainder of the essays in Part One and several of the essays in Part Two as well. As Vivas notes, one can read literature any way he or she chooses, but it is primarily a work of art and *should* be read as such to the extent to which this is possible, given the constraints imposed by circumstance. The primary role of criticism, then, is to lay bare the "meanings and values" that reside in the poem so the reader can return to it with deeper appreciation and sensitivity. The result will be a heightened *aesthetic* response, if the critic has done his job well.

Toward this end Vivas leads the way, as he has since 1938 when he wrote the widely anthologized essay on Theodore Dreiser. Following that essay he has written on a host of other poets whose work he approaches with a deep appreciation that one reader has aptly characterized as "piety."

Coupled with his work on literature "proper" Vivas has always exhibited a concern for tragic poetry and the vision of our world exhibited to us in what he calls "unmitigated" tragedy. When one reflects on the few great tragic poems that can be characterized as unmitigated tragedy, one finds revealed there a "flaw in being." The world exhibits genuine evil, an evil that cannot be explained away by any aprioristic moralizing about heroes and their "just desserts." We are as "flies to wanton boys" and despite the influence of the "gods, justicers above," all is not always for the best in the best of all possible worlds. The strain of cynicism that would lead Vivas to join Ivan Karamazov in "returning Him [his] ticket" characterizes much of Vivas' latest writing and colors his insistence upon the place of value in a world of fact, a world that exhibits genuine goodness alongside ineluctable evil. To this view we must turn in the end, since it is Vivas' "axiological realism," his view that value is real, that grounds his philosophy generally and his aesthetic in particular. And, with few exceptions, Vivas' critics have either chosen to ignore his realism or failed to understand what it entails.

This is not the place to discuss how Vivas' realism can be reconciled with his phenomenalism. I have done this elsewhere.* Suffice it to say that the matter for experience that one works with creatively is given, whether one is a poet or happens to see the world as the poet sees it on rare occasions. The knowing mind constitutes the world out of the raw stuff of experience that is very real in the full sense of that troublesome term— it is independent, obdurate, intransigent, and the rest. The result is a world-for-a-subject, an intersubjective world since all subjects constitute the world in similar ways. That is to say, the world is every bit as "real" as common sense dictates that it is. But it is impossible to speak about "the world" except insofar as it is a world-for-us, an object for a knowing subject. But as an object it is constituted by the mind of the subject who comes into contact with it actively and imaginatively, armed with the schemata provided by the poets and the categories necessary for human understanding. That is to say, even though common sense and the naive standpoint demand *that* there is a world "out there," it is impossible to speak *about* that world except insofar as it is a world *for* a subject constituted by the mind of that subject. Elements of this world have value and this value is discovered creatively by poets (and artists generally) who hand it over to us to be experienced imaginatively in such a way that the poet's way of seeing the world gradually becomes our way of seeing the world. The point has been made rather forcefully by Marcel Proust, who comments in *Remembrance of Things Past* that

> People of taste and refinement tell us nowadays that Renoir is one of the greatest painters of the last century. But in so saying they forget the element of Time, and it took a great deal of time, well into the present century, before Renoir was hailed as a great artist. To succeed thus in gaining recognition, the original painter,

---

*A Theory of Art, Literature and Value: The Philosophy of Eliseo Vivas (New York: Haven Publishing Corporation, 1981).

the original writer, proceeds along lines adopted by oculists. The course of treatment they give us by their painting or by their prose is not always agreeable to us. When it is at an end the operator says to us: 'Now look!' And, lo and behold, the world around us (which was not created once and for all, but is created afresh as often as an original artist is born) appears to us entirely different from the old world, but perfectly clear. Women pass in the street, different from what they used to be, because they are Renoirs, those Renoir types which we persistently refused to see as women. . . . Such is the new and perishable universe which has just been created. It will last until the next geological catastrophe is precipitated by a new painter or a writer of original talent.*

The poet therefore creates culture in giving us, not knowledge, but the possibility of knowledge. Ours is a world grasped symbolically that reveals itself as full of value alongside ineluctable evil. This is the world the poets reveal to us if we take them as seriously as Vivas has over the years.

Hugh Mercer Curtler
Marshall, Minnesota
July, 1980

---

*Volume I, p. 950.

PART ONE

Poetics

Poetry and Culture

1

It is desirable to begin by noting that in the following pages the term *poetry* will be used in its wides acceptation and the term *culture* in its anthropological sense.

On the theory that I have proposed there are four components of culture and a fundamental (or formal) fifth. I put them down graphically in their proper relationships:

The Cognitive	The Religious
The Aesthetic	The Moral
The Fundamental Symbolic Activity	

I shall not attempt to define these modes since I have discussed them elsewhere. But some observations about them are required. The first is that these modes are abstractions from human activity in culture. With the exception of the cognitive, when exercised at its highest level in the sciences and in mathematics, we never observe men acting in a pure way. While engaged in the higher cognitive activities the citizen, with his numerour interests, is crowded out and the knower takes over almost purely as knower. I say almost, because aesthetic considerations enter, as is known, in the formation of scientific and mathematical judgments. While engaged in the other three modes a person acts in a more or less mixed way, in which one of the modes predominates but the others enter. The moral man cannot be purely moral. Knowledge of the situation or problem that he must judge morally is required. This is also true of the religious man, whose response to God or the gods is, one can say perhaps always, compounded of aesthetic and moral elements no less than cognitive ones. A "pure" aesthetic experience is an indispensable abstraction without which the writer on aesthetics is apt to build on a linguistic quicksand. No one, not even

Euclid, has ever gazed on beauty bare. Beauty, or aesthetic adequacy, as we would prefer to say today, when actually encountered, is found freighted with non-aesthetic values.

Knowledge is made possible by an act of aesthesis. The mind that seeks knowledge must first apprehend the object to be known and identify it. This identification of the object in its context in time and space is not in itself an act of knowing but it is the fundamental condition of such an act. It is possible because we human beings possess the capacity to perceive the world by means of symbols. Note that the phrase, "to perceive the world by means of symbols" is pleonastic, for the act of perception is an act of symbolic awareness. Otherwise stated, the term *fundamental,* or *formal symbolic activity,* refers to man's capacity to employ symbols as distinct from signs in order to carry on the activities that constitute his life in culture. Because we can use symbols we are not only capable of identifying the world's contents and of acting more or less successfully as a result of these identifications—other animals do also or they perish—but we discover its order, we make a mental map of it, thus enabling us to alter it in response to wishes and dreams no less than needs, exploring it beyond our direct apprehension of it, extending it and intrapolating it in ways unverifiable by direct observation. This is what our symbolic capacity does for us: It releases us from immediate dependence on direct experience and memory, it liberates us from the world in which we move; but while liberating us it also imprisons us within itself, never permitting a break beyond it to the sources of the symbols. We live in a phenomenal world. In idealistic terms, the mind's symbolic power makes it constitutive of the world but not wholly so. Thus the symbolic activity turns us into metaphysical or para-physical animals, animals that live in a world that we take to be real and for all practical purposes is, but which is in part the construction of our symbols.

To a large extent, it seems, we have cornered the capacity for symbolic activity, probably as a result of our development of language and its derivatives—how far back, we do not know. But contemporary psychologists and students of animal behavior push the claim that other animals are also capable of symbolic activity. There is no need here to examine this claim. For my purposes what is important is to notice that symbols

are not only in fuction but in essence distinct from signs, although symbols may be demoted to act as mere signs. They
produce concepts, images, ideas. Note that the term *idea* is used
here as George Herbert Mead used it, to refer to more than the
psychic events that occur exclusively in the brain. An American's sub-vocal idea of a base-ball bat is more than the image of a
stick specially shaped. It is the psychic response of his whole
body, the whole of it, although part of that response may remain
permanently beyond identification by introspection. Symbols
produce meaning or, when combined properly, are meaningful.
Such proper combinations are language in the broadest sense of
this term. And it is language that is, properly speaking, thought.
But meaning involves more than the relationship of symbols to
that which they symbolize, since the capacity to notice the relationship of something standing for something else is not fur-
nished by the symbol but by the powers of the human mind.
Note also that if the term "idea" is used as broadly as I have
suggested it be, language must be allowed to include much more
than the sort of phenomena that linguists study.

2

Our awareness of the world in a more or less ordered way,
whether distinct or vague, is not only the first but the indispensable meaning of the term *the aesthetic act,* or response, or experience. Within this minimal sense important distinctions must
be made, for the act of aesthesis ranges widely from loose, superficial, unfocused awareness to attention that is narrowly intent
upon an object and that grasps that object successfully in its full
individual identity. The former kind of loose awareness is sufficient to enable us to move about the world, performing our
accustomed taks without disaster. I wait on the subway plat-
for, hear an oncoming train, glance at the head lights when it
approaches, and I know without close attention that this is not
my train. I did not make a mistake. For the most part this
kind of awareness that guides us habitually without error is of
this loose kind, it is unfocused, not at all intent upon the in-
dividuated and relatively unique objects among which we move.
The mind is functioning but it functions by means of stereo-
types, not fully grasping its objects because it is not necessary to

grasp them in their uniqueness to successfully accomplish what we are intent on doing. But consider a man hunting. He is tense. His whole mind, all his senses, are scanning ahead. He notices every motion in the bush ahead. Is that an animal, the animal I want, or the wind that made that noise? Before he brings his gun up silently he has fully realized it is a deer, the kind he is allowed to take.

We have here, then, in theory, two distinct kinds of acts. Since introspection is unreliable it may be difficult in fact to distinguish them clearly but for our convenience it is desirable to separate them verbally. Hereafter I shall call the loose, unfocused act *recognition,* and shall reserve the term *perception* for the focused act. But this is not to say that the act of recognition is inferior to the act of perception. Our capacity for recognition is indispensable because the best endowed person, the most energetic, cannot sustain, all day long, an attitude that is successfully perceptive. If I had to perceive in order to take my shower and shave, I would have little strength left to go down to breakfast. The act of recognition is shorter than that of perception; the latter demands from us energy we do not use normally in the act of recognition.

3

One more distinction is indispensable within the act of perception. In possibly the most common acts of perception context is more or less explicitly present in consciousness during the act. I may look intently at an object in order to see it as distinctly as I can, while comparing it in actuality or mentally with another object in order to establish its identity or the degree of difference between the two. Or I can refer the perceived object to a frame of theory within which I place it in order to find out what its relation is to the theory—whether it fits within it or not. But the perception of an object—as already suggested—can only be accomplished by means of a readily available fund of concepts, notions, ideas, definitions, categories and hypotheses to which I shall refer as *context.* No context, no satisfactorily observable object. The context making a given peception possible can never be brought forth to complete explicitness, since we cannot, either during the act of perception or later, dive down to the bottom of our unconscious in order to identify the factors involved in the constitutive act of minding. The whole body, with its past, is constitutive of perception; and while some of the components are available to awareness and thus open to criticisms, some, no doubt, are never fully available, although they influence more or less effectively the object discovered by attention.

While part of the context is separable from the perceived object in this kind of perception and while in theory all of it is if not separable at least distinguishable from it, there are acts of perception on which the context is altogether or almost altogether absent from our awareness while the act of perception is taking place. Furthermore there are acts of perception in which the mind is so intently focused on the perceived object that the perceiving self also disappears from consciousness and the object alone remains before the mind. The self cannot be excluded, of course; if I may be allowed the expression, while perception is taking place the mind is or we are minding, but there are occasions when we are not conscious of ourselves as minding.

A more extensive discussion of context is not necessary here, except to emphasize that the constitutive mind is the body minding. Because the constitutive mind is the body minding, I cannot separate one from the other. That there is mind—or more exactly minding—that is distinct from the body and some of its processes I am as certain as it is possible to be in such matters. The body carries on in the deepest, utterly dreamless sleep and the belief that the mind (or soul) is able to carry on without the body is grounded on the merest faith. But that I can tell with the confidence of a Cartesian what is the difference between body and mind—that, I am afraid, is more than I can do.

4

Within the type of response to, or experience of, an object in which the context does not appear in self-awareness there is need to make further distinctions. The first step is to recognize that there are varieties of response in the sense in which

Nietzsche recognized two types of response, although he coupled them with two kinds of objects, and more exactly in the sense that William James recognized varieties of religious experience. Since James' days many writers have offered us classifications of these varieties. In spite of the evidence critics make statements to the effect that "we" react to a poem or read a novel in a certain way, leaving out of account who the "we" stands for, totally ignoring those who do not read poetry as the writer reads it. The difficulty only begins at this point because it is not clear whether, because "we" read poetry in a certain way, this is the way in which poetry ought to be read in order to read it properly as poetry.

This is the reason we are led to ask which among the varieties examined by psychological aestheticians is the proper way to read a poem as poetry. It should be obvious that unless this question is answered rationally, reading, criticism, and the docent task founder because anything and everything can be assorted about a text alleged to be poetry but that may not be or may not be read as one.

Several accounts of the varieties of the aesthetic experience by psychological aestheticians are to be found in a book of readings that Murray Krieger and I edited.[1] Among these I find, for my purposes the most fruitful to be Vernon Lee, *Music and Its Lovers.*[2] After an exhaustive examination of numerous responses of music lovers Vernon Lee boiled them down to two types, which she called the hearer's and the listener's. Some people listened intently to the music, were annoyed by breaks in their attention to it, and reported that they were interested exclusively in what was present to them as they turned their mind to the music. Hearers accompanied their attention to the music with imagery that somehow the music aroused and which they enjoyed as much as the music, others told themselves stories while the music played and others valued their affective response above the music because it aroused them emotionally. It should be noted that my poor account of what is to be found in *Music and Its Lovers* altogether fails to do justice to the richness and complexity of Vernon Lee's investigation.

Vernon Lee could not choose between listeners and hearers. All she could do was to anlayze carefully the responses of her subjects and boil her analyses down to the two classes. Although a writer on aesthetics has no authority to legislate for music lovers, I could not rest content to leave the problem where she did, for her conclusion denied all rationality to criticism and the possibility of the docent process. It was necessary, I decided, to provide these activities with a rational foundation. A choice had to be made between hearers and listeners. It was reasonable to call the listener's the aesthetic experience rather than the hearer's, for there is a difference between the objective interest in the music and the subjective responses, uncontrolled or only tenuously controlled, by the music. The listener seeks to have the object that arouses his attention fully before his mind. The bearer, like a river running over a flattish plain, meanders every which way, only partially controlled by the music. He does not try to focus on the music, as the listener does. He is not aware of interruptions because his response is a disordered flow of loosely related interruptions.

This consideration suggested a definition I offered in 1937 to the effect that the aesthetic experience is an experience of rapt attention involving the intransitive apprehension of an object's immanent meanings in their full presentational immediacy. It is attention to an object, fully meaningful but immanently so. The meaning is not referential, it does not point away from or outside the object, it is contained by it. To the degree that the attention is rapt, the object is in full control of the response. The term *immanent meaning* I borrowed from an early paper of John Dewey. He did not use this term in *Art As Experience,* but the notion was central to his exposition of what I call the aesthetic trans-action between an object and a mind.

5

Perhaps the first comment to make about this definition of the aesthetic experience is that it is not a "what is" definition. It refers to an event that takes place when an object, almost any object, natural or artificial—a flower, a piece of driftwood, an apple by Cézanne, Webster's lyric, "Call on the robin red-breast and the wren. . ."—elicits the attention of a mind that responds to it in the way described above. There seems to be no end to the kind of objects and situations that elicit intransitive attention. Those objects that arouse strong emotions or impulses to act, physical repugnance, intense hatred, a heart-rending scene, or a scene that brings forth an uncontrollable erotic attitude—those objects are among the kinds of objects or situations that are likely to impede the aesthetic response. If we extend the meaning of the Greek term *obscene* beyond actions that the Greeks kept from presentation on the stage because they obstruct or impede the irenic mind's contemplation and lead beyond to associations or responses not under control of the initial stimulus, we can state in brief that anti-aesthetic objects are obscene objects. If we bear in mind how widely even members of coherent, well integrated cultures, differ among themselves, we will not be astonished by the large diversity of objects or situations that can bring forth intransitive attention.

Another important comment, one that has brought forth objections to the definition I am advancing, is that an act of rapt attention excludes emotion to the degree that the mind is exclusively focused on the object that arouses it. It does. The self disappears and with it introspective awareness that is an indispensable condition for the registration of emotion. But if I can use the old fashioned distinction between emotion and feeling that was current among nonbehavioristic psychologists when I was working on the subject, intensely rapt attention does not exclude feeling from flooding the object nor does it bring about introspection. Feeling floods the object under attention and gives it a luminous clarity that enhances the observer's interest in it. But note emphatically that it is not my intention to lay it down that emotion ought not to occur. What I am saying is that under certain conditions to which the definition points feeling accompanies the attending mind but emotion does not. If emotion does occur and its occurrence is valued, all the writer on aesthetics can do is to classify the person among the hearers.

The definition I have advanced has been criticized because the term *intransitive* has negative implications.[3] The term does have, but a look at what it points to reveals that it refers not only to what it excludes but also to what it includes, namely, the immanent meanings discovered by rapt attention on the object when it appears to the mind in its full presentational immediacy. Because the experience is a trans-action (a term I have used for decades, often spelling it as I have here in order to emphasize the two way action between object and mind) the aesthetic object does not exist either in itself or by itself. For this reason its apprehension is as positive an act as a person can engage in. The experience has indeed a negative aspect but the positive aspects are clearly central in my description of it. Of course the definition is selective as is the experience itself, or it would include anything and everything for anyone and everyone. As a definition, in theory, it excludes the other three basic components of culture. If the object is to function aesthetically, the intransitivity of the rapt attention will be dominant in the response, while the other components will function in a subdominant way. Notice that the aesthetic experience as defined may never have occurred outside a Platonic heaven. But what it points to is as positive an act as a person can engage in. So positive indeed as to be strenuous.

The definition and the theoretical constructs I have reared on it have been dismissed as arbitrary.[4] After the preceding discussion of the way I arrived at them it is not necessary to waste effort on so ill-informed a criticism. The person who made it did not take the trouble to read what I have written on the subject. Once we recognize varieties of response, the way is open to read a document classified as *poetry* in a number of ways—ways that are as numerous as the distinct interests of readers and their habits of reading. The critic who dismissed the definition I have offered as arbitrary does not advance one that is not arbitrary. But if we can read documents classified by librarians as *poetry* in an indefinite number of ways we need definitions of the aesthetic response and the aesthetic object in order to find our way in the labyrinthine chaos of documents that are alleged to be poetry and criticism of poetry but that are regarded as something else. Too many critics perform their tasks without the restraints of a definition. They travel lightly. This enables them to meander wherever their uncontrolled fancy takes them. They are sometimes "fun" to read, but they seldom throw adequate light on the documents they victimize.

It should be acknowledged that we seldom read the great classics of Western literature for purely aesthetic reasons. It should be further acknowledged that were we to attempt to read novels like *The Brothers Karamazov* and *Middlemarch* purely as art, we would not be likely to succeed. This holds for novels of authors who, like Henry James, made the effort, as we know from *Notebooks* and from his criticism, say, of *Middlemarch,* to create objects of art. So much for your definition, you say? Not at all, I reply, since the definition allows us to be clear about what we are doing when we read books like *The Brothers* and *Middlemarch.*

From the preceding discussion it should be obvious that strictly speaking poetry cannot be read as anything else than poetry. But it is often overlooked that to read non-poetic documents adequately it is desirable to read them first as far as we can as poetry, or to read them as scientists read their documents. Why? Because only when we thus read them can we be confident that we grasp them fully. Proof of this fact can be found by making a comparison of what critics have said about *The Brothers Karamazov.* I refer again to this novel because I am not altogether unacquainted with it. What critics find and what they fail to find in it, shows how they read. I shall not pursue the matter further, except to note that they tear it to pieces in order to prove their commitments to schemes of values that are not altogether congruous with what is to be found in *The Brothers,* including what Dostoevsky the citizen thought he put in it.

Is the view of the aesthetic experience here advanced a revamped version of the old theory of art for art's sake? It has in common with the old view the belief that poetry and art in general are to be cherished for their own sakes. But it differs from the older view in some important respects. First the old view—if we can overlook the variants of the old doctrine—was grounded on the hedonistic assumption, although not always ostensibly so, and it legislated against other uses of poetry. The view here advanced denies that pleasure is the goal of art as art, although it does not deny that it is a frequent concomitant of a successful aesthetic experience and that for some persons it is the sole goal. But then hedonists we'll always have with us. But the belief that pleasure is the goal of poetry *tout court* is obviously a misuse of language. It can hardly be said that the effect, during a successful immersion in a presentation of *King Lear* or a reading of it, is pleasure, although it would take a gifted introspectionist to characterize our complex response to it properly.

These moments of intransitive attention, how common are they? How long do they last? The evidence I offer that they occur frequently to those who know how to listen and to those who know how to see, as distinct from those who only hear or look, is indirect. Vernon Lee's hearers, as noted above, are not aware of interruptions and do not find them objectionable. But listeners, as compared with hearers, are a minority among "music lovers." The statement can be generalized for all the arts, I trust. As to the duration I can only guess; they tend, I believe, to be brief and intermittent. Those rare days in a reader's childhood when he was totally absorbed by an episode, when in the garden he leaned over an insect with untrained curiosity but totally absorbed by it, these moments still occur. But I tend to believe that they occur less and less frequently as the burden of our distractions—for from the standpoint of our capacity for losing ourselves in the objective world they are distractions—and the demands of grown-up living interfere with our capacity for self-less objectivity.

But observe that these two questions that I have just asked are questions of fact which do not jeopardize the validity of the definition I have offered. For while it has been drawn from empirical data, the definition is a logical instrument of discourse and analysis. Without it or without an altogether different substitute that accomplishes more adequately the goals that the definition seeks, it holds that it is impossible to get clearly what people who discuss art are talking about.

It is desirable, here, to bring out explicitly and emphatically the assumption that has guided my comments: I am theorizing. Over actuality a writer on aesthetics has no control. How men should read poetry in order to have intercourse with it as poetry is something about which a pedagogue may inform those who seek his advice. A writer on aesthetics is not a pedagogue—at least not in an obviously direct way. If I have written warmly about the feeling that pervades an act of intransitive attention I have written subjectively. The feeling that floods an act of intransitive attention is part of it and analysis, whether partial or impartial, has to take notice of it.

6

We have seen that an aesthetic trans-action consists of two terms, the object that elicits attention and the mind that responds intransitively to it. The artistic trans-action, on the other hand, consists of three terms, the third being the maker of the object. For this reason an adequate response to an object of art demands knowledge of the tradition that went into its making. But, of course, when fully assimilated, this knowledge does not function explicitly during the transaction between a mind and an object.

As regards the object of art the aesthetician has little to say and that little he can only state in the most general terms. The analysis of art objects is the province of critics and historians. All the aesthetician can point out is that the classical notion of variety in unity has generally been considered an essential feature of an object that can be grasped aesthetically. Whether this condition still holds is a question for critics to decide. The requirement of unity applies—or used to apply—with greatest adequacy to paintings that can be seen as wholes, to short stories, and to objects that can be perceived in their entirety. When applied to novels, as the reader of Henry James' criticism must know, the term *unity* must be modified, for the object is not grasped perceptually in an *Augenblick* but mentally or ideationally, as the object is reviewed by the mind and seen to hang together. Indeed no act of aesthetic perception takes place instantaneously. The aesthetic experience is an act of perception that requires time, even in the case of a miniature. It is an act of absorption in an object. Fully aware of the misunderstanding to which these remarks have led, I set them down, nevertheless, but with great diffidence, because as already noted, I am not writing about what people actually do who enter into commerce with what they call art but not always is, but about what some people do when, knowing what art is, they seek commerce with it and not with something else. In his famous essay, "Poetry for Poetry's Sake," A. C. Bradley wrote that poetry can be read poetically, clearly implying that it can be read in other ways. But Bradley was concerned with one problem, the relation of substance to form, which he rightfully held could not be perceived separately in the act of poetic reading. He paid no attention to the question how the reader of poetry as poetry had to read a poem in order to read it poetically. In this essay I am concerned, among other questions, with the question that was of no interest to Bradley.

For this reason it is necessary to call attention to a number of requirements that are needed to bring about the proper response to poetry when we seek to read it as poetry. Some of these requirements are so obvious that one hesitates to state them lest the reader be offended. But I have good reasons to believe that even the most obvious ones are often overlooked. No one is born with knowledge of how to listen or see or properly read for the sake of a full exploration of an object before him. It takes training to listen or see or read properly, as one who has taught others how to read or see can testify. As noted, it also takes energy and freedom from distracting pressures. I just mentioned that it takes knowledge of the tradition to which the object belongs. The aesthetic experience of which I am writing is not for the lazy, the ignorant, or the person preoccupied with distracting concerns. Neither is it for the person chiefly concerned with himself and with the external world only in so far as it has some relation to himself. Serious interest in art is not for narcissists.

I recently came across an instance of narcissism. A reviewer —his name does not matter and the distinguished medium in which he advocated his irresponsible reading is of no interest— writes that novels encourage a variety of counters—I am following the statement almost *au pied de la lettre.* Some of these counters, the writer continues, are located within the novel. Other counters we fill in ourselves, as it were, dictated by what we are given, always inclining to go too far, restrained by the sense of reasonable possibility elaborated in the formal constraints of the novel.

Notice, it is "we" who read this way, not "I," the writer of the piece. There could be no objection to the statement if it were intended as a confession of how the writer reads novels. Nor is he an uninhibited narcissist, since he recognizes the formal constraints of the novel. But he asserts his freedom to read as he likes, introducing "counters" not found in the novel. Our language gives us away. For the writer, novels contain "counters." One of my dictionaries defines the noun *counter,*

as "a piece as of metal or ivory used in reckoning and in games."
To use it, of course, it must be made previously to its usage,
and when used in reckoning or in games counters are, as often
as not, likely to have lost the face value engraved on them. We
then recognize them by size or shape or color, and use them in
reckoning or games without paying much attention to them
individually. One would like to know more than the writer tells
us about his counters. But we are told enough to suggest the belief that his reading is not fully controlled by the text, for some
of the counters he fills in himself. How far does he go? What
makes him stop his meandering and return to the text? Above
all, how does he know that what he fills in by himself is related
to the text and how does he know what relation it has to it?
Overlook the fact that into a serious novel a great amount of
effort and skill, knowledge and concern, for the whole and for
its components, has successfully gone into its production. Is it
not clear that a reader filling in counters by himself lacks respect
for the novel? Henry James' strenuous efforts—we have ample
evidence from his *Notebooks*—were wasted because his work is
allegedly full of counters and because it is read by readers who
supply their own counters, gathered from who-knows what
corner of their undisciplined minds. On this view a novel is an
elastic bag capable of expanding to contain an indefinite number
of counters supplied by the reader. Contrary to this view it must
be asserted that if the novel is worth reading it is because of what
it has to say to the reader, not the reader to it. Displaying no respect for the work of the poet, our narcissistic reader uses the
novel as a tool to bring out his uncontrolled associations.

7

As regards the maker, and suggested by the view that novels
contain counters, the first statement to offer is that to the extent
that the object is a work of art it is the product of a mind that is
creative, which is to say, a mind that does not bring to its task
ready-made counters. Hence the well-known fact that the object to be made does not yield to the conscious intention of the
maker and offers him an obdurate resistance which indicates that
it possesses a kind of autonomy that a serious maker is not easily
able to overcome. The clarification of the maker's original inten-

tion demands changes. Back of what the maker brings to his work is his talent and trained skills, back of these the whole content of his psyche, his moral character, his religious political and personal commitments. But these powers and factors are not altogether under the dominion of his conscious intention and of his plans as he had formulated them before he set out to make the object. They are more or less submissive to the emerging exigencies of the object. Between the maker and the emerging object there is tension, struggle. Vestiges of the tension can be discovered in the note books of makers. Perhaps in the case of Mozart there was no tension. Or so, I take it, the legend has it. He stands aside beyond the reach of the guesses that one dares make about the creative artist. But of the rest one can say without fear of exaggeration that to make is not merely to dominate but to yield.

In so far as this is the case the doctrine of expression, interpreted as Karl Popper does, in a simple way, is as utterly in error as Popper says it is. The artist expresses himself but what he expresses, the matter for his art, is not open to inspection by the maker or any one else after the transmutation has taken place. The maker expresses something over which he does not have completely self-conscious control. The Greek myth of inspiration—the possession of the maker's mind by a god or muse alien to him—comes closer to the truth about art than any other formula that one could put in its place.

At this juncture in the exposition it would be easy to slide into a swamp of obfuscation by appealing to explanations that are ultimately mystical. The maker is of course in control in a plain sense. No alien god or muse descends on him and takes over. But we can easily be misled by reference to the maker in the singular, as if he were a homogeneous psychic entity, all of one kind of soul-stuff. He is not. Because he is more creative within the range of his activity than most men, whose activities, such as they are, may show creativity in their own fields, the maker is, in respect to art, more or less split, and he may have— the great poets do indeed have—a deeeper psyche than non-creative men. While in one sense the whole man, then, contributes to the emerging object, the question whence the matter for the maker's art and his in-forming forms come seems to be anybody's guess. For all I know both matter and forms may

arise in part from the accumulated experience of remote ancestors lying in the maker's collective unconscious. I know the
Jungian hypothesis is abhorred by well brought up rationalists.
But how can we account for the genuinely creative contributions
of the maker? That they are genuinely creative I have no doubt.
But much less easily than to believe in Jung's notion I find it to
believe that the genuninely creative matter and forms are acquire-
ed by the maker after his birth. As Leibniz replied to Locke,
there is nothing in the mind that does not come from experience—except the mind itself.

But this is not a question that must be settled here. It is
enough to advert to it. What calls for attention here is the fact
that the object is not altogether submissive to the maker's self-
conscious wilfulness. From this fact a matter of the greatest
importance follows. To bring it forth it is necessary to draw a
distinction between *the poet* and *the citizen* in whose body the
poet dwells. The citizen may be present among the *dramatis
personae* of the poem, but to the extent that the poet is gifted
the citizen is not able to dictate what matter the poet in-forms.
This does not hold for artisans or mechanics who bring into the
making of their objects ready-made counters or blueprints. For
this reason it is a radical misreading of a poem to assume that we
can find in it a character who is a spokesman or mouthpiece of
the poet. Both terms are used by Isaiah Berlin in The Romanes
Lecture of 1970, "Parents and Children," on Turgenev. No
doubt Turgenev the citizen introduced a spokesman or mouthpiece into the stories he wrote. But a poet of Turgenev's talent
has no spokesman or mouthpiece in his stories other than the
whole poem—which sometimes says less but usually more than
the citizen wants to say through his spokesman or mouthpiece.

The belief that the writer is represented by a mouthpiece
or spokesman arises from the assumption that the citizen is in
control of the poet's work. He is not. It may also arise from the
unexamined assumption that the citizen is more fully the man
than the poet. My own conviction is that the poet comes closer
to being the full man than the citizen, for the latter lives on the
surface while the former has connections with depths the citizen
may not even suspect. We should go farther, for it is possible
that the use of the singular term *the poet* may not be accurate,
since the poet may be, indeed can sometimes be shown to be,

made up of several semi-autonomous personalities more or less in conflict among themselves.

8

Considered by themselves, none of the four basic components of culture requires extrinsic justification. Since each is a way of being human, to ask for a justification of any one of them is to call for justification of living itself, something that in ultimate terms is meaningless—unless posed as a theological demand. The need that leads some makers, critics, teachers of the humanities, and aestheticians to justify the artist's work by an appeal to other than the intrinsic value of art and the exercise of the creative power of the artist is a moral need.

Today art is justified in terms of the morality it fosters or threatens or the knowledge it yeilds. Social intransigence often demands that art serve political ends, but this is part of the moralistic demand. The moralist assumes the suzerainty of morality over the other three components of culture. But the election of morality as suzerain is an arbitrary choice if made by fiat. One person or group may decide that morality is primary—for himself or itself. But to decide it for others by ukase is an intolerable act of despotism. When one of the four components of culture takes over despotically the result is a deformed society. Two instances of such cultures come readily to mind: The Spanish world for several centuries after its great age and the world of the New England Puritans. I have pointed out elsewhere that the Cathars could not have built a civilization to rival the world in which they lived and repudiated. This holds also for a world—were it possible—built by a Herbert Marcuse. A good world is a world that seeks to approach Santayana's notion of the life of reason, in which all basic human needs find a more or less satisfactory means of fulfillment. An external proof of the fact that artistic activity is one of the basic components of culture is found in Franz Boas' *Primitive Art,* in which he points out that no group of human beings living socially neglect art.

On the other hand there can be no objection to the demand that artistic activity conform to a moral scheme—no objection, that is, so long as the demand is properly qualified, defined and advanced, not despotically but rationally, and so long as it is a demand that it conform to, but does not ask that it promote a moral scheme. In view of the ease with which moral despotism tends to take over, it is not superfluous to note that the demand that art conform to a moral scheme rationally involves allowance for the freedom of the individual members of the society. Members of despotic societies are bullied into accepting moral schemes that are alien to them. In our free world it is not possible to impose by force the scheme of any one person or group on others.

Before bringing this topic of the relation of poetry to morality to a close it is desirable to make two additional observations. The first is that the demand that poetry should have a compelling moral interest or it fails to contain seriousness and the profundity that, it has been claimed. T. S. Eliot associates with moral preoccupation—this demand, I say, is a hardy survival in reverse of the views of men—Timothy Dwight was one of them —who held that the language of Shakespeare was the language of vice and the theatre was the antechamber of the brothel. The view—and this is the second observation—stems from a faulty philosophical anthropology that fails to reckon with the basic components of culture.

9

Perhaps more widely accepted than the moralistic thesis today is the view that the function of poetry is to give us knowledge. One frequently runs into critics who write about the truth of art but who seldom warn the reader that the term *truth*, as they use it, does not mean the same as the truth of Euclid or Newton or a philosopher. Take this statement by a contemporary writer: "Autobiographies are very enjoyable to read so long as you realize that there is not a word of truth in them. Novels, on the other hand, are full of truth." Very clever, but there is not a word of truth in the witticism, since the word *truth* is being bandied about irresponsibly.

That poetry can yield knowledge cannot be denied. But

what kind of knowledge does it yield? The kind of knowledge poetry yields is seldom good, although it may often be the best that under the circumstances we can get. I remember reading a critic some time ago who asserted with admirable aplomb that Balzac gave us exact and comprehensive knowledge of his world. Since the writer was a literary critic and not a historian of nineteenth century France, I took the assertion to be irresponsible. What he probably meant was that Balzac gave him a feeling of exact and comprehensive knowledge of the Frenchman's world. But how true was that feeling our critic had no means of knowing.

Although poetry can and does give us knowledge, if of a kind its primary or residential function is not to give knowledge but to present an object, which is to say, to offer to awareness an object that can be perceived, enjoyed, and subsequently, if desired, inquired into. But to perceive a presentation and to derive knowledge from it are two different acts. The patois I am using here is technical and is employed for the sake of economy and precision. The poet selects from his experience as human being and by subjecting that which he selects to the creative process he transmutes it as he in-forms it into a poem. I use the term transmute in its alchemic sense, for the operation is the conversion of base metal, if not always into gold, always into a higher metal than the experiential ore from which it was transmuted. The transmutation produces an object that is radically different from the matter for poetry that the poet selected. Given a poem of quality and a reader who knows how to read, the poem becomes, more or les unwittingly, part of the categorial scheme by means of which the reader grasps his world. In its absence, in the absence of the arts in general, the world lacks the organization and the definition that it has when they function categorically. Thus it is false to assert that poetry as poetry gives us knowledge. What it does is to offer us the means to obtain knowledge. Whether he fully knew what he was saying or not, Oscar Wilde was right and Aristotle and his followers throughout centuries have been wrong. Nature imitates art.

10

As a conclusion it seems desirable to summarize the thesis presented in this paper. Poetry and the arts in general make an important contribution to our world by serving categorially to constitute it. From the world that is constituted to a large extent by poetry and the arts our knowledge starts. The world in which Galileo lived contained churches in which lamps swung. Galileo's observation of the swinging lamp was one of the steps— or so legend has it—in the development of classical mechanics. Galileo began from the common sense world familiar to him and his fellow citizens. They thought they had knowledge of their world, and they did have some or they would have been worse off than they were. But mixed with that knowledge was much falsehood, much nonsense, many myths and traditional notions that they took to be true but were not. It hardly needs to be pointed out that today physicists do not start, as Galileo did, from the world in which they live. They start from an accumulation of hypotheses that they correct and to which they add, that is quite far from the dramatic world in which men live and that we normally, and not altogether in error, take to be the real world. At the bottom this world and its social agencies is possible because we human beings are endowed with the fundamental symbolic capacity used to perform the element or formal act of aesthesis that is constitutive of the four basic omponents of culture.

NOTES

[1] *The Problems of Aesthetics. A Book of Readings.* Edited by Eliseo Vivas and Murray Krieger. New York, 1953, 296-304.

[2] Vernon Lee, *Music and Its Lovers. An Empirical Study of Emotional and Imaginative Responses to Music.* New York, 1933, 23-34.

[3] In *The Reader, The Text, The Poem. The Transactional Theory of The Literary Work,* Louise M. Rosenblatt. Carbondale and Edwardsville, 1978, p. 30.

[4] By Gerald Graff in "Reply to Some Commentaries," of his "The Politics of Anti-Realism," in *Salgamundi,* No. 42, Summer-Fall 1978, p. 104. In a sense, of course, all definitions are arbitrary although some of them are real; for they point to an area the definer has chosen to discuss and the choice is prompted by interests that can be called arbitrary. However, ignorant of what was behind the definition my critic could not had had anything but impatience with it.

The Constitutive Symbol

The term "constitutive symbol" has three distinguishable meanings: It may refer to the elementary means we use to grasp the world perceptually, the means which Kantian philosophers call categories, and which give the world the basic order it has for us. Or it may refer to the more or less sophisticated works of art we find in all cultures, however primitive these cultures may be. Or it may refer to components of works of art. It is this third sense of the term that centrally concerned me in the chapters on *The Rainbow* and *Women in Love,* because one of the reasons these two great novels have their high artistic value is that constitutive symbols are among their components. But we cannot discuss this third meaning of the term "constitutive symbol," without first discussing the other two.

In order to make clear what I mean by the term, I shall begin by quoting a statement made by Lawrence which I found in the useful volume edited by Mr. Beal. In an article entitled, "The Dragon of the Apocalypse," Lawrence says: "And gradually we realize that we are in a world of symbol as well as of allegory." A few lines later he continues:

> You can't give a great symbol a "meaning." Symbols are organic units of consciousness with a life of their own, and you can never explain them away, because their value is dynamic, emotional, belonging to the sense-consciousness of the body and the soul, and not simply mental. An allegorical image has *meaning*. Mr. Facing-both-ways has a meaning. But I defy you to lay your finger on the full meaning of Janus, who is a symbol.[1]

The hasty explanation Lawrence gives us of this pregnant distinction I would reject in some important respects. In the absence of a full explanation the distinction remains no more than a passing, although a brilliant, *aperçu.* But it is perhaps just as well, since his theoretical efforts, as I have already indicated and as he himself was aware, were more often than not of little value.

A reference to the constitutive symbol, no less suggestive and just as incomplete, is found in Mr. Leavis' study of Lawrence. He tells us that "significance in Lawrence's art is never a matter of a mere intended 'meaning' symbolized; it works from profounder levels and in more complex ways." A few pages further on, discussing Gudrun's wanton provocation of the highland cattle and the violent encounter between herself and Gerlad (in Chapter XIV of *Women in Love*), Mr. Leavis writes:

> To sum up the significance [of this incident] is another matter:
> the whole remarkable chapter is very complex, closely organized,
> and highly charged. It will be noticed that I have avoided the
> terms "symbol" and "symbolism" in this discussion: to suggest
> that the rabbit and the cattle "stand for" this and that would be to
> suggest much simpler ways of constructing and conveying signifi-
> cance. . .than we actually have.[2]

I subscribe to these statements with the following qualification: For the "never" in the first quotation I would substitute "not always," making it read: "significance in Lawrence is *not always* a matter of mere intended meaning symbolized." When significance is only a matter of meaning symbolized, I shall refer to the symbolic device as a "pseudo-symbol" or a "quasi-symbol," and I shall contrast it with those devices which I call "constitutive symbols," and which are considerably more than a matter of intended meaning symbolized. Observe, however, that scenes that are more than a matter of intended meaning symbolized or constitutive symbols, must perforce be very rare, even in writers of the highest genius. To produce in a long book a number of "highly charged" constitutive symbols, like those that called forth Mr. Leavis' pregnant statement, is to expect much more of a creative artist, however powerful his genius, then he can give us.

Because the word "symbol" does not have a univocal and recognized acceptation in the English language, there can be no harm in calling the device a "constitutive symbol," although we must recognize that Mr. Leavis' objection to the word is well-founded. Whatever terms we choose, the choice itself is arbitrary and the use of terms a question of stipulation. If what the terms are intended to mean in this essay is defined with a modicum of clarity, they will do as well as any we can invent or find in a dictionary. In order to lighten the presentation, when there is no risk of confusion it is best to speak of the device merely as "symbol." A symbol is to be contrasted with a quasi-symbol or a pseudo-symbol, in which something stands for something else that can be grasped independently of the sign vehicle. Another term for quasi-symbol is "sign" but I prefer the two terms I have adopted in order to distinguish this device from traffic signs, old-fashioned shop signs, and other non-verbal devices of this sort. Our problem, now, is clearly before us. We must try to obtain a working idea of the constitutive symbol in abstract terms and to answer some of the questions the notion raises.

Were a philosopher to ask me what I mean by the term, "constitutive symbol," I would answer that the constitutive symbol is a creative synthesis of empirical matter which manifests itself in dramatic and moral terms and which functions categorially. But I would emphasize the words "creative" and "synthesis." For the constitutive symbol is not arrived at by a mere reshuffling or rearranging of the matter of experience. It is *creative* and it is a *genuine synthesis.*[3]

This is true of the constitutive symbol in any of the three meanings that have been discriminated in the first paragraph of this appendix.

Let us turn to the first of these meanings. A more usual term for it is "category." We have learned from neo-Kantian philosophers, particularly from Cassirer, that the categories with which we grasp the world are not fixed, innate forms, as Kant took them to be, universally valid and susceptible of a neat arrangement in a table of four classes made up of three each. It is best, therefore, to call them "symbolic forms," as Cassirer called them. The world is grasped through, or by means of, symbolic forms.[4] Whether or not there is an a priori element in them, or whether some of them are a priori, is fortunately a question we need not answer. I would suggest that the answer to the question awaits a satisfactory resolution of the mind-body problem. The closer we come to interpreting mind in terms of body, the closer the relationships of perception to

apprehension and of experience to somatic grounds are speci-
fied by psychology, the more readily must we expect to find in
the physical structure shared by the human animal qua animal
innate forms that are universal although susceptible of variation
through the influence of cultural factors.

A constitutive symbol, in the first meaning, is a symbolic
form by means of which the world is apprehended. But in this
sense, the symbol is a basic and elementary form. By virtue of
its relations to other forms, the world is apprehended as orderly
—or, more exactly, as containing such order as the interrelationships among the forms used to apprehend it allow. The apprehension gives the world *meaning*. But the *meaning* that it gives
the world is not that which the scientific semiotician is interested
in. The semiotician uses the term "meaning" for a relationship
in which there are three terms: a sign, a thing that the sign
stands for, and the mind, for which the sign functions as sign.
But before a mind can make anything stand for something else,
both the sign and the thing signified must be grasped by the
mind for what they are, each must be given identity, each must
be discriminated from other things. I cannot say that a certain
kind of pole signifies a barber shop for Americans, unless I
recognize the pole and the barber shop as each being what it
is in itself and as distinct from one another and from much else.
A thing must mean itself before it can mean something else. I
have to be able to distinguish it, I have to be familiar with it,
before I can use it as sign. And if the scientific semiotician
should ask how a thing can mean itself, how meaning can be
immanent, can be reflexive and not referential, the answer is
that terms like "meaning" and "significance" are legitimately
used in two different senses at least, and no one can impose on
others his use as the only one that is permissible. One of these
senses of "meaning" is that of the scientific semiotician. But his
theory assumes that the thing signified by the sign and the sign
itself can be grasped directly, independently of any means whatever. And this is indeed the case as regards both sign and thing
signified in a realistic epistemology. But the writer holds that
both signs and referends must themselves be grasped by means
of symbolic forms before anything can be made to stand for
anything else. And here the epistemological realist and the
neo-Kantian disagree radically. For the latter, the process of
perception and apprehension is complex and involves a creative

synthesis within a universe of discourse which functions implicitly when that to which the mind turns is grasped as significant or meaningful.

We grasp a thing as significant in a variety of ways: by discriminating it from other things and learning to apprehend it clearly as the thing it is, by learning its use or how it is made, by discerning its position in a chain of familiar events. It may be at bottom a matter of familiarity—but a familiarity acquired through some kind of relation to the thing. However a thing becomes meaningful or significant to us, ordinary things and events attain significance apparently without much effort, and when they attain it we can use them and know their place in our world. This knowledge may be unclear and more a matter of handling the thing or performing the event than the kind of knowledge sought for by the philosopher or the scientist. But for the purposes of ordinary living it is sufficient. When an African native learns to drive an automobile, he has knowledge of the machine without the least knowledge of the physics that makes it possible. He may even acquire an elementary knowledge of the mechanics of internal combustion engines without anything but the most inadequate knowledge of the physical principles that control their operation. Familiarity makes a fork and a chair intelligible under ordinary circumstances. But change the light or setting and they may become puzzling. We refer a familiar object to a context and it is meaningful. For us that thing is a fork and that other is a pencil. The Australian aboriginal who has never seen a fork or used a pencil will be puzzled by them and will initially find them meaningless. An object that enters our purview is instantly categorized, although all too often unsatisfactorily. The Australian aboriginal, I imagine, is not altogether happy calling a fork and a pencil whiteman's thingumajigs, for so long as they remain thingumajigs and nothing else, they remain challenges to his curiosity and sources of irritation to his intelligence. They cease to be challenges and sources of irritation when they become more adequately categorized.

It is at this point that the activity of the poet, the maker of constitutive symbols in the second sense I have referred to, becomes of interest to us. The world in which we live does not consist merely of physical objects that must be discriminated from one another and identified verbally in order that we may live. Ours is a complex world of institutions, values, subtle human relationships, of which we must have knowledge or we run into trouble. To grasp our world in its full axiological density, to acquire a viable sense of our place in it, of the destiny it permits us to achieve, to grasp it as adequately as we grasp a chair or a fork, requires a process of categorization which is both dramatic and moral. We accomplish it, of course, with the same unconscious ease as we acquire the complex forms of our native language. But the actual ease with which we come by the world (and I do not mean, of course, to minimize the difficulties of growing up and of learning to adjust to our social environment and to our own inward demands) should not hide from us that before we can have a world out there, for us, we have to reduce it to order: we must learn what are the direction and force of its energies, what are the values and instrumentalities which are at our disposal, how much room we have and how we can move within it. And all this, let me reiterate, not merely at the physical level but at the level of human relations, which is to say at the moral level. These remarks apply to ourselves as much as they do to the external world, indeed even more so, since self-knowledge may be more painful. Should we fail, or rather, to the extent that we fail, to discover what are the energies and what are their direction and force, we are confronted with failure—a failure we may believe we escape, but the consequences of which are inexorable, since it makes itself felt in our lives not necessarily as punishment but as omission, by reducing our opportunities to develop into the fullness of our humanity as provided by our society. Success, or such success as we achieve in living—and I am not thinking of worldly success, of that which is approved by the world, although I do not underrate the value of this kind of success, I hope—depends, fundamentally, on our ability to make experience whole, to make the world and ourselves intelligible to ourselves and to some extent to make the world and ourselves amenable to control.

My claim is that the world in which we live is made whole when the poet, the maker, subjects its matter to a creative process.

The process of apprehension or the aesthetic process is prior to the artistic process and the latter presupposes the former. For that reason the constitutive symbol, in the second meaning of the term, functions categorially: *it is the means by which we grasp our world at the basic level of ordinary practical living.* When the constitutive symbol is achieved, there is an interinanimation between it and the thing or process it symbolizes, a kind of permeation so that for us the world is a world grasped not only *through* the symbol but *in* the symbol also. This is the truth which motivates the efforts sometimes made by critics (in my opinion, erroneously) to find a correlation between the sounds of a line of verse and the things said in it. In the sense of creating constitutive symbols, we are all poets—which is to say, *makers*—but those whom we call poets are more conscious and more skilled makers than the rest of us. And this is the poem's basic and indispensable function: it gives us the world. We read into the world the poem's order and intelligible action; and the nature of the actors and their destinies become the means by which we understand ourselves and our fellows. Note that the poem is a dramatic and a moral category or, more precisely, an organized complex of dramatic and moral categories. It is dramatic in the original sense of the term, since it refers to deeds or acts; and it is moral in the sense that the actions and the judgments of the actors are presented as instinct with values which have a bearing on our weal or woe.

A work of literary art taken as a whole, then, is a constitutive symbol. This is the reason I took pains to show that even an autobiographical novel like *Sons and Lovers,* which appears on the surface to be a faithful representation or imitation of actual events, is the product of a creative act in which not only the selection and organization of its component parts are products of creativity but the rendering of the parts themselves is the product of creativity. In the second sense of the term, any work of art as a whole, whether it contains constitutive symbols within itself as components or not, is itself a constitutive symbol, even though it may appear to be an imitation of reality.

This is more easily seen on a small scale, in short stories for instance, than on a large scale, in novels or dramas. "The Rocking Horse Winner" is a story that critics of Lawrence have tried to interpret in discursive terms. But the attempts, ingenious and even speciously convincing as they may be, in the end must fail. Lawrence wrote a number of short stories which, because he could not finish them, were failures. After carrying the story at a high level of creativity he could not keep up the effort and descended to a lower level, adding material that had not been transmuted thoroughly by the creative imagination. I am thinking of stories like "The Captain's Doll," in which, in order to wind up the story, Lawrence falls back on dreary autobiographical material totally unlike the substance of the firrst part of the story. This is also true of "The Fox." In this story he starts with an authentic and potent constitutive symbol and ends with the old song and dance about the need of the female to submit and be passive in the sexual act. But if we take the earlier part of this story we find that to assign an external meaning to the fox, and the relations of the girls to it, is to be satisfied with an interpretation of the story that is inadequate. The doll, the fox, the rocking horse are, in the last analysis, beyond elucidation by discursive language. They are constitutive symbols.

The nature of the constitutive symbol is easily grasped not only in powerful constructions like "The Rocking Horse Winner" and "The Woman Who Rode Away" (a story that does not suffer from the faults of "The Captain's Doll" or "The Fox," but which I do not admire because its substance, although wholly transmuted matter is, as I have already noted, wholly negative and masochistic), but in works of larger scale like Kafka's novels. A large number of the efforts to "interpret" *The Trial* or *The Castle* are wholly ridiculous. But even those that are not must in the end fail: if the critic is looking for an exact conceptual statement of their meaning, and one fully congruous with the novels themselves, he is bound to be disappointed. And the reason is that in these works Kafka is offering us a presentation. It is through them that we grasp reality and not the other way. We cannot grasp them through reality. I am overstating my case, for after all without some experience of life, art is meaningless. But there should be no serious harm in an exaggeration that brings to light the important function of art.

We next turn to the third meaning which, as I have already indicated, is the one which is of greatest interest to us in this study: This is the symbol that is a component of a work of art. What I have said about the second meaning of the term applies with very little alteration to the third. It is a complex situation or scene, such as those to which I have called attention in the text and on which I have tried to throw some light, which gathers the significance of events preceding it and illumines the scenes or situations that follow. The scene in which Gudrun slaps Gerald and that in which the rabbit officiates at their marriage in an obscene rite are nucleii that exhibit Gudrun's corruption and power as contrasted with Gerald's corruption and specious power. In the novel the corruption of the woman is not rooted in her lust for sexual excesses. Gudrun is corrupt because she sides with the German artist, who accepts industry. She is stronger because Gerald needs her while she can do without him. Gerald is corrupt because he worships the machine and fails to acknowledge the Eros of the sacred mysteries, as the organizing force which would have enabled him to give his life genuine meaning and character. The moon scene plays a similar role in respect to Birkin. As I tried to show, it reveals the radical predicament in which Birkin finds himself. It is true that Birkin's cogitations the day after the moon episode do not clarify a number of questions they suggest. But the constitutive symbol of the moon episode gives us a powerfully vivid image of the difficulties from which Birkin suffers.

But we do not come to a full understanding of the constitutive symbol until we contrast it with the pseudo-symbol or the quasi-symbol. The meaning of the mare episode can be adequately elucidated in discursive terms and it is, indeed, fully elucidated within the novel. The introduction of it gives the reader the full commitment of Gerald to the ethics of productivity and the concommitant need to achieve dominion over men, animals, and things which that ethic demands.[5]

2

A large number of important questions of diverse nature arise when we consider the constitutive symbol. Some of these refer to extremely technical epistemological problems—for instance the question as to the ground on which we know there is a reality that exists prior to, and independently of, the symbol. Since reality appears to us only by means of (through and in) symbols, what evidence do we have for the belief that there is something beyond them? I cannot consider this question here, since it has no proper place in an essay on literary criticism. It has been discussed by professional philosophers and those interested in it are referred to the literature on the subject.[4] However, it must be indicated with emphasis that this problem is a legitimate one, and a critic who accepts the concept of the constitutive symbol must either solve it satisfactorily or must know where to go for a solution of it. Otherwise his critical observations and judgments lack the theoretical basis that I would be the first to insist criticism must have. To be responsible, criticism must be based on an aesthetic which in turn must be based on a complete philosophy, including an epistemology. Criticism that cannot claim such a basis or that is grounded only a syncretistic hodgepodge of theories picked up *en passant* without regard to their fundamental coherence is not responsible.

Although I can, with good conscience, dismiss the epistemological problem that the notion of the constitutive symbol gives rise to, there are others that cannot be so dismissed and the elucidation of which will throw light on the nature and function of the symbol. (1) Is the constitutive symbol a formal or a substantive device? (2) Is there a relation between the constitutive symbol and the so-called heresy of paraphrase? (3) Does not the function that has been assigned to the sumbol overlook the fact that some non-literates have no poets? (4) What, if any, is the relationship between the constitutive symbol and Jung's archetypes?

1) In the organismic theory of art on which the contextualist bases his practical criticism, the answer to the first of these questions is that the symbol is both a formal and a substantive device and not exclusively either. For the organicist, the distinction between form and substance can be made only in mind—one cannot be actually separated from the other. Form cannot be formulated in the manner in which the rhyming scheme of a sonnet is formulated, by means of letters. We can direct attention now to form, now to substance. But the form we attend to is always substantial or substanced form and the substance is always informed substance. Unsubstanced or pure form is something that only the Platonic mystic, and he but rarely, can *aspire* to apprehend. This much at any rate I believe we can with confidence assert: common folk do not claim to have had such experiences. And of course matter utterly free from form is chaos and cannot be thought at all. The symbol is a *formal* device in

the sense that we can analyze several component symbols making up a poem and discover how they differ from one another in the roles they play and in the substances they inform. It is a *substantial* device in the sense that the poem or the symbols that may be among its components are constitutive, which is to say that they inform substance that, as Mr. Leavis says, is "highly charged"—with significance, as I imagine he means.

One qualification, however, is desirable. Because the constitutive symbol works from profounder levels and in more complex ways than the quasi-symbol, it is not appropriate to say of it that it is a way of "constructing" significance. Working below the level of consciousness, the constitutive symbol comes about, it grows; the verb "to construct" suggests a mechanical operation like bricklaying or carpentry. For a similar reason I have used the word "device," *malgré moi*. It is hardly the word to employ to refer to the product of that essential mystery which is the creative process. For what do we know about it? The observable steps that psychologists have sorted out, what do they tell us about the dark gestation, about the matter that goes into the formation of the organism that is the poem, about the manner in which the creative mind adds and takes away from the experience that it struggles to inform?

2) The relation between the work of art which is a constitutive symbol and the so-called heresy of paraphrase is easiest to elucidate if we recall that some works of literary art, some poems, do not contain as components constitutive symbols in the third sense to which I have referred. Devoid of constitutive symbols as components, they may be, nevertheless, great works of art. I am thinking, for instance, of the novels of Jane Austen. Her novels seem to give us a report of the actual world in which she lived, nothing ever happens in them that could not have happened to her or her friends. Her readers seem to be at home in the world of her novels. Allowing of course for obvious differences of time and customs, Emma and Mr. Woodhouse could be English relatives of neighbors of ours. This is true of all of her novels. The Bennets of Longbourn are, like the Woodhouses, people we might have met. Jane Austen's novels could be called "naturalistic" or "realistic," and the theory of imitation *seems* to apply to them so obviously that only academic pedantry would challenge its application to them. Stendhal's epigram,

"The novel is a mirror carried along the high road," seems to apply to all of them if we are allowed to qualify to the effect that the notion of Jane Austen carrying a mirror along a high-road is incongruous. "Three or four families in a country village" is what she turns her mirror to. But if we remember what I took pains to bring out in connection with *Sons and Lovers,* it will be granted that the notion that Jane Austen's novels are "reflections," or "imitations," of the world in which she lived is false. Her novels have the high quality they have because she was a *creative* artist and in so far as she was one, her work cannot be a copy or an imitation. It is truer to say that the world imitates the novels than to say the novels imitate the world. They are constitutive symbols—the means through which we organize our experience.

We are now ready to come to the point and explore the relation between the constitutive symbol and the "heresy of paraphrase." Since the literary work of art is a presentation and not an imitation, its meaning is immanent and not referential. It can be apprehended but it cannot be subjected to analysis by which we can distinguish tenor from vehicle and exhibit each separately from the other. This is, of course, as already noted, a matter of degree. For indications can be given as to how to grasp the poem, how to distinguish its form and how to apprehend its substance, although the form is substanced form and the substance is informed substance. But just as in the Leibnizian universe the principle of the identity of the indiscernibles holds throughout so in the organismic theory of art that has controlled the writing of this essay, the autonomy and contextual self-identity of a literary work of art must be asserted. For the individual work of art there can be no substitutes. There are, of course, similarities and classes, so that the historical taxonomy of art is not an arbitrary affair. But to the extent that a work of literary art is excellent, to that extent it is unique and no substitute can be found for it. This holds, of course, for all works of art in any medium whatever—although how it holds for music is a problem of such difficulty, that it is fortunate I do not have to discuss it here. If you take *Emma* to represent or imitate life, a discursive account of it can exhaust or come close to exhausting the novel, and a translation into another language is possible without loss. But according to such theory the creative element that *Emma* contains is implicitly denied or overlooked and it is the novel that is tested by the world that it imitates and not the world that is tested by the novel. Assert, however, in all seriousness, that the novel is a constitutive symbol, the product of genuine creativity, and what you say about the novel is in the last analysis something which is wholly inadequate to the novel. The novel is beyond satisfactory translation or the possibility of paraphrase. Let me repeat that all sorts of indications can be given the reader as to what he will find in the novel. But ultimately he has to go it alone and enter into the kind of transaction with it that is the aesthetic apprehension of the intransitive and the immanent grasp of its meanings.

A number of important qualifications, however, are called for. The first has already been noted: the question as to whether a poem can be translated or not, which I have treated as if it were a question of either/or, is always a question of more or less. The second qualification is that I do not mean that novels we may call "realistic" give us a world as real as ours or more real than works like *King Lear* or *The Trial*. While the world of a novel by Jane Austen is more like our world than the world of novel by Kafka, Jane Austen's novels are just as fictional as the novels of Kafka, although they possess a sense of actuality that we cannot attribute to the two great novels of Kafka. In this respect there is no difference between one work of art and another.

I would like to add a further qualification, namely that while I am using the term "the heresy of paraphrase," and on other occasions I have referred to "the intentional fallacy," I do so because the labels are in wide usage. But it goes against my grain to speak of "heresies" or "fallacies" in the realm of aesthetics and criticism. In such fields, in which there are as many self-appointed, authoritative revelations as there are writers, and in which councils of bishops cannot be called in order to read out of the church these individuals whose theories differ from ours, to claim for a theory the catholicity or orthodoxy that alone could give us the right to hurl our anathemas against those who disagree with us is to give an impression of egregious presumption. On the theory of imitation it is not heretical to paraphrase or translate a poem, and on a simple two-dimensional theory of mind such as pre-Freudians hold, it is not fallacious to consider the intention of the writer as adequately represented or embodied in what he says about his work.

3)   The question as to whether there are or are not poets in non-literate societies is one that will interest anthropologists as well as critics and aestheticians.   And it is one that I welcome because it will enable me to further clarify the notion of the symbol and what I take to be the function of poetry.

It is of course true that in non-literate societies there are no poets in the sense in which we find them in ours: there are no men or women who employ their full time and talent in the manner in which Shakespeare, Donne, Jane Austen, and D. H. Lawrence employed theirs. If by the term "poet" we mean the specialist or the professional, it is possible that there may be non-literate societies that lack poets and poetry. But there are no societies that lack the artist, and in making this statement I am backed by the authority of Boas and Robert Redfield. It is possible that in some of the societies that lack poetry—in the sense of linguistic objects—other arts take its place: the dance, elaborations of religious ceremonies—although it would be difficult to conceive of the latter activity carried on without the aid of language.   Again, it is also possible that in small, non-literate societies that do not have specialists their absence is made up for by the fact that everybody or nearly everybody in the society is a kind of poet, carrying and passing on the myths in which the vision of life of that society is embodied. This is a question of fact and not to be answered a prioristically. But I find it difficult to believe that there are societies that altogether lack some sort of rudimentary vision of life expressed in myth. Boas some time ago pointed out in his book on primitive art that all peoples have artists, no matter how hard a struggle they have to keep alive. Energy they can ill afford is routed from the job of survival and put into the creation of works of art, which from the standpoint of survival may seem useless. And Redfield shortly before his untimely end wrote the following:

> The peoples studied by anthropologists, taken as whole groups acting and thinking over long periods of time, show a creativeness beyond the demands of subsistence and mere survival. In such a group, however meager its resources and however hardpressed it is to survive, we see some production, an accumulation of generations, in which are expressed imagination, a sense of coherence, a progressive building of some "work of the mind."[6]

Since Redfield had stated earlier in the essay from which I have quoted that man individually and as a group grasps the world as intelligible, I can drop the discussion at this point, for what I am concerned to assert is that it is the poet or the proto-poet, or that faculty in men that constitutes their poetic talent, that is essential for the creation of a world view.

I have been speaking, then, of the poet in two senses: the self-conscious writer of novels or verse or plays, on the one hand, and the myth maker on the other. The former is possible only in certain societies. The latter is to be found in all.

4) The question of the relation between the constitutive symbol and Jung's archetype could, if pressed, lead to perplexing problems of an exasperatingly controversial nature. For this reason I would like to make clear that in the present context I am not interested in the question of whether Jung's genetic interpretation of the archetype and of the manner in which it functions in the process of individuation is valid or not. As is known, Jung traces the symbolic archetype to the primordial experience of the human race and further back to undifferentiated cosmic sources of energy, which he boldly claims the archetype expresses. To the majority of our contemporaries, for reasons we need not go into here, these speculations of Jung are disturbing and even repugnant, although there is nothing in the naturalism that is the reigning philosophical temper of our age that renders these speculations inadmissible—except perhaps that they are speculations as to origins. Fortunately we can avoid these controversial issues, and turn to the similarities and differences between the archetype and the constitutive symbol.

For Jung's definition of symbol we must turn to Chapter XI, entitled "Definitions," in *Psychological Types or The Psychology of Individuation.*[7] Here we find a full discussion of the distinction between what Jung calls a "sign" and a "symbol." The discussion shows that Jung's distinction is, in some important respects, very similar if not identical to that which I have tried to make. The object to which the sign refers is independent of the sign and can be presented or exhibited with full adequacy either by another sign or by direct presentation, whereas that which the symbol conveys or expresses cannot be conveyed in any other manner than by the symbol—or, more precisley, *in* the symbol. Jung also holds that that which the symbol conveys cannot be exhausted by explication, because it is relatively unknown. The symbol, so to speak, is bottomless. The word "tree" refers to a certain thing to which I can point with my finger by taking you to the window and saying, "That, there, is a tree." In Spanish a tree is *un arbol,* and in using the Spanish rather than the English nothing is gained or lost in discursive communication about the thing that both words designate.

But while the sign points to the known or the knowable, and is not incarnate with that to which it points, so to speak, this is not the case with the symbol, which according to Jung expresses or embodies something relatively unknown, something the mind does not fully grasp, having depths that no sounding will ascertain satisfactorily. The symbol, for this reason, is pregnant with meaning—but not the meaning of the sign. The word "meaning" has changed its meaning. The meaning of the symbol is for Jung ultimately a pre-individual, collective experience and finally cosmic energy which it channels into expression. Because they express pre-individual, collective experience, the symbols or archetypes, are fully "charged"—to fall back again on Mr. Leavis' useful term. But charged with what? With the pristine reactions of early man and his animal forebears which the symbol expresses for them and still expresses for us? To understand the charge of the constitutive symbol we either have to accept Jung's genetic speculations or substitute our own for his, for the charge must be explained, and it would appear that it has something to do with the depths of the personality, those dark bottoms beyond accessible reach by direct conscious inspection. The fact of the charge, however, and its nature, cannot be put in question, even though we may be at a loss for an adequate explanation of the source of the charge. The charge consists in the power to arouse deep, perhaps totally formless emotion, or if the symbol does not arouse it, to express it objectively, so that we cannot mistake it. And the nature of the charge must be defined, in part at least, by the fascination in exercises, both of fear and attraction, by the sense it carries with it, the ambivalence and the confusion it brings to the surface.

There is an important difference, however, between the constitutive symbol and the archetypal symbol, and this difference is so clearly and precisely stated by Ira Pragoff that all I need do is quote his words:

> Cassirer proceeds with the idea that man is essentially a symbol-making creature. It would be correct to say that Jung holds the same belief. The difference, however, is that Cassirer understands symbols as instruments which arise out of man's experience in his efforts to further his purposes in communicating with other men and in thinking more efficiently. The question of symbols has, essentially, an epistemological meaning to him. Jung, on the other hand, interprets symbols in terms of the inner functioning of the psyche. Symbols do not arise out of experience as a means of communication in society, but symbols arise out of the spontaneous creativity within the psyche. There is thus a basic difference in the conception of the ways in which symbols function. To Cassirer they are effective as means of knowledge in relation to outer experience; to Jung they are effective in the depths of personality as autonomous channelizers of psychic energy. Symbols operate on a more fundamental level for Jung. When they are understood only as means of communication, they are on the level of consciousness, which is the surface of the psyche; but as autonomous and spontaneous creations carrying large sums of energy, they operate in the unconscious and express basic psychic processes. They are thus much more dynamic factors than mere means of knowledge, and this difference has far-reaching consequences in the two approaches to man.[8]

The difference can be put in a single sentence: Jung is a psychologist and Cassirer is a philosopher whose central concern is epistemology. But the two interests, those of the psychologist and those of the epistemologist, are not necessarily incompatible with one another. In fact, the symbolic archetype, whatever its source, functions in literature and in religion as a kind of means of communication, and this is the reason that so many critics have been so powerfully attracted to Jungian psychology and that Miss Bodkin has written a whole book on the subject of. . . to which so much space was given in an earlier chapter.

NOTES

[1] *D. H. Lawrence. . .Criticism,* ed., Beal, p. 157.

[2] Leavis, *op. cit.,* p. 220 and p. 230.

[3] Since I am speaking to a philosopher, the terms must be taken in their technical acceptation.

[4] *The Philosophy of Ernst Cassirer,* ed., Paul A. Schillpp (Evanston, 1949).

[5] The contemporary, sophisticated, Anglo-American mind is so deeply instinct with the scientistic spirit that it finds repugnant as well as inadmissible the notion of symbol here advanced. But the need for such a notion has long been felt by many students working in many fields. However incomplete or even defective any formulation of the notion may be—and I concede in advance that the one here proposed is likely to have more than its share of error and lack of clarity—the various formulations of the phenomenon which students are trying to elucidate, each from his own standpoint, cannot be a projection of an idiosyncratic, merely obscurantist mind. In his argument against Bultman's effort to demythologize the Christian religion, Jaspers asserts that myth is not a "cloak" or "disguise" that we put on general ideas, "which can be better or more directly grasped intellectually." (I myself would not use the phrase "grasped intellectually," because myth is as much a product of the intellect as theoretical physics or Mozart's music; it is one of the modes in which the intellect functions.) Jaspers goes on to point out that myths are the carriers of meanings that can be expressed only in their language. "Mythical figures are symbols which, by their very nature, are untranslatable into another language." Karl Jaspers and Rudolph Bultman, *Myth and Christianity. An Inquiry Into the Possibility of Religion Without Myth* (New York, 1958), pp. 15-16.

[6] Robert Redfield, "Anthropologicl Understanding of Man," *Anthropological Quarterly,* Vol. 32, No. 1, January 1959, p. 18.

[7]C. G. Jung, *Psychological Types or The Psychology of Individuation* (London, 1923), pp. 600-610.

Reality In Literature

1

In this paper I am asking whether, and in what sense, we can speak of the reality of works of literature—works to which I shall refer hereafter by the generic term of "poetry." We have before us two problems, both of which need to be treated with circumspection. Therefore, I must treat them in an abstract, purely theoretical way. The problems are of two quite different kinds: one is psychological, and the other ontological. But although distinct, they are, nevertheless, intimately related, as I hope to show towards the end of the paper.

In representative art the psychological problem does not seem to present extraordinary difficulties. In poetry, representative painting and sculpture, the object of the work—what the work is about—bears some sort of resemblance to the furniture of the daily world: to men and their actions, to the things they use, and to the ambient medium, artificial and natural, in which they live. For this reason we have to say in the case of poetry and of representative art, that their objects symbolize the same kind of reality as that actually possessed by mental objects. Insofar as this is true, we have no unique problem. A problem arises when the claim to perception is seriously entered. Sometimes our transactions with poetry convey a heightened feeling of reality, a feeling that the ordinary world does not usually convey. It is an experience difficult to give an account of. It may be a close relative to the mystical experience—I do not know. At its peak, the reader disappears, and all there is, is the "thereness" of the object of the poem. I call the event a revelation, in the etymological meaning of the term: a tearing of the veil, a presentation of intense vividness of what the poem is about. The work before us stands out radiantly, with an effulgence that claims that we have taken a step upwards, into a reality that is usually hidden from us in our daily world. The semitransparent film that stands between us and the furniture of the world in which we live daily has dissolved. We move up, to yield with anticipation to the increasing radiance that shows itself to us. The claim that the revealed object makes—and I am using my words with some care—cannot be disregarded, however we choose to interpret it. Let me press into use for our purposes a vivid phrase that William James used in his discussion of the sense of reality in a slightly different context: "a man's soul will sweat with conviction" when "his entire faculty of attention is absorbed" by a poem. Its object seems, as he puts it, more "utterly utter" what it is, than at other times. Thus James is one of our witnesses for the fact that poetry can convey on the occasion of total absorption in it a sense of superior reality. And kindly note that while I have modified slightly some—not all—of James's words, I claim to be swimming, so to speak, in the mainstream of his thought on this matter.

The actuality of this sort of experience has been denied by some writers and ridiculed crudely by others. But in addition to the testimony of William James that of many other writers could be added: That of Vernon Lee for instance, and of Henri Delacroix. Indeed, except for some critics, whose exclusive interest in poetry seems to be to make it raw material for their professional activity, the experience is not totally uncommon, although rare, to readers of poetry and people interested in the other arts.

In view of the evidence, then, the question does not seem to me to be about the actuality of the heightened sense of reality. Are we faced, let us ask, with a claim somewhat similar to that made by Plato in *The Symposium* and in *The Seventh Epistle*? Or with that made by Rudolph Otto when he writes about the experience of the numinous? In still different terms, is the claim that in rare aesthetic transactions poems disclose to us ontologically different kinds of reality than that possessed by the stones that the cultivated philistine kicks? Or can the experience be explained psychologically? My answer is that while much of the "utterly utter" sense of reality of the object of the poem can be explained successfully by the same means used by James to explain the results of intoxication with nitrous oxide, the claim cannot be exhaustively explained, in the case of poetry, by this means. Otherwise stated, I am going to show that the ontological problem cannot be altogether dismissed, however far psychology can go towards an explanation of the sense of reality given us by the poem. If we pursue the problem of the informed substance of poetry far enough, without regard to regnant philosophical orthodoxies, and come at the problem from a different standpoint, we shall run into complications that call for a metaphysic or ontology that is forced to posit at least one realm besides that of existence or the spaciotemporal realm—the only realm allowed us today by the dominant climate of philosophical opinion.

2

I wish I had not found it necessary in the past to reiterate what I am going to say again. The iteration cannot be avoided, since it is at the heart of my doctrine. When a poem functions as poetry, it functions as a presentation, which is to say that it does not refer explicitly beyond itself. It is autonomous because the privileges that govern it—or if you prefer, the loose conventions that guide its making—are not imposed by external authority but are the result of intrinsic exigencies acknowledged by the maker and his readers. Besides being autonomous, the poem is also self-sufficient, but in a qualified sense. The qualification may appear to be a silly tautology. But the failure to consider it leads to the misinterpretation of the nature of poetry. To read a poem with full enjoyment calls for an arduous preparation. This should go without saying it. One needs to know first the language of the poem. But his demand is not one that is easily met. Consider that most of you have taken a lifetime to learn the language, and those who have not learnt it at their mothers' knees can never compete in some important respects with those who did. Learning the language of a poem will often include learning special languages—that of Shakespeare, for instance. It includes a full, concrete, detailed knowledge of whatever is to be found on a page. Indeed, adequate knowledge of a language can hardly be distinguished from knowledge of the culture for which the language is a medium of apprehension, communication, and communion. Given knowledge of the language, a poem can be there, for the reader, to enter into a poetic transaction with it, that may lead to the poem's taking full possession of him. His grasping it thus needs lead to no other act than that of his dwelling on it, as we may dwell on a bouquet of flowers or a stalking cat. Stendhal left us a phrase that, however interpreted, is false: "Beauty is a promise of happiness." But beauty is not a promise, but a bestowal, not to be enjoyed elsewhere, later, but here, now. This holds for the poem when read as poetry.

This is to say that a poem is a complicated tissue of meanings and values expressed in and through the language by means of straight denotation, psychological connotation, imagery, allusions, and the large number of devices critics have studied, not the least important of which are the theme's organization and the aural quality of its language. To say "expressed in and through" is to utter a pleonasm for, at least in my *papiamento*, the word "expression" refers to the use of language not merely to point to things external and independent of the language, but to present things that are dependent on the language.

That the meanings and values expressed by the poem do not make external references seems to be an offensive notion to some critics. Years ago a very logical logician objected to Mrs. Langer's notion of a presentational symbol because it was a contradiction in terms. Of course it was, and so was Kant's disinterested interest. C. W. Morris borrowed the term "icon" to convey the same notion, but failed to do what he set out to do. Linguistically odd also is Dewey's notion of immanent meanings. These are all efforts—call them desperate if you will—to draw attention to the essential peculiarity of poetry, its capacity for possessing exclusively internal reference. Read as poetry it is intrinsically meaningful, but denotation external to the poem is not encountered in it. This is not peculiar to poetry. We frequently look for the sake of seeing, as when we fix our attention on the stalking cat just mentioned. And pure mathematics is a body of knowledge, the noblest of them all, some think, that does not refer to a world outside itself.

3

Although what I have just sketched is a repetition, as I said, of doctrine that is to be found in print, I had to review it here, in order to ground the statement that the self-sufficiency of poetry accounts in part for the sense of reality it conveys to the captive reader. His captivity is made possible by a number of factors analyzed by critics when they focus on the poem's unity. But also, and most importantly, by the nature of symbolic language. In the chapter from which I quoted James's vivid phrase, Chapter XXI, Vol. II, of *The Principles of Psychology,* he points out that we live in several worlds. James described seven of them, but pointed out that the number is of no importance, nor does he expect us to agree with his list. What is of importance for us is his comment. He wrote: "Every object we think of, gets at last referred to one world or another of this or some similar list" (II, 293). In the list, under No. 5, he places the worlds of poetry. Compressing the account, No. 5 reads as follows:

> (5) The various supernatural worlds. . . . Each of these is a consistent system of definite relations among its own parts. . . . The various worlds of deliberate fable may be ranked with those worlds of faith—the world of the *Illiad,* that of *King Lear,* of the *Pickwick Papers,* etc. (292)

At this point he attaches a footnote that is, for our purposes at least as important as the text. He writes:

> Whilst absorbed in the novel [Ivanhoe] we turn our backs on all other worlds, and for the time the Ivanhoe-world remains our absolute reality.

4

Note that it is James who writes "absolute reality." The statement needs qualification. The Ivanhoe-world is our absolute reality if we are absolutely absorbed by it. But while absolute absorption is common, I suspect, with children of bright minds, in adults it occurs along lines of specialized training, and our capacity for it diminishes with age. We have ample evidence that the feat of absolute absorption in art or an absorption close to it, is apparently one that the majority of people are incapable of. Even for those who can perform it, the realization of it depends on many external factors that I cannot pause to enumerate here. In the same footnote to which I have just referred,

James goes on to say that

> When we wake from the spell. . .we find a still more real world, which reduces Ivanhoe and all things connected with him to fictive status, and relegates them to one of the subuniverses grouped under No. 5.

So far as his explanation goes, James is right when he implies that the sense of reality conveyed by the absorption in a poem does not give the poem an ontological status identical with the status possessed by the ordinary world. But while, for his purposes, this is all that James needs to say about the worlds of poetry, as contrasted with the world that for James and for the great majority of mankind is "a more real world," if we label the worlds of poetry "fictive," we shut the gate on the inquiry, precluding much needed enlightenment.

For us, the problem does not arise from the fact that absorption in the poem yields a sense of superior reality. My acknowledgment, a moment ago, that there are those who sweat with conviction, does not give me the right to say that the poem, or something in it, has or does not have a status in being, similar or different from that which the objects of language have. Again, for James's purposes, all he needed to do was to distinguish the conviction with which the poem makes us sweat from the greater reality of the world when the sweat ends. Our purposes, however, demand of us that we indicate that we are faced with two different senses of reality. The conviction of reality with which we sweated a few moments ago, is to a large extent accounted for by our total or close-to-total absorption in the poem. The senses of all other realities have been effectively excluded while we were sweating in the captivity of the poem. The only world there was, then, for us, was that of the poem. But how can we sweat with the conviction of the reality of the object of the poem one moment and immediately upon escaping from its captivity, dismiss that reality cavalierly by calling it a "fictive" world? The world of the poem made us sweat. Dripping with sweat, we step out of it without trouble and enter the ordinary world, which James calls "the more real" world. But although more real, it does not put us to any strain whatever; in it we are as cool as if we were in an over-refrigerated room. Note, however, that the psychologist's hand has been quicker than our eye, for James switched from the puddle of conviction created by our sweating—a conviction that may or may not be correlated to knowledge—to a more real world, but one that in spite of its greater reality does not even cause our collars to wilt.

Put in different terms, the word "fictive" is not self-explanatory. And this is one of the reasons we have a problem. We want to know what it is that makes the worlds of poetry "fictive." But there are some kinds of answers that I, at least, have rejected after analysis. I do not want to be told that fictions are the work of the imagination. This old gimmick of inventing faculties to explain phenomena—the dormitive virtue of Montpelier, the explanation of the obscure by the more obscure —leads to interesting verbal disputes that graduate students must be acquainted with, but that throw no light on the problems by which we are puzzled. Another answer I cannot accept is one in the other direction, given us by The Philosopher, when he tells us that poetry is more true than history because the former is about universals. This statement is inadmissible for a number of reasons. I'll mention one: It can only be advanced by a man who believes that all of us think abstractly and that what a poet does is to dramatize, put concrete dramatic flesh on the conceptual abstractions that he originally thought of.

Poetry has also been said to be appearance and illusion. But neither of these characterizations advances our quest, since for a phenomenon to be an appearance there must be a reality of which it is the appearance, and the same holds for illusion. It is fairly obvious that what these theories assert is what is more clearly asserted by the theory of imitation. Not that I do not know that there are a number of interpretations of the view expounded by The Philosopher in the *Poetics*. But I believe we can finally reduce these to two. The sophisticated view of imitation includes creativity as one of the powers of the maker and, hence, novelty in the thing made. I fail to see anything in the pages of The Philosopher that warrants such *ad hoc* patching. In any case it turns the theory into an attenuated form of the expression theory. The other version is true imitation, copying. This is the meaning that The Philosopher had in mind. A contemporary Aristotelian has stated it as follows:

The artist separates some form from the matter with which it is

joined in nature—not, however, the 'substantial' form, but some
form perceptive by sensation—and joins it anew to the matter of
art, the medium he uses.

All that needs to be said about this account of the making
of a poem is that its crudity is incredible: all the more incredible, when we remember that it was proposed by one of the three
or four greatest philosophers that our civilization has produced,
and has been transmitted to us in the above words, at this date,
without a warning about its crudity, by a man with a scholarly
reputation. This account, I would suggest, applies to what I
imagine is the making of a death mask: it also applies to the
work of Rosa Bonheur and, specially, to the work of Nazi and
Socialist realists. It also applies to the type of reportage that the
demiliterates of our society take to be genuine novels. I argued
some time ago that when it is said to apply to music, all it does
is expose the fatuity of one who believes that the pattern of our
great compositions is like the pattern of human emotions prior
to their information by the musical composition. Nor does any
interpretation of imitation that I have ever come across apply to
architecture. But that it applies to the making of a genuine poem
—whether great or small—is inconceivable, and can easily be
shown to be seriously in error. But it is not here possible to pursue this topic further.

                                5

While I have been considering imitation, I have been suggesting in passing—as the reader has already realized—what the various theories of expression seek to emphasize, each in its own
philosophical context. We have long known that the act of expression is not a pressing out, as squeezing toothpaste from a
tube. It is a synthesis in which the experiential matter that goes
into the creative act, and the form or forms that inform it, are
completely altered in their natures by interaction among themselves and with that which the creative mind adds out of its own
spontaneity. The experiential matter is the stuff of life as the
poet has lived it, including of course his experience with art and
in our case, especially with poetry. A. C. Bradley analyzed this
problem in his famous lecture, "Poetry for Poetry's Sake," but

his termnology is somewhat fluid, and for this reason I have adapted to my own needs Dewey's term, "the matter for art." This is transmuted into what I call the informed substance, that is the finished poem, the public object that the poet and his readers read. Since the informed substance is the product of the creative activity, it is of course unlike any of the ingredients that made it up. The result, then, is a work of art, a poem that contains a modicum of genuine novelty.

On this view, what I must examine is not the status in being of those ingredients of the poem that are left more or less untouched by the creative activity of the poet. These, as already indicated, have whatever status in being is claimed by ordinary mental objects. The ingredients of the poem that require examination are the genuinely novel ones. At the outset, however, I should call your attention to the fact that I believe that all symbolization, however ordinary or commonplace, is constitutive.

Let us turn our attention for a moment to the nature of symbols, for everything depends on our understanding them. The word "symbol" is used in Cassirer's sense. To do so, we must first distinguish symbols from signs. This usage can be taken as stipulative, but the distinction is real. Symbols are constitutive, and they never function in isolation; they always function as members of a system to which they usually have explicit relationships, but always have deeply rooted implicit ones. Signs denote that to which they refer in an extrinsic relationship, which is to say, that we can apprehend, or believe we can, the thing denoted, independently of the sign by means of which we refer to it for the purposes of apprehension and communication. But symbols and what they symbolize are inseparable from one another, and not fully distinguishable. That is what was meant above when I said that the poem expresses its object in and through itself. One can speak of expressing what is symbolized—but the phrase is pleonastic. That what the poem expresses is expressed through its language creates no trouble, or seems not to. When it is asserted that the poem also expresses its object in the language, the statement gives trouble.

Let us turn our attention therefore to what is expressed in the language of poetry. Here we face the central question. But a sufficient elucidation of it would call for a long discourse on the theory of constitutive symbols. Beyond the *ex cathedra* statement that symbols are constitutive, which is to say that the world is what it is for us because of the symbols we use to constitute it, here I can say no more. I can call attention to the fact that, in very general terms, this is a well known hypothesis, advanced by psychologists, ethnolinguists, and philosophers other than the one in whose footsteps I am, at this point, following, Cassirer. But since there are those who refuse to believe that the language of poetry expresses the object of the poem in as well as through itself, two tests can be suggested to show that those who reject the constitutive nature of symbolic structures are in error.

The first test is to compare a poem, an English one for us, with a translation of it. I shall not undertake the analytic comparison here since it would lead us off on a road I do not want to travel, away from a purely theoretical, abstract, exposition. But it is one of the commonplaces of our day, and a true one, that poetry cannot be translated satisfactorily. We can give the argument of the original poem in a foreign language, but over and beyond this we cannot successfully go. To try it turns the *tradutore* into a *traditore*. We can also create a new language, as was done by Urquhart and James Mabe. But the Rablais of the one and *La Celestina* of the other, can only "convey the spirit" of the originals. We put it in this way to be kind to the *traditori* and let them off with a suspended sentence. This is very, very old hat. What has not been indicated is why this is the case. And the reason is that regnant theories of meaning have been theories of signs and not of symbols, and have failed to make clear why and how language, all the more so the language of poetry, is constitutive.

The other test works on the same principle: Try to alter radically a piece of English verse, by changing the informed substance while sticking closely to the argument. You may come up with something better than the original, but not with anything that can be called an exact equivalent of the original. Old hat again.

6

We return to our question: What is the status in being of those ingredients of the poem that are contributed to it by the creative act? If one denies genuine spontaneity, novelty, the question was answered in the second paragraph of this paper. If one affirms spontaneity, one is in deep trouble, because the only solution to the problem—at least the only one I can see—is one that is profoundly repugnant to the majority of our contemporary teachers of philosophy.

In broad strokes, the solution runs something like this: The symbolic medium of language presents to us the informed substance of the poem. Like all media, language is ephemeral. But the informed meanings and values that constitute the object of the poem, in one sense are not ephemeral, for they do not have their source in existence, in the spacio-temporal realm. We all know that Galileo banished from what he called the real world— the world of classical mechanics—those qualities that later came to be known as secondary and tertiary. They have been kept out of this so-called real world by strong philosophical traditions. If we believe that values are functions of human life and can be explained exhaustively in psychological terms, the only kind of creativity that we can accept is that which comes from shuffling the components of experience. We are thrown back on John Locke's notion of mind—a *tabula*, before the birth of the child, so *rasa* that the fingerprints of an angel can be seen on it. On this view the dignity of poetry and the other arts is denied, for they are denied indispensability and, to come to our problem, on this view we cannot fully account for the sense of superior reality imparted to some of us by a poem.

It is desirable to state candidly that, with Croce and Cassirer for guides, what I propose is to point the way back to some sort of platonism. I have written "some sort of" and write "platonism" in small case, because I do not want to make the greatest philosopher of our civilization, who also was one of its great poets, responsible for my views; and that, for two reasons: the first is that I have neither the learning nor the temperament to be a Platonist in capitals; and the second is that I cannot accept the psychology on which Plato—insofar as I understand him— grounded his theory of our knowledge of the forms. Plato believed that we are endowed with the faculty of Reason, which trained in the proper moral and cognitive manner, could be brought to apprehend forms in their immaculate purity. Note that the platonic theory of forms that I am alluding to here is a simplified travesty. It is mentioned only to make the point that while I believe it is necessary to assert that forms have status in being that is more than nominal, I cannot agree with Plato that all forms can be apprehended by us in their full purity. When we come upon them, we find them informing matter. It is the substanced form, or the informed substance, that the poet offers us for our perception. Neither can a philosopher get at any other kind of poetry. The beauty of the *Iliad, King Lear,* and not to quarrel with James's taste, even *Ivanhoe,* is the only kind of beauty that we'll ever be able to grasp. Or perhaps I should say, that the majority of men are ever able to grasp: for Plato seems to have been capable of an experience not given to the majority of men. Pure forms, untainted by matter, pure intelligible objects, are objects fully accessible to men. But ordinarily we would hardly call them beautiful. If, as it seems, such objects were for Plato the highest form of beauty, ordinary men would say they can hardly be expected to emulate such severity. But you have already noted that this is too rough and simplifying a way of disposing of the difficult and unyielding problem of the beauty of intelligible objects—whether in mathematics, metaphysics, or wherever they are to be found. That beauty can be claimed for them I do not wish to deny; indeed, I affirm it. But they do not fall within the purview of ordinary aesthetics because they lack what Prall called aesthetic surface.

7

The critic may reply: informed substance as an object of contemplation is not something over which there needs be quarrel. The question that is going to divide us is the source of the forms that do the informing and of the substance that is informed. How did they come about? In short, what do you have to say about the creative experience, to make us take seriously the claim you make for genuine spontaneity in the mind and genuine novelty in the object?

I am going to tell you a story about the act of creation. At present, I believe, that is the best that can be done in non-mechanistic terms. And it is because little is known about that aspect of the act of making a poem, as distinct from copying, or of anything else for that matter, that takes place below the level of consciousness. It is below this level where I believe the genuinely creative part of the act takes place. If for any reason, we do not like the notion of the unconscious, we will have to say that the creative act—or that part of it hidden from inspection—takes place in our organism, chiefly perhaps in the brain. I believe much is lost and little gained—if anything at all—by pushing the act of creation from the psychological to the physiological level. For all the troubles we have with the notion of the unconscious, it does help to tie up a lot of phenomena that before its Freudian meaning came into use, remained uncorrelated. But the unconscious I have in mind is, if you like a bastard unconscious, not the pure-blooded, rigidly deterministic, nineteenth-century notion Freud left us. The creative act is an act that involves some spontaneity, genuine creativity. Below the reach of self-awareness, the miracle takes place. And if anyone charges that the dirty word I just used, the word "miracle," puts me among the obscurantists, I will ask him to give us a non-mechanistic explanation of the creative act. When he does, I shall withdraw the word "miracle" and apologize for using it. In the meantime, I beg you to remember Freud's words: "Before the problem of the creative artist analysis must, alas, lay down its arms." Freud of course meant psychoanalysis, but the statement applies to behavioral analysis all the more, or any kind of analysis so far known.

It should be noted that I have been considering the creative activity and not its occasion. A poet may undertake to make a poem on order, or because "the germ of the story," in Henry James's phrase, is suggested to him at a dinner party; or because a friend dies by drowning or is killed in the bull ring; or quite accidentally, it is suggested to him as he dips a bit of cake. Nor do I want to convey the idea that the act takes place entirely out of the reach of consciousness and somehow free from the trained skills, the accepted conventions, the rules if you allow the word, and the rest of the multitude of guiding habits formulated or not, that direct the poet in his choosing and rejecting forms, themes, images, and the rest of the components that criticism tells us make up the finished object. But the conscious process is not wholly unknown, as I believe the unconscious is. I have referred to the conscious activity in passing, under the rubric of the labor of the file, because I am chiefly concerned with emphasizing the unconscious activity in order to focus on the status in being of the meanings and values that the creative act discovers. The thesis, if I may repeat, is that if we take the creative act seriously, the values and meanings that in one sense must be said to be the product of discovery are in another sense the product of genuine creativity. It is the novelty imported by creativity that in part elicits the conviction of reality with which we sweat. Thus, if status in being at the spaciotemporal level, at the level of existence, were the only realm of being, my problem would not be susceptible of solution.

The poet creates meanings and values, since before the act of making the poem, he knew nothing about them, or very little, and what he knew, if anything, was obscure and inchoate-which is to say he did not really know them. But to create them he had to dive to the very bottom of his mind, way below the level of awareness, in order to discover them. A better metaphor than that of the diver would be the following: The creative mind somehow stirs its own bottom, roiling what has been turbidly settled on it, thus seeking to bring up to the surface of awareness what it has disturbed. It wants something although it does not know, or does not know clearly, what it wants. But the other metaphor is easier to handle in a succinct manner. The poet dives into the darkness. He feels what he is looking for but does not really know what it is; it is something, matter without form, and forms free from the substance they are always found informing at the level of awareness. Stuff without shape and shape without stuff: here are two basic ingredients of the creative act. But we have to add the power of the poet's mind that we may assume brings about the synthesis. We call it his creative energy, or the primary imagination. I would not talk about the act by saying it was a rehearsal of the primordial act of creation, but there is no objection to saying that it is a repetition in the finite mind of the eternal act of creation. This language has been used, not to conceal our thought, but to camouflage our ignorance. There is no objection to using language in this way as long as we keep vividly before our minds just what we are doing. The trouble begins when we take these verbal disguises to be genuine explanations.

Much more light is needed on the most puzzling aspect of creativity. To the mechanistic mind, of course, the light is not considered anything but obscurantistic darkness. Again, I do not claim the following remarks to be an explanation. Like Coleridge's words, they represent an effort to catch a bird that is not there by putting salt on is tail with an empty saltshaker. Let us imagine a spider that has been forced to produce thread beyond its capacities by the food we have given it. Such is the creative mind. It produces out of itself beyond the matter and forms for art that it has taken in. What it finally produces comes both from formal and material resources that have been imported and also from that which is contributed by the poet out of his own private, home-made resources. The spider has been fed, but the food it took does not account exhaustively for the amount and quality of the thread it produced. It is this, the poet's own, totally idiotic, contribution, that gives his product the brilliant power of absorption that is its novelty. The feeling of reality turns out to be more than mere feeling. It comes to the object not merely because of the subject's near absolute absorption in the object, but also because the object possesses, as the result of a genuinely creative act, much more than is available to the rest of us prior to the poet's making of his poem.

Nominalistic and scientistic minds will find this story ridiculous because John Locke did his job so well that in spite of Leibniz, who demolished the first book of the *Essay,* Locke convinced the empiricists, British and French, that the notion of innate ideas was philosophically deplorable. And why? It does not take close reading to see that Locke's theoretical argument against innate ideas was in error, because he did not understand what the term "innate idea" meant, and that the gravamen of his criticism was purely ideological—innate ideas were the refuge of absolutism. But Leibniz's answer was the basis of a more adequate notion of the mind than that of the British empiricists. There is nothing in the mind other than that which comes from experience, said Locke. Yes, nothing, said Liebniz, except the mind itself.

We all know that the guards of the *tabula rasa* orthodoxy have kept in line a large number of thinkers in England, the

United States, and at least in the eighteenth century, in France. The faith in it is strong and the sanctions against those who stray from the orthodoxy are harsh. The contrary belief has recently-been called "disgusting" by a reputed teacher of philosophy. Nor is he the only one confronted with heresy, to display the irenic temperament of a rational mind. However, at this very moment, as you know, the faith in the *tabula rasa* is threatened by a few rebels from a discipline from which, I dare say, the regime expected no trouble—the linguistic. But I feel that while in philosophy one can't look gift horses too closely in the mouth, and that the help against the entrenched orthodoxy brought us by some linguists is welcome, we did not really need this help. Long before it arrived some of us were confident that the *tabula*, even John Locke's own baby *tabula*, had never been entirely *rasa*, but had many scratches on it before old Locke let out his first baby wail. It is however gratifying, if to nothing else, to one's vanity, to be able to greet the linguistic volunteers who are helping us push the *tabula rasaists* into the cave of paleo-empiricism.

Concerned with advancing a theory of the genesis of the "matter for Art" used by the human mind that was not mechanistic, Jung told a different kind of story than the one I sketched above. He was interested in the philogenetic side of the problem. And to make some headway into the puzzle he had to introduce some weird characters into his story: a collective unconscious, a racial memory, and numerous archetypes. Why these characters should have brought down on Jung's learned head the implacable contempt that has been heaped on it, is a story that does not exactly belong here. Enough to say that it is one of the many proofs we have of the open mind of contemporary thinkers.

I have introduced Jung, not to declare my agreement with him but to point out that we are faced with a genuine problem. Stories do not solve it. But at least they indicate with some clarity where mechanistic, scientistic explanations fail.

We must still ask the question: Does the diver, of whom I was speaking above, use ingredients that he did not create in the making of his poem? I return to this question to emphasize strongly that the creative act does not create altogether out of nothing. Probably the largest amount of informed substance is discovered. But the poet manages to alter what he finds or discovers, as well as what he creates. In the making of a poem there is creation and there is discovery. The individual talent does not work outside a tradition.

I hope that this story has done what stories sometimes do, that is, throw light on the act of creation, by pointing out why genuine creativity remains so far unexplained. Trusting that it did, we are now able to finish our discussion.

We have seen that a psychological explanation accounts to some extent for the conviction of reality that a poem sometimes elicits. But this conviction arises also from the revealed meanings and values that the reader grasps. These are, to some extent, at least, new for the reader. And to that extent they lend radiance to the object of the poem. The object of the poem, more "utterly utter," is the product of genuine creativity.

We have arrived at the end of the tour. I do not claim originality for the views I have presented to you. In philosophy, originality is somewhat suspect. I can easily name some of the sources from which I have helped myself generously. Croce, the Bradley of the inaugural lecture, "Poetry for Poetry's Sake," Samuel Alexander, and other thinkers, the majority idealists, like the John Dewey of *Art As Experience.* The doctrine I have put before you is offered as a sort of Platonism. It may not be the real Plato, for scholars are still fighting as to who is in possession of the true mummy. But there is something about my Plato that gives me confidence that I have presented to you a somewhat recognizable portrait, and that is his bushy beard. If you remember how that formidable philosopher, Quine, as he was recently called, and a large majority of contemporary teachers of philosophy, cordially detest the bushy beard of Plato, and with hands devoid of piety would shave it off, I flatter myself that the beard is bushy enough for my picture to be true Plato. May I close by claiming with diffidence that whether I have presented to you the real Plato, or a pseudo-Plato, or no Plato at all but the product of my ignorance exclusively, it has been with the aid of someone I have taken for Plato that I have tried to get at the complexities of poetry that neither the defenders of the *tabula rasa,* nor the champions of positivistic philosophy of science, nor nominalists, nor linguistic analysts can approach.

PART TWO

Critical Theory

The Objective Basis of Criticism

Criticism seeks, legitimately, to perform several functions: it tries to guide and improve public taste, to disclose the relations of art, considered purely as art, to non-aesthetic activities and values, to determine the comparative worth of the aesthetic qualities embodied in objects which may compete for our attention, and to enlighten the artist on the true nature and meaning of his created object, since the artist may do better or worse or quite differently than he intends. To its many ends contemporary American criticism is well equipped. Critics approach their tasks with no small measure of sensibility, discriminative power, historical knowledge, and by and large a proper feeling for the importance of art. Yet contemporary American criticism suffers from a serious defect: it ignores, sometimes truculently, the need for a systematic philosophy of art. The fault, it must be said in fairness, is not entirely the critic's, since contemporary aesthetics tends to be an autonomous discipline concerned chiefly with problems of philosophic method and with epistemological issues, and to ignore the problems of criticism and the contemporary situation in art. But it is my impression that aestheticians today are more apt to learn from critics than the critics from the aestheticians. Be that as it may, often it appears as if critics were enemies of theoretical consistency.

What aesthetics should be able to offer the critic is not an academic discussion of purely philosophical problems of method and of epistemology, although these cannot be altogether avoided, but an examination, carried on in technical terms, of the underlying assumptions that the critic must and does make about such problems as the nature of art, its relation to other modes of activity, the categories with which it can be approached, its function. Such an examination must remain in the nature of the case a dry, abstract, purely theoretical analysis. Critics, impatient with the difficulties of technical inquiries whose relevance to their work is not immediate or obvious, tend to scorn them and to fall back on a shabby hand to mouth pragmatism which does not avoid but merely ignores them and which therefore inevitably generates confusion. Contemporary critics, with a few notable exceptions, do not have a clear idea of the theoretical foundations of their discipline, in spite of the serious sense they have of the importance of art for human life.

Nowhere in the field of criticism is the need more urgent for an adequate theoretical clarification than as regards questions about the validity of the judgment of comparative merit. What validity or justification does the critic have for his judgments? Does his judgment express merely his own taste, his sensibility, his own private knowledge and wisdom, or does it claim somehow to discriminate, by means of such equipment, values that are objective and about which one can fruitfully dispute? And if he does make the claim to objectivity where do these discriminated values reside: are they located in the object or is the latter merely a means to bring them into existence through the satisfaction the object gives to the spectator? The complex problem which these questions formulate is, of course, a very old problem. But for all its antiquity its solution is no less urgent today than it ever was, for without some sort of clear opinion on it, the critic's practice is apt to be characterized by the inconsistencies and ambiguities which are the usual consequence of unexamined assumptions.

No matter what he takes his function to be, the validity of the critic's analysis depends on the validity of the aesthetic judgment that he must make. For even if he should not be interested in pure aesthetic values, but should seek to discover the relation of the art object under analysis to other interests, he cannot discriminate with clarity the relationship between art and anything else—whether it be politics or morality or religion or science—unless he has a clear knowledge of the value as art of the object whose relationship he is seeking to disclose. To assume, as moralistic or sociological critics seem sometimes to do, that the moral or political value of art can be decided independently of its aesthetic value, is simply absurd. For if an object acts on us morally in total independence of its aesthetic value, it is not as art that it thus acts, but as a moral object; and the specialized aesthetic discriminations of the art critic are totally irrelevant and may even be in the way of his apprehending its moralizing message.　But if it acts on us morally by means of its aesthetic quality then a clear examination of the latter would seem to be a prerequisite to an adequate examination of its moral efficiency. The critic of art then, however he may conceive his task, depends for the success of his activity on the validity of the aesthetic discriminations he is capable of making.　But the converse is not true.　For an object may function solely as aesthetic and in the discrimination of its aesthetic value no other considerations need then enter than merely aesthetic ones. It may be, of course, that since we are human beings and not exclusively aesthetic animals, interest in purely aesthetic objects may be an incomplete diet for us, incapable of sustaining our complex and heterogeneous needs.　Indeed a wise critic would recognize this as elementarily true.　But the fact is no justification for confusing aesthetic values with moral, religious, social and any other kind of values.

But what does the validity of the aesthetic judgment itself depend on if not its objectivity?　For an avowedly subjective judgment is one with which no one in his right mind would undertake to quarrel theoretically, since all it asserts is a private and arbitrary preference.　You may point out to the subjectivist the consequences of a given preference and, on this basis, you may seek to dissuade him from opinions you take to be dangerous to him.　But you cannot find a rational argument against a preference that claims no rational ground and demands no jurisdiction beyond itself.　But how can we, in view of the stock arguments of the subjectivist, defend the objectivity of the aesthetic judgment?

The aesthetic judgment is objective in the sense that it asserts the presence in an object of an aesthetic value-trait which is open to public inspection.　This view is rejected on various grounds. Mr. Pepper, for instance, rejects it on the ground that the value of the object depends on the observer's taste, and C. I. Lewis on the ground that the value of the object consists of its potentiality for giving immediate satisfaction in experience.　In this discussion such issues cannot be gone into and it must be assumed that the presence of aesthetic values in objects is a matter of prima-facie experience.　When I say "Jane is beautiful" it is of Jane I am speaking, of the beauty that somehow resides in the shape of her face, he eyes, mouth, in her fresh skin and in her neck, and not of myself; her beauty is certainly not in me, nor in my reactions to her, although, of course, I cannot discover it unless I somehow react to the features in which it resides. If beauty reveals itself only to an individual and does so in an incommunicable way, so that no one else can discover it, nothing more can be said about it, except that, unless the person who claims to descry it is a liar, it is there for him. Correction of such taste is impossible. But the objects of art with which criticism busies itself are not of this kind. And the critic, in engaging in his activity as critic, asserts thereby tacitly that they are not, but that they are values that are discoverable by others besides himself. Otherwise why does he publish his opinions? It may well be that the critic will discover in the objects of his preference, after analysis has done its best, an ineffable quality which helps give the object the specific value that it has for him, but which somehow eludes his power of analysis. But if the critic starts with ineffables instead of ending with them when he can do nothing to exorcise them, he condemns himself to emotive grunts of no interest to anyone but himself.

Now an objective judgment of an object not only refers to a value trait, but does so because the object possesses some sort of discriminable structure on which the value depends. This is so by definition, for art involves material that possesses an inherent capacity of organization, shaped intentionally by the artist in order to capture a determinate congerie of aesthetic values. If the presence of the value is not controlled by the object's structure, there is no question of art and the object is of no interest for criticism, although such an unanchored value may be within the grasp of enraptured and immediate apprehension for some men. But, you may object, why could we not talk of values that reside in objects but that do not depend on structure for their presence in them? If and when one finds them, he can no doubt talk of them, but he could not share his experience with his neighbour unless the latter had already, by the same happy accident, apprehended the same values. No artist could have controlled their presence in the object; nor could critics make objective reference to them. For it is only through reference to the structure to which they are anchored that reference to aesthetic value is possible; otherwise the presence of a value in an object is altogether fortuitous and miraculous, to be apprehended only by those who do so accidentally and forever closed to those who do not.

That values reside in objects and that they depend for their presence in them in the latter's structure seems to me a matter of common experience although often denied by philosophers. But it is also a matter of experience that values reside in objects independently of their structure. Consider for instance a picture of a "Virgin and Child" almost utterly devoid of aesthetic value, such as one sees in religious store windows, and which no doubt appears to some believers as beautiful as well as holy. It seems to be a difficult question as to how values which are not, so to speak "anchored" to the structures of objects, get to reside in them. It is usually said that they are "projected," and with this utterly inadequate problem-begging metaphor many aestheticians and psychologists seem to be satisfied. But this is fortunately not a problem which we need to discuss here, for whatever answer we give to it, it remains a fact that "unanchored values," so to call them, are on examination found to be different in kind from those which depend on the object's structure for their presence in it. It is true that some aestheticians have held that all aesthetic values are projected; but even if they are, they cannot be indifferently and arbitrarily projected upon any object, and on this theory the critic still has the problem of discovering those structures which are hospitable to aesthetic values. The point is, obviously, that there is a relationship of some sort between aesthetic value and structure, even if no one has yet successfully formulated it. A faded snapshot of a dead child may wring the same feeling from his mother as a portrait of his done by an artist of distinction. The value of either object, for the mother, need not depend on its intrinsic structure but may entirely depend on the extrinsic and purely accidental power it may have of reminding her of her lost child. In an aesthetic object, however, the structure subtends the value and communicates it, irrespective of purely accidental relationships between the subject who will grasp it and the object on which it resides. Indeed an aesthetic structure is one which successfully excludes the irrelevant values and controls rigorously the values and meanings it communicates.

The assertion of the possibility of objectivity of aesthetic judgments does not mean that such judgments are absolutely correct but merely that they are corrigible. The correction of judgments involves greater difficulties in art than it does in science, where techniques of abstraction, isolation, quantification, and controlled experiment enable the inquirer to confine his attention to the precise phenomena to which the judgment refers and to exclude idiosyncratic irrelevancies. In art, in the absence of such instrumentalities, corrigibility takes place through the give and take of criticism of the object. In such give and take the criteria of criticism are themselves open to criticism. And only by means of a criticism of such criticism is the presence of a value in an object isolated and related to its structure. Through such a process the specific nature of the structure is itself defined by critical analysis, the value it subtends is isolated, and the criteria which governs its presence in the object exhibited. Thus the utterance of the judgment "This object is beautiful" is in a sense the least important part of a critical effort, since challenge of the judgment involves an examination of its basis, and this examination may disclose that the judgment rests on insufficient grounds. If the "verification" (a most inappropriate term to use for these activities) consisted, as some simple-minded positivists hold in respect to moral judgments, merely in the statement of formulae expressing intrinsic values and the logical deduction of specific valuations from these, discussion would be futile and criticism would consist in the clever conditioning of another's taste by one's own. This is in fact what criticism often undertakes to do: arbitrarily to recondition another person's taste. But discussion of beauty is also addressed—although of course it rarely is—to the discovery and exhibition of values subtended by aesthetic structures which for some reason we have either overlooked or misconstrued. The assumption on which such discussion is carried on is that the exhibition of the structure will allow the value to come forward and that its presence will then draw forth our interest. For value exists prior to interest and more often than not creates it. This is always the case as regards non-inherited interests, all those, that is, above the biological level. But even congenital or inherited interests do not create value, they merely discover it. The correction of criteria is possible because the determinate structure which subtends value and which controls our perception of it can be appealed to. The criterion is an inductive statement of an empirically discovered normative transaction between a mind and an object embodying a value, but once stated the criterion enters into the situation and acquires normative force, clarifying and governing taste. In no case however is it more than empirically related to the situation over which it rules. Our formulated criteria are susceptible of correction because a pre-existing structure, conflicting judgments about the value it subtends and the very examination through which both structure and values were discovered can be appealed to in order to correct each of the factors involved in terms of the others when the presence of conflicting judgments reveal the need for such correction.

Value judgment, then, is objective, first, in the sense that it refers to a quality of an object and not to the subjective quality of satisfaction, fulfillment, enjoyment, or pleasure which may be derived from its grasp. One of the most frequent forms of the subjectivistic fallacy consists in confusing the value of an experience with the value of an object in an experience. Both object and experience of it may be endowed with value. But to deny value to a thing because it does not happen to enter into an experience, is to fail to make distinctions essential to the clarification of our subject matter. Aesthetic value is not the quality of an experience but of an object in an experience; the only value experiences can have for the subject undergoing them is moral value, although objectively viewed one man's experience may have aesthetic value for another. It is true that the aesthetic object is always an object in an experience, but so are all other objects which may be the objects of judgment; the predicament holds of scientific objects and not only of aesthetic objects. Of course the adequate possession of a positive value should in the majority of cases involve subjective satisfactions. But when these are present they are by-products of the activity which resulted in the possession of the objective value, and if such satisfactions are also considered by the subject in possession of the objective value as adding to that value, as they indeed do, the critic must insist on the distinction between the value of the object, and the added values in terms of satisfaction that its possession brings with it. The residence of the aesthetic value in an object can be ascertained through the fact that it is available for public inspection. The judgment is valid to the extent that it can justify itself to those adequately endowed judges who are interested in discovering the value to which it refers; but it is not objective in that it can do so but because it can: I mean that it is objective because it refers to objective traits but we ascertain their presence publicly and only by thus ascertaining them can we be sure that the values are there.

But—and there are of course several "buts"—the word 'beauty' is much more ambiguous than words which designate physical properties, since, first, that to which it points is not apprehended by but through sense; and second, and this is the source of the worst trouble, the discrimination of beauty, as resident upon specific structure, depends on our ability to descry in the object's construction, its aesthetic purpose. Our failure to discover in a poem of Hopkins the beauty so readily found in one of Keats is not infrequently caused by the fact that we approach the former with expectations acquired through our acquaintance with the latter. Modigliani will not give you what a Titian will nor does Picasso try to do what Goya did. How then shall we determine the artist's aesthetic intention? Will we discover it from what he says in his letters or from Boswellian records that we may be fortunate to possess? Even if we had such records for all artists we could not use them without checking their statements against the artist's work considered in the context of the aims and directions of his tradition or school. What artists say about their work all too frequently depends on aesthetic theories which may not be relevant to their practice, or if they are, may not have been fully elucidated, or may not be consistent. In any case the artist's statements are only a part of what he had to say and, as artist, not necessarily the most important part. What he has had to say is best found in his art. The criteria of validity of a statement about an object must be whether the statement represents the object truly. The artist's statements about his object must certainly occupy a preferred place in our decision about his intentions. But they cannot be accepted at face value.

Examination of the object with adequate knowledge and sensibility may yet reveal no value in the object for one examiner, although for another it may be there. I can agree with you that the structure was conceived for the purpose you ascribe to it and agree, as far as discrimination can carry it, as to the structural traits you so perspicuously describe. But for all that I do not find in the object the value that you find in it. On the very grounds that you find value I may even find the very opposite, a disvalue. Does that mean that it has value for you but not for me? Does it now follow that we both are right? This conclusion would legitimately follow from complete knowledge about yourself and myself; until we possess such knowledge the source of the failure must remain an open question. The disagreement may mean that factors as yet undiscovered—either in you or in me or in both—are interferring with an objective grasp of what is there to be grasped. You may be "projecting" values on the object which are not truly there; or I may be made blind to them by my lack of sensibility or ignorance or by deeply grounded prejudices; or we both may be at fault and may be perceiving more and less than the object's structure subtends. And the reason for this is of course that judgments of value, as uttered, are never beyond challenge. The law says that a man acquitted at court can never be tried a second time for the same crime. But his value judgments do not have the same privilege he has and they can always be called a second, a third, and a fourth time, to justify themselves. Error does not thereby impair the objectivity of the judgment. What objectivity requires, besides the objectivity of the value, is not that we have consensus, but that we have on hand means of checking the validity of our judgments. Infallibility is not possible but it is not necessary either. And the means to check the validity of conflicting judgments are difficult of application, inefficient, and take more time and patience than we usually have at our disposal. But they are there to be used if we want to use them. This is a most important point and it would be well to dwell on it longer, at least to the extent of suggesting that a theory of objectivity cannot be made responsible for the sins of omission and commission of specific judgments. A certain subjectivistic aesthetician not long ago made a historical study on the basis of which a very famous Italian painting has been praised by various critics since Vassari; and because of the heterogeneity of the demands clearly made by the various critics which he studied he concluded that there is no way of choosing between the various conflicting modes of criticism. But the conclusion is a total non-sequitur, since it has assumed that there is no way of criticizing across the boundaries, so to speak, of incompatible conceptions of the intention of the artist. The analysis assumes, as all subjectivism seems to, that each individual's reaction is absolutely valid, and we must take it at its face value.

The claim of objectivity depends, then, secondly, on whether it is possible to disclose the means by which conflicting judgments can be corrected when discrimination has done its best and has, through a perspicuous analysis of structure, called forth contradictory value judgments. We have already noted that in cases where seemingly inerradicable disagreements are encountered neither of the conflicting judgments can claim initial superiority or validity over the other. By what means then shall we correct these judgments? Notice first that the rational correction of judgments involves, as a guiding condition, the desire to arrive at the truth. In practice this is an ideal more honoured in the breach than in the observance. But unless the condition is assumed no further discussion of the problem is possible. And in practice to the extent to which we fail to realize this ideal there can be no possibility of correcting conflicting value judgments, not because the techniques for so doing have failed, but because other objectives have been substituted for those of rational inquiry.

But, the reader will press, what techniques do you have in mind? The answer, I am afraid, will disappoint lovers of novelty as well as those addicted to scientistic methodolatry, for the techniques in question are those which were used by Socrates in his own moral inquiry: the mutual interrogation of claims and counter-claims in order to elicit from them the evidence on which they rest and the clarity on which they count; in short what Plato called a "dialectical" inquiry. In the give and take in which a dialectical inquiry consists, the judgments in conflict are corrected by confronting them with the facts to which they pretend to refer, and the principles on which the judgments are based are themselves subject to criticism by reference to the objective values, as critically apprehended, to which the inquiry is addressed, and which remain the ultimate basis of appeal. It is important to notice, however, that what is purely idiosyncratic—whether in the artist or in the judge of his work—is irrelevant to an objective judgment, and gradually emerges when the conflictint judgments are put, in Plato's phrase, through the gauntlet of the argument. Criticism seeks to reveal the aesthetic value of an object, to relate it to the structure that sustains it, and to relate the object to the traditions to which it belongs and define the intention of the artist. Thus the critic tries to put himself in a position from which he can evaluate objectively an artist's achievement in relation to the achievement of other artists who may be members of his tradition and even of other traditions. The total process, carried on against all comers, results in the gradual crystalization of opinion from which the errors of subjectivity have to some degree been expurgated. This doctrine may be maintained while admitting freely that the process is not one from which error can be thoroughly removed.

The foregoing account will no doubt seem to be infected with circularity to those readers who, not adequately acquainted with the actual complexities of criticism, will think of the problem solely in abstract terms and will demand logical rigor and elegance above fidelity to the complex facts. But the account is not circular since it holds that the criticism of the judgment and of the criterion which rules it is always controlled by objectively given facts to which final appeal is made. First hand acquaintance with the actual procedure of criticism will reveal it to be characterized by inefficiency and confusion, but not by radical circularity. In the give and take of criticism, through which gradually the true values embodied in objects emerge, the intention of the artist is more or less clarified, and his contribution to taste is slowly digested.

One criticism that has been made of this account must be met. The doctrine has been called conservative because, it has been argued, it calls for a criticism which is guided by the criteria of well established taste. But this is not a fair interpretation of what the view intends, since established taste is not on this theory a fixed affair to which art must conform. If however it should be insisted that the theory is more likely to give comfort to a conservative artist than to a revolutionary one, since it seems to put so much emphasis on established taste as a source of criteria of value, it were well to remember, in justice to it, that taste itself is not treated in this doctrine as if it constituted the final criterion, since taste is held to be responsive to values presented, to beauties actually embodied. If it is open to criticism, it is not because it is conservative, but because it sounds like Deweyism. But the similarity is specious, since the final criterion is held to be the objective value, the beauty embodied, or the abortive failure before us which somehow suggests the intention of the artist. These are held to exist prior to their discovery and to be regulative of taste. We can depend on taste only when it is impeccable; but any serious challenge to it immediately puts it on the defensive. It often happens that taste for some reason ossifies; in such cases the error carries with it its own punishment, since the tradition it sustains soon dies instead of developing. If on the other hand, taste becomes too fluid, too ready to welcome all innovation, as is the case in our day, the error also carries with it its own punishment, for it becomes distracted, queer, eccentric, unintelligible. In such periods those to whom art should minister become even more distracted than they already are by contemplating objects that are hermetic puzzles and keep the secret of the artist's intention within themselves against any serious and honest effort to wrest it from them; and men who need art wander starved amidst the plenty. Art, one of whose most important functions is to bring order, harmony and lucidity into a man's vision of his world, adds to the chaos and speeds up the social disintegration that produced it. The individualistic intuitionist, the man who repudiates all tradition on the authority of his inner voice, condemns himself and, in so far as he is influential, his fellows, to shallow experimentalism. Such a man acts as if he carried in himself his own self-validation. But the very conception of self-validation is a contradiction. For this reason, while we must agree with Philip Blair Rice who has insisted that private factors do in fact enter into valuation, and must add that they serve to individuate one's taste, we cannot agree with him in so far as he seems to suggest that they ever "justify" it. When a judge falls back on them he has withdrawn his judgment from all criticism and has asserted that he is interested in the expression of his arbitrary will rather than in the objective justification of his taste. Note however that if the argument of this essay has been made clear the phrase "objective justification" should be taken as pleonastic, since the effort to justify a judgment consists precisely in exhibiting the objective and sharable basis on which it rests.

It is also necessary to remember that the notion of tradition, as T. S. Eliot has pointed out in his well-known essay, "Tradition and The Individual Talent," does not call for an inert and frozen past in terms of which we must judge the present irrespective of the differences in interest and orientation which may be found to exist between yesterday and today. Eliot pointed out that the appearance of a new poem involves a reinterpretation of the tradition. He writes as if the past changed—and that involves a conception of time that commits us to a weird metaphysics. But if he allows us to read him as if he had meant, not that the past changes but that our interpretation if it changes, I would willingly subscribe to all that he says in the first part of his essay. Now the literary humanists—I mean, Irving Babbit and his now almost totally extinct followers—as I read them, bring the present to the rigid norm of the past and instead of judging it, in Eliot's distinction, they amputate it. For them the differences between the practice of the modern artist and that of the ancients was traced to contemporary aberrations and the devils of modern history, Bacon and Rousseau. The complimentary error, that of the individualist, because more virulent at present, is much more dangerous today than that of the humanists. The individualist denies the jurisdiction of the past over the present and assumes the right of the artist to unrestricted originality. It ignores the fact that we owe loyalty to our past because we are absolutely nothing without it. The repudiation of the past is justified on a philosophy of history according to which there can be a radical break between our age and another. The repudiation of the past involves a misreading of history which is both egregious and obvious. Those who have contempt for the past counsel us to bind ourselves to wilful, upstart movements which express the transient needs of men without piety, restrained by nothing but the limitations of their own willfulness. We need expect nothing from *guerilleros* either in art, in ethics or in politics; we are much better off if we take our chances with the tradition than if we appeal to the latest *appart,* whether it be positivist, instrumentalist, or Marxist. In contrast with these two extremes, a genuine empiricism allows for the progressive transformation of the past in terms of the present, even to the rejection of aspects of the tradition that can be shown to be genuinely in error. But it also insists that the past must judge the present, for we cannot define our own contemporary norm without its aid.

These remarks cannot be taken as an exhaustive treatment of the problem of aesthetic revolutions nor even of those minor revolutions which are frequently accomplished—as it would seem —by your strong individuals and which result in a marked deflection in the direction of taste. A complete treatment of this phenomenon would take us far afield, and would involve investigations of regions so far unexplored, as far as I know, in order to discover the relationship between the social processes and artistic creativity. Nor do these sketchy notes touch on another problem, a much more difficult one, and one which an exhaustive treatment of the problem of aesthetic value would have to face. For moral phenomena cannot be satisfactorily elucidated unless we distinguish between the conditional and the categorical moral imperatives. But in art we do not find, so far as I can see, a similar dualism.

We are now in a position to gather our results: the discussion has been grounded on the belief that it is of the essence of truth to give an account of its grounds, submitting these without strings to criticism. In the exact sciences, discussion is carried on in terms of techniques and procedures that in part are devised in order to locate the idiosyncratic in observation and the ambiguous in formulation. In art these techniques are not available, but through persistent discussion and criticism failures and limitations of commission and ommission on the part of the artist and his critics emerge, and their exhibition constitutes the process of corrigibility. If judgments are corrigible, or rather in so far as they are, they are objective. But it would be impossible to speak of corrigibility if the discussion had not sought to make clear what is meant by asserting that value traits are objective and dependent on structures which can be discriminated objectively and which can be intentionally devised to subtend a complex of values. However, the connection that we have discovered to exist between a physical structure and the value it subtends is a purely empirical, a *posteriori,* one. If such a connection does not issue in subjectivism it is because, in spite of cultural conditioning which tends parochially to blind a man to the alien, an earnest inquiry into alien values will frequently reveal to him that those values are objectively present. In aesthetics however, the desirability of arriving at uniformity of judgments remains and is likely to remain in the realm of the possible, whereas in ethics— not in moral judgments—uniformity and universality of agreement is in fact a reality, at least among those men who have not been, as Bishop Berkeley put it, debauched by philosophy. The empirical, contingent connection, then, between physical structure, embodied value, and a spectator's capacity under favorable conditions to discover it, makes criticism an intelligent objective activity, which is capable of guiding taste and correcting the artist's practice. We also saw, in passing, that criticism entails a complete theory of aesthetics, since it operates on a notion— whether explicit or implicit—of the function of art and of the meaning of the purely aesthetic. The failure to define the purely aesthetic and the function of art is what gives the subjectivist a plausible ground for his belief that about values there can be no rational dispute. This paper was based on the assumption that in concrete critical activity the purely aesthetic can be isolated, and that the resident function of art can be distinguished from its non-resident functions. That a discussion of the basis of criticism—to which an essay on the aesthetic judgment really is addressed—depends on a general aesthetic theory is worth while pointing out because in no field does a hand to mouth pragmatism seem to be more entrenched than in the field of criticism. But serious and responsible criticism would acknowledge freely its dependence on the wider philosophic enterprise which is aesthetics. Our criticism is bound to remain erratic and inconsistent in so far as it is informed by embryonic conceptions of the uses of art and of the validity of the critical judgment.

Intercourse With Art*

1

In a recent essay entitled "Literary Criticism and Aesthetics," I examined the lack of cross-fertilization between criticism and aesthetics in our age and argued that criticism not grounded on a coherent aesthetic runs an almost certain risk of being itself incoherent, while an aesthetic that ignores the concerns of practical criticism is almost certain to address itself to "problems" that are generated by the autonomous philosophical perplexities of the aesthetician and are not likely to be of interest to persons concerned practically with art.[1] In that essay I was writing about literary criticism and theory of literature, but the thesis holds for all the arts and for aesthetics in general. In this paper I shall take for granted the need for an intimate relationship between aesthetic theory and practical criticism and shall seek to show by means of examples what happens when the critic lacks the control of aesthetic theory or fails to ask himself what art as art does in contrast with what conceptual or discursive thinking does.

Since it is not likely that "Literary Criticism and Aesthetics" will be widely read I should note here that it did not advo-

---

*This essay, appearing here under the title I originally gave it, was published in *Humanities Symposium,* Winter 1972, Vol. 1, No. 1, under the title "In The Presence of Art," which suggests the contrary of what I sought to expound in it. The Editor objected to my title because it suggested to him sexual intercourse with art. Having changed my title the editor unfortunately died when the magazine—it is my guess—was in the process of going to press. At any rate I was not consulted and the first time I saw the title was when I received author's copies. Had I seen proof I would have withdrawn the piece.

cate a given theory or a given mode of critical practice. Almost any theory will do, so long as it is coherent, in order to control any mode of critical practice. Nor did the essay argue that the controlling theory had to be explicitly formulated. What is indispensable is that the theory, whether explicit or not, control the practice in order to reduce, if not altogether do away with, incoherence. It ought to be here emphasized that at the basis of a controlling aesthetic theory a notion of "pure art" is indispensable, whether we believe that in actuality such a thing exists or not, and whether the critic believes that the actual function of art, however defined, is in fact useful or detrimental to the good life, however the latter be conceived. A perfect circle does not exist, it has no locus in actual space, but were we not able to define it and thus distinguish it from other conic sections, our practical, no less than our theoretical, efforts would be subject to disastrous errors. And so with the notion of "pure art." We need the notion if we are to grasp how our concern with any other mode of activity than the aesthetic, when blended with the latter, extends or restricts our experience.

The distinction, however, between "pure art" and actual objects of art is rejected by some critics who seem to believe that criticism is not bound by the exigencies of clear thinking. But whether or not the critic acknowledges the need for clear thinking and seeks to achieve it, he is sometimes apt to fall into one of two errors. The first consists in the confusion of the concept of a thing with the things of which it is a concept. Obvious as the fallacy is when stated abstractly, it is systematically incurred by many critics who fail to see that a definition of pure art does not entail the existence of art objects that can be said to be altogether pure. But it is the case that we cannot speak with a modicum of clarity about what an object of art is supposed to do unless we have a concept of the object and keep the distinction between the concept and its object clearly in mind.

The second difficulty is more grave. For we must acknowledge that we cannot consider anything, whether it be a physical thing or a thing of the mind, except by means of, or rather, in and through a concept. From which it follows that for each one of us poetry is what he takes it to be. It is at this point that our distinction between concept and thing offers us its first service. For the chaos that reigns in aesthetics arises to no small extent from the fact that we have no generally accepted concept of the work of art as distinct from a moral or religious or cognitive object, as we have of barometric pressure and of the criteria of a Beauty Queen.

The remedy for the second difficulty is obvious. We must submit our notion of the art object and the grounds on which we arrive at it to public criticism. Before I advance a concept of an art object—which is to say, my own idiotic notion, proposed for full citizenship—let me assert what I take to be the two most important of several conditions that a definition must meet. The first is that for the sake of elementary clarity we must close the term to be defined, even though we know that the closing is arbitrary. The closing of course limits or defines our discussion, it puts a fence around those objects that fall within the definition, and says nothing whatever about the nature or value of those that are excluded. It is important to emphasize this point, because the notion that aesthetic concepts are "open concepts" has been hailed as a liberating proclamation in many quarters. Aside from the fact that what is new about this doctrine is only the label, for criticism it is a mischievous half-truth—the other half being that the critic who wants to avoid confusion closes his notion and states its referents with full candor, so that his readers know what he is talking about and what he has decided to neglect.

A definition of art must also take into consideration that objects of art come into being only in relational complexes and cannot be defined, therefore, outside such complexes. In the relational complex (s - R - o) the spectator—as I am forced to call him—is the s or subject term and the o, the art object, in a specific relation R to the spectator and *vice versa*. I have reasons to believe that the meanings and values that make up the informed substance of an art object have status in being independently of their being terms in relational complexes. But they function as ingredients of an object only in a relational complex. Vary the subject term however slightly and the object term varies—in actuality. And I say "in actuality" because the concept of an art object, since it is an ideal term, or abstraction, or construction, does not vary.

The concept of art I arrived at long ago is this: an art object is a symbolic structure, embodying immanent values and meanings, so organized that the whole elicits and sustains rapt attention upon itself exclusively—or as I prefer to put it, intransitively—in its full presentational immediacy.[2] Equal emphasis must be put on the kind of attention paid by the spectator and on the unity of the whole that elicits it. For it is only by means of the unified object that the attention achieves intransitivity. It is also important to note that the means and values funded in the object are presented *in* as well as *through* symbols, and not merely by means of signs or representations. The difference between a symbol and a sign or a representation is that a sign or a representation seems to point to something capable of being apprehended independently of that which does the signifying or representing, whereas that to which the symbol points can only be apprehended in the symbol as well as through it. It is necessary to emphasize "seems" for complex technical reasons that cannot be expounded here. Suffice to say that all mental apprehension is symbolic, although some of it seems to be signific because symbols in common usage become so stereotyped and transparent that we assume that we apprehend their referends immediately, which is to say without the aid of the symbolic means in which as well as *through* which, we apprehend them.

This definition can be grouped for the purposes of criticism with a definition in terms of sympathetic attention, offered by other aestheticians, only by a hasty misreading of both. If the definition is to be classified with other definitions—and I am not one to make claims for the originality of my views—it is to be grouped with the Kantian disinterested interest. A man aiming at the merely verbal pseudo-clarity that is the goal of so much contemporary philosophizing either dismisses Kant's paradoxical expression as a mere contradiction in terms, or translates it by reduction to mean mere disinterestedness or disinterested and sympathetic attention. In either case he fails to see that the expression vividly calls attention to a difficult, complex, and important substantive problem.

2

I shall try to show, next, what happens sometimes when the

distinction between the aesthetic response and ordinary attention is disregarded.

One critic has told us in all seriousness that when one reads a poem his attention is not controlled by the poem. In disregard of the variety of modes of aesthetic response of which we have empirical knowledge, this writer, like so many others, takes his own undisciplined habit of reading to be typical. If "type" means the average, he is probably right. But if "type" means the ideal or the lawful (and these two are not the same) he is wrong. Nor does he seem to be aware of what a devastating confession he is making about his unbuttoned habits of reading. For him the reading of the poem is not controlled by the poem. The poem is the occasion for undirected ramblings guided solely by fortuitous associations. According to him the reader indulges in a loose relaxed excursus. Not for him the sharp focusing of attention upon the immanent meanings in their full presentational immediacy, which is forced upon the mind that seeks to discover what is there—that seeks avidly the whole, in its organized unity, that is there. No wonder that such a critic has nothing to say about how the reader's mind seeks the organization that the poet struggled so hard to achieve and to some extent achieved. There is one thing, however, that must be said for this kind of reading: although these lazy meanderings may contribute nothing to the mind that indulges in them, they do not tire it either. In any case, between the relaxed response to the poem and the intransitive attention the definition refers to, there is an important difference, whatever value we may end up by putting on the relaxed way of reading over the taut reading called for by my definition.

Besides the relaxed, unbuttoned snatching at chunks of poetry for rumination, in disregard of their mutually sustaining organic unity, there is another transitive mode of response to works of art which is often encountered. Consider Heidegger's way of looking at van Gogh's painting of a pair of shoes.[3] The picture of the shoes is introduced by Heidegger to establish the distinction between tools or equipment and works of art. This is important because I am going to show that Heidegger uses the picture as an instrument. In a well-known passage Heidegger tells us:

In van Gogh's painting we cannot even tell where the shoes stand.

> There is nothing surrounding this pair of peasant's shoes in or to which they might belong, only an undefined space. There are not even clods from the soil of the field or the path through it sticking to them, which might at least hint at their employment. And yet.

And yet what? And yet, for Heidegger there is much more to the painting of the shoes. The picture tells him, as it would have told Sherlock Holmes of Baker Street, a lot that it cannot tell us, unimaginative Watsons that we are. Besides finding that the shoes are those of a female peasant Heidegger discovers a great deal more:

> From the dark opening of the worn insides of the shoes the toilsome tread of the worker stands forth. In the stiffly solid heaviness of the shoes there is the accumulated tenacity of her slow trudge through the farspreading and ever-uniform furrows of the field, swept by a raw wind. On the leather there lies the dampness and saturation of the soil. Under the soles there slides the lonelieness of the field-path as the evening declines. In the shoes there vibrates the silent call of the earth, its quiet gift of the ripening corn and its enigmatic self-refusal in the fallow desolation of the wintry field. This equipment is pervaded by uncomplaining anxiety about the certainty of bread, the wordless joy of having once more withstood want, the trembling before the advent of birth and shivering at the surrounding meance of death. This equipment belongs to the *earth* and it is protected in the *world* of the peasant woman. From out of this protected belonging the equipment itself rises to its resting-in-self.

This is what the painting of the pair of shoes seems to present to the seeing mind. Heidegger does not tell us which one of the pictures of shoes by van Gogh he is writing about, although he knows that there are several of them. Remembering but vaguely one that he could have had in mind, we could be carried away by his eloquence. But if we look at the picture—and reproductions are easily available—we see that it presents much less and much more than Heidegger tells us. One need not be a student of van Gogh (I am not) to know that the pictures of shoes are not among his great paintings and that they are probably pre-Arles pictures and not among those works in which van Gogh, after he moved south from Paris, showed in a splendid manner the full energy of his mind, eye, and hand, the brilliance of his palette, the power of his art. If these paintings are interesting it is chiefly because they were painted by van Gogh, a man whose genius only a little over a year later burst into the flowering that made him one of the great painters of modern times. Had van Gogh continued to paint shoes and peasants as he did until 1886 no one, not even Heidegger, would be today interested in his work. Why then did Heidegger choose the picture of the shoes to comment on? Why did he not choose one of van Gogh's great canvases? The chances are that we shall never have a satisfactory answer to this question, but it is probably not far off the mark to suggest that one possible reason, among perhaps others, was that Heidegger knew what he could do with the shoes when he got to work on them with his unfettered *angstvoll* imagination.

How did our Sherlock find all that he tells us he sees in the shoes? He merely states what he finds. He does not tell us by what process he discovered the shoes to be a woman's, and what in them told him that under the soles he could somehow perceive the loneliness of the field-path as the evening declines. We have to admit that for Heidegger van Gogh's painting of a pair of shoes turns out to be a marvelously eloquent. . .eloquent what? What is it? Is it a painting-cum-poem? Or is it merely the instrument to produce free association prompted by an anguished pair of shoes? I aks, with due respect of course, what does this association show us, besides a capacity for writing a prose poem on the occasion of looking at a picture of a pair of shoes by van Gogh? What it shows, I submit, is lack of knowledge about how to look at a picture, and a systematic confusion of literature with painting. These are two distinct defects but they support each other. A painter puts before the eyes of the beholder an infrangible visual object, something to be ravished by the eyes. He does not put before the beholder an occasion for a poem.

It is easy to show that Heidegger does not know how to look at paintings. In order to do so we must remember some of the things we know about the pictures of shoes left us by van Gogh. There are at least three of them that I know of, but since one is a pair of city shoes—the old fashioned kind with elastic on both sides—that one we can dismiss entirely. The other two could be peasant shoes. There is one in Amsterdam in brown and another in Baltimore in blue. We know that the Amsterdam picture was painted early in 1886 and this means it was painted in Paris. This places it at the very least fully one year before the painting in blue that is now in Baltimore and is signed *Vincent* and dated 1887. The latter is therefore closer to the Arles period than the Amsterdam one. We also know that the Amsterdam picture is a painting of van Gogh's own shoes. The Baltimore picture is a painting of the same shoes. Neither is therefore the picture of shoes belonging to a female peasant. But we need not display the profound erudition I have given evidence of here (gathered from a museum catalogue and a quick glance at the three volume edition of *The Complete Letters of Vincent Van Gogh*) since all of us have seen many drawings and paintings of peasants by van Gogh, and we know that they are always represented as wearing wooden shoes. I do not remember a van Gogh peasant wearing leather boots.

The eye of a man interested in painting is ravished, not because the canvas tells his mind a story—which it may or may not do, and still remain as aesthetic object—but because it was painted by a painter of great ability; which is to say by a painter who, endowed with inborn talent, developed that talent by applying himself to the techniques of the painter, techniques of a draftsman and colorist, seeking in and through them to express in color on canvas whatever he sought to express. And just as a poem cannot be translated or paraphrased, neither can a painting be rendered in words. What can be rendered in words are the facile quasi-metaphysical associations of the man who, standing before the painting, deceives himself that he is looking at the painting, when what he is doing is using the painting as a stimulus for an exercise of his literary imagination.[4]

What does Heidegger tell us about the painting as a painting? Nothing whatever. It needs to be repeated: *nothing whatever.* On the basis of what he says about van Gogh, how can we distinguish the work of, say, Millet (who was also interested in peasants and in whom van Gogh was interested) from the work of van Gogh? And will anyone who has not read Heidegger find that under the soles of the shoes "there slides the loneliness of the field-path as the evening declines"? Why not the dawn? Why not the August sun, beating fiercely at noon? If Heidegger discovered the values and meanings in the shoes he ought to be able to tell us how he did it. I confess that I remain unconvinced and

amused. Unconvinced by the emotive outpourings of our philosopher; amused by the fact that men, men endowed with rest-
less intellects and experience of the world, can fall for the spiel;
and further amused by the fact that no one, reading our philosopher, seems so far to have broken out in irreverent Gargantuan
guffaws.

It is true, of course, that the eyes see in depth or they do
not see at all. We interpret what we see, and the interpretation
is something we perform by bringing to bear on what is present
to the innocent eye the totality of our experience. This is the
fact to which Dewey referred when he spoke of "funded meanings." We do not see sense-data. But eyes that know how to
see paintings, yield themselves to control by what is there in
front of them and find what is there worthy of seeing. Not
Heidegger. Confronted with a painting of a worn pair of shoes,
he undertakes a remarkable act of metaphysical *Einfühlung* that
enables him to find in the shoes whatever he feels like reading
into them.

But to deliver metaphysical solemnities in the manner of
Heidegger is not the only way to disregard a painting. Another
is to write a poem about a painting—a poem inspired by it and
full of historical allusions—passing that off for a verbal description of it, without being aware that it has as little to do with
the painting as Heidegger's emoting about first and last things
has to do with van Gogh's picture. This is the job Walter Pater
palmed off on us as a description of a painting by Leonardo of an
Italian wench with a smile that generations of critics have agreed
to call enigmatic.[5]   Since Pater was a gifted writer of prose
poetry, his rhythmic euphonies, like those of Sir Thomas
Browne, or of Newman, or of the Joyce of *The Portrait,* ravish
the ear and reverberate in the mind of those who love such
sonorities. Pater's paragraph about La Gioconda is beautifully
cadenced. Indeed it exhibits Pater at his paterish best. But the
paragraph is not about Leonardo's picture nor about the woman
who sat for it (about whom, if I am not misinformed, we know
only the very little that Vasari has told us). Pater's paragraph
is a concoction of the not altogether exiguous historical resources
that could serve a *fin-de-siècle* imagination on the loose.

Note that there is no law, civil, aesthetic, ecclesiastical,

Platonic or any other kind, forbidding a writer to write a poem
inspired by a painting, any more than there is a law forbidding
the writing of a poem inspired by another poem—by a translation, say, of Homer. But that is not what is at issue. What is at
issue is the fact that Walter Pater wrote a poem, inspired by the
painting, never warning us that it has very little to do with the
painting. Of course I do not believe that he was aware of the
deception he practiced on himself and on his readers.

These considerations should make clear that there is a difference in kind between intransitive attention to a picture or a
poem—or to anything, for that matter, to a piece of driftwood,
or to a can of soup or a picture of one—and the transitive attention I have exemplified in connection with pictures by Leonardo
or van Gogh. As for the meandering of the first critic we con-
templated, very little can be said about it, since that kind of
mental process would elude transcription even by a Joyce.

Note that what I said above about "pure art" applies to
intransitive attention. I have written about a conceptual entity
and not about actual experience. How often and how close to
such a concept our actual responses come is a question that cannot be answered in general terms. I have evidence that responses
of a fully intransitive nature actually occur. They seem to be
rare and fleeting, but they do take place. But were the evidence
to be rejected, it would not damage the argument. Note also
that a number of varieties of transitive attention have been classified (by Henri Delacroix and Vernon Lee, for instance, and
other writers as well), although varieties of response have usually
been examined in order to arrive at relativistic conclusions that I
do not accept.[6] Note, also, that classification of varieties of
transitive response must necessarily be fluid, since a given response acquires its identity from the interests that stimulate it,
and our interests in objects of perception are as complex and
multifarious as they are heterogeneous. But the responses of the
three writers I have looked at are enough to make the point.
And that is, if I may be forgiven the iteration, that there is a difference in kind between what I have called the aesthetic and
other modes of perception. To erase the difference has serious
consequences for aesthetics, for criticism, and for the docent process. For this reason the iteration should be forgiven. The thesis
that the function of art is to serve as a cognitive instrument, or as

a tool of socio-political indoctrination, or as a means of moral or religious edification—which of course it can—arises from a nest of confusions, the chief of which, I suggest, is the failure to distinguish at the theoretical level, our modes of perception.

Because a large number of misunderstandings are current about the nature of the intransitive experience, it seems desirable to dwell on it further. What it involves is a kind of response that anyone acquainted with the demonology of our regnant philosophical orthodoxy ventures to characterize only with the greatest reluctance, because the *mot juste* for it is one of the faugh-words of our sophisticated vocabulary—a term that roils the stagnant minds of a large number of our "modern" contemporaries. The experience is *ecstatic.* But all that is meant by the term (*ekstasis*) is that we are led to *stand out* of ourselves. In those rare, fleeting moments when the mind takes full possession of an aesthetic object we reach fullness of awareness, and it is just as correct to say that the object takes possession of the mind as to say that the mind takes possession of the object. Captor and captive become one. All there is during the precious moment is an object in its full effulgence and compelling fascination. The mind for which the object is there has undergone an eclipse, it is fully gone, it has disappeared completely. Where has it gone? The object with which it has merged, in which it has lost itself, by which it has been embraced and devoured—this object has taken it, and one's awareness of oneself is no longer there. The awareness of our identity and of our body, the more or less constant awareness of ourselves, the more or less distinct feeling of selfhood that we normally carry with us in varying degrees of conscious awareness, is no longer telling us that we are there. All there is is the object by which we have been captured. And at this point in the transaction we can say that the object is present in itself and by itself, and is not—not at the conscious level, that is—an object in a relational complex of which the *s* term is a functioning term in awareness. This statement will make a lithic mind cry, "Contradiction!" And for that kind of mind the statement no doubt does seem to contradict what I have said about the transaction.

But if the self has disappeared, how do I distinguish the object which is there for a mind in the successful aesthetic experience from the merging of the soul with God in the mystic trance, or the Platonic contemplation of the Good of which we are told in the *Symposium* and in the Seventh Epistle? I can only guess without confidence the answer to this question, since it has never been given me to undergo the mystic or the Platonic experience—assuming that they are two and not one, as they most likely are. But if I can go by what mystics tell us, there is a difference between the aesthetic object that is before a mind that has merged with it, and the blinding flash (or is it a long moment?) of illumination and relief that must take place when the mystic achieves his consummation. However this is a subject on which I do not care to exhibit my ignorance.

It may be objected that when one reads a poem as history or psychology one is not reading poetry but history or psychology, and yet when one reads a poem as poetry, one reads it in the same way one reads history or psychology, and that there is therefore no need to invent a distinct mode of response and to call it aesthetic. At least two replies must be made to this argument. The first is that the distinction between transitive and intransitive attention was not invented but discovered—by Vernon Lee, for instance, who did not use the terms as I do and, as suggested above, arrived at conclusions I deem inadmissible. The second is that the denial of the distinction sets us back to the pseudo-clarification of the man who denies the reality of the aesthetic experience. The difference between the transitive and the intransitive response is that between a man who looks at a painting of a pair of shoes to undertake an act of psychometaphysical *Einfühlung,* or at a painting of an Italian wrench in order to write an historical poem about it, and the man who looks at a work in order to see (with whatever scrupulous care he can bring to the act of seeing) what is there and only what is there.

The next point is that the denial of an identifiable aesthetic experience must go still further than I have taken it. It must either deny that there are any such things as aesthetic objects altogether or it should assert that they exist by themselves and in themselves and can be apprehended as aesthetic by anyone who attends upon them in any old way. The first assumption does not seem to me worthy of serious consideration. The second could easily be challenged by asking the man who makes it to submit a definition or description or account of an object that functions as an aesthetic object in and by itself, irrespective of the way in which it is approached.

Further, to assert that we read a poem in the same way we read history and sociology is to assert that there is no difference between the mental processes involved in our response to an aesthetic object and the processes of ideation involved in thinking through scientific problems—the selection of the proper data for observation, the making and testing of hypotheses, which is to say, the application of the proper scientific methods to phenomena. Nevertheless the writer who denies the difference between transitive and intransitive attention distinguishes between the objects of scientific inquiry and aesthetic objects. Since he does not distinguish them in terms of the response elicited by stimuli functioning as a whole in a certain way, he must distinguish them by traits the stimuli possess *in* and *by themselves,* the presence of which in one set and the absence of which in the other, enable him to make the distinction. But if objects of cognitive inquiry or aesthetic objects possess such traits *in* and *by themselves,* how can we use the same object—the same canvas, say—now aesthetically and now as a cognitive document? Take "The School of Athens." To the man interested in art it says one thing, to the historian of philosophy it says quite another. But in one sense it is the same thing: the same canvas, the same lines, pigments, composition, and the rest. The transitive spectator tells us that his response to it is the same whether he looks at it as a historical document or as an aesthetic object. What then has changed in the thing that enables him to say that the same thing is now an historical document and now an object of aesthetic contemplation?

Here, then, is the challenge to any one who dismisses the aesthetic experience as non-existent. These are questions to which he has to turn.

One last observation on this topic: The aesthetician who says that there is no such thing as a distinctive aesthetic experience, in spite of empirical evidence adduced by those who would define it in terms of intransitive attention, seems to be arguing that because he has not the faintest notion of what an intransitive experience is, there is none. These are people who cannot see that others may not suffer from their own limitations. Indeed they belong to a well known subspecies of human animal: they are the descendants of those sapient Aristotelians whom Galileo invited to look through his little tube and who replied that they did not have to look because they knew there was nothing to be seen.

3

There are a number of qualifications and reservations to be appended to the concept of art I have advanced, some of which ought to be dwelt on. The first is this: What can it mean to read a poem of the length of *The Brothers Karamazov* intransitively? One can read a short lyric intransitively, and look at a picture of not too large a size in the same way, and listen to a piece of music of moderate length. But the nine hundred and more pages of a complex novel? A long symphony? A picture of the size of Rembrandt's *Night Watch*? Hardly, says the critic.

The question assumes that what is meant by "intransitivity" is "all at once," or "instantaneous." If this were so, I should have to acknowledge that large objects, whether in a spatial or temporal sense, cannot be perceived intransitively. For one cannot read, in a sustained single act of attention, a novel some nine hundred pages in length. And one cannot see in an *Augenblick* a canvas the size of Rembrandt's *Night Watch*. And of course the same holds for a symphony or a concerto.

The answer is that it is not possible to respond aesthetically in an instant to any object, however small. To grasp what is involved we must recall the distinction made by Dewey between "recognition" and "perception." Recognition is a response that approaches automatic, stereotyped or purely conditioned SR behavior, by means of which we hastily and not too distinctly 'place," as we call it, an object—by means of which we name it, or distinguish it roughly as of a kind, or in some way or other mark it off. "Perception" is intently exploratory and takes time. It is deliberate. It seeks to grasp in full an object present before the mind in its full identity as a gestalt. It seeks to grasp this object in its uniqueness and not as a kind or as a member of a kind. Aesthetic perception—and here I may be parting company with Dewey—seeks to grasp the immanent meanings that constitute a unified whole. And it dwells, when successful, with such rapt attention on the object that we can say in an almost literal sense that the subject's self-awareness (the reflexive sense of ourselves we always carry with us) disappears. If we must say of the object that it is there for a mind, it must be added that we know this before and after the experience but that at its peak we cannot say it. During the experience, all there is is the object; nor is there, for a consciousness which is crowded by the object, a self which can assure us that it is there. The self has been captured and erased. In order for the object to effect its capture the captive mind contributes its intense, focused attention upon the object. And in its unified organization the object performs the capture, erasing self and ambient world in one successful eradication, leaving the object.

But, of course, in reading a long novel or listening to a long composition we do not have the object before us all at once, any more than we can have a painting wholly and fully there all at once. The work comes to us as an organized object that we survey in our minds, with the difference that surveying a painting of, say, no more than six by three feet, is achieved by a mere shift of the eyes: whereas surveying a novel, in order to discover its organization, involves an act of concentrated recollection in which we perhaps select prominent episodes and characters, and put them forward in our memory while keeping in the background others that we consider of minor importance. But we have a sense, however vivid or vague, of the wholeness of the object, and it is to this sense of its wholeness that we refer aspects or components of it when we wish to test whether our organization is adequate.

The organization of the object is the reader's responsibility and one beset with pitfalls. The test of whether we have succeeded—and it is always, of course, a matter of degree—is to ask ourselves whether we have found the interrelationship of the various components of the object to one another and to the whole they make up. If we seek the organization of a novel, we grasp episodes, scenes, events, and agonists in their mutual interrelationships as we progress to a determination of the relative order of rank they attain in the developing action. If we use the novel for rumination—as a springboard for our own associative ramblings—we may be enjoying a most valuable experience, but we cannot be said to be enjoying the object, for the object is hardly in possession of our mind. If we agree with Henry James about Dostoevsky's and Tolstoy's novels we cannot read them as poems. For in principle it is impossible to discover the organization of large, loose, baggy monsters or fluid puddings. When James thought about them, his aesthetic sensibility was outraged. But the vast continent that is *The Brothers* can be grasped as a whole if one is willing to discover its unity and not to ask that it have the kind of unity one seeks to achieve in one's own work. *The Brothers* does not have the tight unity of *The Ambassadors* or *The Portrait of a Lady*. But it is not without its own kind of unity. In order to bring this topic to a close all I need do is quote D. H. Lawrence, who said about his own work: "They want me to have form, and that means their pestiferous, ossiferous, skin-and-grief form, and I won't." James' form is not a pestiferous, ossiferous, skin-and-grief form. But neither are Dostoevsky's and Tolstoy's novels the large, loose, baggy monsters or the fluid puddings that James thought they were.

I mean it seriously when I assert that the wool-gatherer may be enjoying a most valuable experience—for him. All I am entitled to assert is the difference in kind between the experience of the wool-gatherer and that of the intransitive attender. The relative values of these experiences cannot be decided by the aesthetician. This is a distinctly moral question, by which I mean that it is a question dependent upon moral criteria that enable a man to place certain experiences high on a value scale and relegate others to a lower place. I am of course entitled further to assert that whatever the value of the wool-gathering experience, however highly it may be placed in a moral scale, even if it be placed higher than the value of intransitive attention, the wool-gatherer cannot claim to enjoy or realize the values of the man who attends intransitively. Those are unique to the mode of attention given to the latter.

But what is the value of attending to art as art, I may be asked, when I have acknowledged that it can be attended to with profit for a large number of ends other than the aesthetic? The answer is that it is only when we attend to an art object as art— when we have fully grasped as an organized unit its immanent

meanings in their full presentational immediacy, in rapt attention—that we find out what the object presents. Until we achieve
such a grasp we do not know whether we have merely selected
from the object those aspects we are sympathetic or unsympa-
thetic to. This is what liberal and conservative critics, both, do
to Dostoevsky, when they read him as if he were arguing for the
ideology that he espoused as a man. He attempted to do so in
The Possessed, coming close to doing what he set out to do and
what his critics, liberal and conservative alike, expect of him. In
the other three great novels, I believe it can be proven that Lawrence's dictum applies:

> Oh give me the novel. It's the novel I want to hear.
> As for the novelist, he's usually a dribbling liar.

I want to know what the work of art presents, the whole work,
as distinct from those aspects of it I abhor or agree with, because
I am convinced that as a general rule what a successful work of
art imparts is something that cannot be grasped without its aid.
When the rule is refuted, when my insight is superior to that of
the poem, I can look for the fault, not in myself, as I usually
try to do when I find fault with an object of art, but in the work.

These statements do not seem to me to require further
elucidation. When we consider them carefully they turn out to
be an analytic assertion. How can we claim acquaintance with an
object of art, or knowledge, or possession of it, unless we make
the effort to get acquainted with it and to some extent succeed?
If we are interested in taking possession of an object, there seems
to be only one way of doing it, and that is actually to get as
thoroughly acquainted with it as possible. And this is done when
we ascertain how it is put together, out of what materials, according to what design, and for what end. It may be possible
to become sufficiently acquainted with a theory to justify the
claim that one knows it, by making raids into its interior from
various points at its perimeter, without carrying on an organized
and thorough exploration of the whole territory. I doubt it, but
I shall allow it because I do not want to argue the point here.
However that be, I am confident that it is not possible to achieve
the end of the aesthetic experience—if the end is full possession
of the object—by using the object as an associative device, or by
attending to it in any other way than the intransitive mode. To

gain a full grasp of an aesthetic object we must grasp it as an organized whole.

4

It should not be difficult to see that the concept to art that I have presented here is a highly restrictive one. I do not apologize for this fact but put it forward, rather, with pride, for I find no use for conceptual schemes or definitions that include anything and everything and exclude nothing. Such definitions set no ends, they limit nothing. The purpose of a theoretical organization of a segment of experience is to clarify it and to distinguish it from other segments. This involves excluding those objects belonging properly to other segments of experience that do not belong properly to the segment to be analyzed—or in which, for any reason, we are not interested.

Among the kinds of objects that we normally think of as imaginative literature and might include in a definition of poetry, there is a kind that the concept of art here advanced necessarily excludes, and that is satire. A satirical work says something about our world, it is referential and didactic. What ends satire may seek to achieve I cannot stop here to consider. Enough to acknowledge that if it is read intransitively we prevent it from fulfilling its end. It ceases to be satire and turns into something else—into pure art.

Is this possible? I do not see why not. I do not believe I could do it any longer, but I once read *Gulliver* with an innocent mind. It was a child's edition in Spanish and to me, then, *Gulliver* was a delicious tale that fascinated me, held me captive, and that I fully enjoyed. It was not until quite a number of decades later, when I read it in order to teach it to a class, that I read the *Gulliver* that Swift wrote for mature readers. The innocence gone, both from the book and from the reader, I read *Gulliver* the way it was intended to be read: as the powerful, the savage, indictment of man that it is.

But how do I answer the arguments of those critics who are said to be trying to reinstate historicism? I do not know how to answer them for the simple reason that I have not been able to read them. However, I do not see how, in one sense, history can be kept out of our attention to objects of art. If what we want is full possession of an object, we have to be fully familiar with its symbolic conventions. It is probably the case that a student today reading Hemingway, let us say, needs no knowledge of the American language other than that which he brings with him to his reading. But neither the student nor his teacher can read Shakespeare without a glossary. The mature teacher may no longer need it. But once he did. The student certainly does, and will continue to need it for a long time. It is my impression that students who read *Emma* do not run into serious trouble with the language of the novel. This is of course true only in a very superficial sense. There are only very few words in the novel that they do not know. "Landaufarouche" is one of them. But beyond the surface it is not history that is required for taking full possession of *Emma*. What is required is an ear for the complex felicities of Jane Austen's language, a discerning mind for the ironies, and considerably more, all of which must be imparted to the student before he is in a position to read *Emma* with profit in the intransitive mode.[7] But it may be desirable to bring out explicitly the fact that I have been discussing the point on the assumption that the teacher and the student are interested in coming into full possession of a poem. There are arduous preparations to be made towards that end. But the goal is the full intransitive experience.

This is not to say that a work such as *Emma* cannot be placed in historical perspective, whatever that may mean and however that may be done. Nor is it to deny that it can be used as a historical document, nor to deny that it can be used as a springboard for the reading of an edifying lecture on the ungenerous attitude of Jane Austen and her class towards the men and women who were building the wealth of England at the time. Emma's attitude towards Mr. Martin and towards Augusta Hawkins is not generous. Jane Austen exposed Emma's attitude towards the young farmer. But she justified Emma's rejection of Mrs. Elton. It can be argued that she probably felt threatened by the class to which Mrs. Elton belonged as well as outraged by its vulgarity. Thus Mrs. Elton becomes a "representative of a class," and the teacher is in a legitimate position to speak of the class structure of England at the beginning of the last century.

He can follow up with a discussion of the threat that the new wealth presented to the genteel landed gentry that Emma Woodhouse and her future husband, Mr. Knightley, represent. Where the teacher goes from here depends on the resources of his knowledge, his time, and, alas, how little he cares for literature and how much for facile social history.

If, then, the only way to take full possession of an object of art is to take possession of its meanings as an organized unity, in full presentational immediacy and by means of rapt intransitive attention, it would seem to follow that whether our interest is in the object for its transitive meanings and values, whether sociological, political, moral or any other kind, the first and indispensable step is to take possession of it as fully as we can, which is to say, to take intransitive possession of it.

NOTES

[1] Published in *The Philosopher Critic,* ed. Robert Scholes (Tulsa, 1970), pp. 13-39.

[2] *Creation and Discovery* (New York, 1955); reissued as a paper back by Henry Regnery Company (Chicago, 1966). *The Artistic Transaction and Essays in Theory of Literature* (Columbus, Ohio, 1963). "Dostoevsky: Philosopher or Novelist," *Modern Age,* Vol. 9, No. 3 (Summer, 1965), pp. 302-309. "Philosophy of Culture, Aesthetics, and Criticism: Some Problems," *Texas Quarterly,* Vol. LX, No. 1 (Spring, 1966), pp. 231-241. And "Reply to Some Criticisms," in *Criticism, A Quarterly of Literature and the Arts,* Vol. IX, No. 2 (Spring, 1967), pp. 123-141.

[3] Martin Heidegger, "The Origin of the Work of Art," in *Philosophies of Art and Beauty, Selected Readings in Aesthetics from Plato to Heidegger,* ed. Albert Hofstadter and Richad Kuhns (New York, 1964).

[4] One need not be a van Gogh scholar to know that he was not a follower of Clive Bell or Harold Rosenberg. He endeavored to express in his paintings considerably more than one can find in painters who exclude literature from their canvases. In a letter to his brother, Theo, he writes about a picture he would like to send him:

> I have tried to make it clear how these people, eating their potatoes under the lamplight, have dug the earth with the very hands they put in the dish; and so the painting speaks of manual labor, and how they have honestly earned their food. I wanted to give the impression of quite a different way of living than that of us civilized people. . . .

And he continues:

> All winter long I have had in hand the threads of this fabric, and have searched for a definite pattern; and though it has taken a rough, coarse aspect, nevertheless the threads have been selected carefully and according to certain rules. And it may prove to be a real *peasant picture. I know it is.*

In his letters to Theo we find a number of similar references. But note carefully that it is van Gogh who underlines the last few words. The defender of Heidegger could argue that while Heidegger might have gone too far afield in his description of what is to be seen in the picture of the shoes, he is following the intentions of van Gogh. There are a number of points to be made in reply to this defense. The first is that van Gogh writes of searching for a pattern and following rules. This is to say that in his letters—and not only in the one from which I have quoted—he speaks as a painter, a craftsman, trying to do in color on a canvas certain things. In Heidegger's account there is no hint at all of this important fact. And it is here that we would have to look for the difference between reading literature from a canvas and looking at a picture as a picture. Consider next that it is a question as to whether van Gogh could have succeeded in painting what he writes Theo he set out to paint. He could have painted gnarled hands that have done hard work. But whether he could have distinguished the hands of a peasant that have dug the earth from those of a city worker who handles a monkey-wrench to earn his living is questionable. He could have done it iconographically, but van Gogh did not use iconography to tell more than painting could, in a purely graphic way, tell. The last consideration is that the argument has overlooked the fact that I am comparing Heidegger's associations with the paintings and not with van Gogh's intention as expressed in his letter. The question is whether in the painting we can find what Heidegger first reads into it in order to take it out. Anyone who has read van Gogh's letters can extrapolate from them. It takes common knowledge of van Gogh's life and sympathies. Possessed of knowledge of van Gogh's sympathy for the peasants and of the life he lived in the Borinage, we can read all sorts of stories into the canvas. Van Gogh's life and interests as a painter are pitifully rendered in his letters. See *The Complete Letters of Vincent van Gogh, with reproductions of all the drawings in the correspondence.* 3 vols. (New York Graphic Society, Greenwich, Connecticut, n.d.) or a more accessible but smaller collection, *Dear Theo, The Autobiography of Vincent van Gogh,* ed. Irving Stone (Garden City, 1946), p. 342.

[5] I would not insult the reader by directing him to Pater's famous paragraph. But it is not an insult to remind him that Yeats cut up into uneven lines part of the paragraph and printed it as verse in his *The Oxford Book of Modern Verse.*

[6] A number of these are found in Vivas and Krieger, *The Problems of Aesthetics* (New York, 1953), pp. 277-304. Of course every account of the aesthetic experience is an account of a mode of response. The importance of taking account of the varieties, and the problem to which the

varieties give rise, I discussed in "Contextualism Reconsidered" in *The Artistic Transaction*, particularly pp. 189-193.

[7] I discussed this problem in "Criticism, Intrinsic and Extrinsic," *Creation and Discovery*, pp. 161-173.

Critical Assizes

1

A number of the theories that control criticism today, particularly the theories of critics that believe no theory of criticism is necessary to practice their trade, are open to radical objections on theoretical grounds. They do a great deal of harm to our proper intercourse with literature and therefore to the humanities and, as a consequence, to the quality of our life. A few of these will be examined here. The examination was prompted by the recent reading of a discussion of the relation of literature to philosophy in which no awareness was discernible of the indispensable requirements that must be met to achieve an acceptable elucidation of the problems the book took up. The reading of this book brought to mind other theories that I have long thought were in error. I need not mention the name of the author who started me off on these animadversions or the name of his book or the names of the other writers but one whose views will be criticized, because in one formulation or another, these views are widely current and are found controlling a great deal of the criticism we read. Since the remarks that follow are not personal, I need not mollify my expression for the sake of the courtesy I acknowledge one writer owes another with whom he disagrees; I can say bluntly that the theories here scrutinized, particularly those that initiated this essay, can hardly be called serious.

They are not serious because questions about the functions of literature are philosophical questions and cannot be discussed unless the writer accepts the strictures to which philosophers submit without bridling. To answer the question about the nature of literature and its functions a fully worked out aesthetics is required—as I have had occasion to point out elsewhere.

It is desirable before beginning to make a prefatory remark:

the different conceptions of the function of literature defended or presupposed by critical discussions of works of literature are determined by the different interests of the critics; in our society, interests cannot be controlled by critics, aestheticians, or anyone else. Is the aesthetician's job, then, solely to point out the pluralism of functions, to ascertain the interests that determine them, and to add that about interests there can be no more dispute than about taste? Yes, if he is an aesthetician and not a moralizer or legislator this is all he can do. But it must be borne in mind that a complete description of a function includes an account of the benefits that it brings with it and those that it excludes or undervalues.

2

The first view to be examined is the belief that philosophical positions can be found in works of literature. If philosophical positions are unsupported formulations of some sort such as those uttered by the characters or the author editorially, we have to grant that they are also found in works of literature. For instance, we find in *The Possessed* and in *The Brothers Karamazov* one of the articles of faith of Dostoevsky-the-man. In *The Brothers* the idea appears at least four times. As Father Zossima puts it, "every one is really responsible to all men for all men and for everything." But this unsupported statement is not a philosophical position, and to support it one would have to write a treatise on Christian ethics, for asseverations are not philosophy. In the novels nothing like this requirement is met. However seriously Dostoevsky-the-man took his views, the novelist was not interested in giving us a reasoned and sustained argument in favor of his belief, although the man thought that *The Brothers*, for instance, established his faith and "answered Ivan." Philosophy is not to be found in Dostoevsky's novels. Philosophy is an activity through which illative conclusions are reached. Otherwise put, statements claiming truth value come in systems, in the absence of which all that can be said of them is that they are mere opinions. Theologians claim that there are truths of faith—in the epistemic sense, not in the sense of trust—which are possessed by the recipients of grace. All I can say here about this claim is that if there are, they are the only kind of truths that can be formulated in an unsupported statement.

The assumptions, the categorial scheme, the definitions, and the method that are required to obtain philosophical knowledge are not supplied by art to the literary man; what art supplies him with are the means worked out by his predecessors, which added to his own talent and the matter for his novel, enable him to write a story. Readers who are not interested in a serious analysis of the relationship between literature and philosophy frequently take the feeling of vividness, of lucidity, of force, and sometimes even of splendor that literature elicits from them to be a sign that what they read is true; but what they are enjoying is a conviction, a feeling.

Another aspect of the same defect appears when one considers the author's belief that there are views or attitudes that are found in works of art expressed in language that is not philosophical but that can be put into philosophical language by the critic. One is led by this assertion to wonder what the author means by philosophy. Clearly he believes that the philosophical nature of a view or attitude depends on its linguistic wrapping. Take a thug to Saville Row and he becomes a gentleman. Take attitudes or views and dress them up in philosophical language and they become philosophical. But is there a philosophical language? I'll grant a proposition that, without careful qualification, is doubtful; still, what makes a position philosophical is not the language in which it is expressed but the way it is supported, the reasons given for its tenability. These may be drawn from any school, and the language can be academic English, Papiamento, or the Taki-taki spoken by the blacks of Guyana. So long as reasons are given for the statement, it can with full justice claim philosophical status. Philosophy is philosophizing; there is a radical difference in kind between philosophizing and mere asseverations.

3

Take next the assertion that works can be masterpieces of philosophy and literature at the same time and in the same respect. This is not true, although it is true that one can read some works of philosophy as literature—Plato's *Phaedo* and *Symposium,* to cite two unimpeachable instances. There are works about which experts disagree, some people taking them to be philosophy and others a species of conceptual poetry. *Thus Spake Arathustra,* is an instance of this kind of writing. However we classify books like *Zarathustra* the need remains, before we can discuss the relation of philosophy to literature, of defining the way we intend to use the terms. These definitions can be no more than stipulations of usage; but without them we have no way of distinguishing works like *The Imitation of Christ,* the prose writings of San Juan de la Cruz (not the *Cánticos*) from *A Treatise of Human Nature, Notes From the Underground,* and *Middlemarch.*

It is necessary to distinguish these classes of works because a work of philosophy like *Phaedo* or *Symposium,* is read in an entirely different way when it is read as literature than when it is read as philosophy. Let me say parenthetically that I am speaking here, as I shall be for the most part throughout, in ideal terms. To return, the point is so important that I beg to be allowed to call the reader's attention to it with emphasis. Although the same book can be read as literature and in an indefinite number of other ways, if philosophy is systematic argument no work of literature can be read as philosophy; arguments found in it do not function as arguments but as components of the drama. No one wanting knowledge about the relation of church and state in Russia in Dostoevsky's time would go for such knowledge to the brilliant chapter in *The Brothers Karamazov* in which Ivan's essay on the subject is discussed.

Today, if I am not mistaken, the most popular way of reading literature is not as philosophy but as sociology, although it may be that the psychoanalytic way of reading rivals the sociological. Indeed, today the difference between literature and sociology has intentionally been erased by writers of books that librarians classify as novels and by critics who tell their readers what to find in the books they read. I have a vague memory of a discussion by a critic a number of decades ago about the threat of sociology to the novel. The threat can only be felt by people who cannot make the necessary discriminations.

That the different ways in which a book is read turns it into different kinds of objects would not be the case if we accepted the assumption that what is to be found in a book, its content, is there by itself and does not require the mind, with its equipment and its diverse ways of approaching a text to apprehend it.

4

In the book that has prompted these comments we are told that literature has always had a fundamental moral purpose, however discredited authors have been as bearers of moral vision. This is a simplistic statement and we need to make important distinctions in order to understand the relationship of literature to morality.

Works of literature can be judged to be moral or immoral most obviously because they are believed to modify our character and our scheme of values or because they may be factors in the lifelong process of *paideia.* There may be critics who honestly believe that literature has no effects on the soul; these people are ignorant of the way in which literature affects character, usually indirectly and subtly. But many who deny the effect of literature on character can hardly be taken at their word, for they are sophisticated persons. The men and women—including a bishop—who testified at the trial of *Lady Chatterley's Lover* either did not know how to read and in all honestly did not see what is to be found in the book or were aware of what is to be found in it and decided that their duty as witnesses for the defense was to defeat the prosecution for the sake of doing away with narrow moralism. If the latter, the conflict between the witnesses for the defense and the prosecution was not a literary issue but a conflict of moralities carried on in literary terms.

That literature, or nearly all of it, has moral effects on the soul is something that I do not put into question. Whether all the arts have moral effects we need not ask here. The evidence for my belief was not gathered systematically, by sociologically approved methods, it is the crystallization of haphazard but fairly close observations of students, conducted throughout a long teaching career.

But although literature has moral effects on its readers, we know that it does not affect all readers in the same way. Indeed I go farther and hold, on grounds I cannot present here, that literature is ineffaceably, indefeasibly, and infrangibly ambiguous. Other factors than the text itself contribute to produce its effects on its readers, effects that are seldom direct and obvious; they are subtle and, because they are mediate and not easy to discern by the individual who enters into a transaction with a work of literature, and much less by others, must be classified as "non-residential." If I am right, a writer does not have complete control over the way his work will affect his readers, since he does not have control over the type of persons they are. The contemporaries of Aeschylus and Sophocles, by and large, were in agreement with these two poets about the moral quality of the effects of their poetry, since the two writers and their public made up a relatively homogeneous group and their audience expected instruction and the poets attempted to give it. But if the writer does not have control over the response his work arouses in his readers, the moral purpose of art cannot be considered to be fundamental.

The phrase, "the moral purpose of art" may also mean that in literature at least, and in some works of graphic art—let us say, in a still life canvas of flowers of Renoir—since "the matter for" the in-formed substance of the works consists to an appreciable extent of meaning and values, it is to the same extent made up of the very stuff of morality. *Middlemarch*—to refer superficially to a profound and complex novel—consists of the relationships of conflict and agreement of Dorothea and Lydgate and the members of each group, relatives and friends; this is the stuff of moral activity and discourse. In this sense one can say that the moral purpose of this novel is fundamental; and this is probably true of a great majority of works of literature. But in one respect only is the in-formed substance of the novel moral; in another respect it is as fundamentally made up of the stuff of art, the forms and devices and means of novelistic expression used by its maker. Whether this is the case with all art I do not believe it is desirable to stop to consider here at length. Goya's *Los estragos de la guerra* no less than *Middlemarch* may be said to be fundamentally moral in purpose in this sense. But what is the fundamentally moral purpose of a canvas by Jackson Pollock?

There is a third sense according to which it may be asserted that some works of graphic art contain, as components of their in-formed substance, meanings and values, although these are not presented by means of iconic signs. This holds for other arts, although whether it holds for all of them I do not know; but it is especially true for literature, music and among the graphic arts, at least painting, although the different arts affect different individuals differently. A still life of Cézanne—no more than a few apples on a table covered by a wrinkled tablecloth—gives some viewers a feeling of values and meanings present on the painting to which I can find no better way of referring than by saying in a somewhat stuffy way that they seem to symbolize non-iconically something of cosmic import. Whether this sense or feeling is an indication of something actually in the canvas for the viewer— I believe it is—or of something we are reading into it which is not symbolized by the in-formed substance, is a question very much worth exploring, but one to which I cannot turn without going far afield.

5

There is a view presented in the book under consideration that, when I first read it, I could not believe my eyes that I had read it correctly; I went back several paragraphs to be sure that I was not being misled by a misinterpretation of the context. I was not. We are told that the role of "the philosophical critic" is to express "in language suitable to philosophy. . .views and attitudes which are found in the work in a totally different form, and which are therefore not quite philosophical." The statement is followed a few lines below with the following assertion: "one may extract from Dante's *Commedia* a conception of an orderly universe within which justice and piety reach their fulfillment." The reader is begged to note that the word "extract" is the author's. A number of pages later the same idea regarding the task of the philosophical critic is put in different words, expressing more fully and as a result, in a more blatant manner, the writer's conception of the task of the philosophical critic. One reads that "the task of the critic or interpreter. . .is to bring into the open —often by the intentional sacrifice of the aesthetic qualities, the architectonic structure, the force of the work he is dealing with—

the intellectual theses, positions, and justifications that are rather obscured in the work of art." When one comes upon the second statement one is no longer shocked or astonished, for it is quite clear by then that the author's attitude towards objects he takes to be art permits him to practice the kind of criticism that consists of dismembering the object he criticizes. Had he told us that the dismembering was performed in order to gain a deeper and more comprehensive grasp of the object than before it was performed but that the ultimate objective was to view the object as a whole, he would not be open to criticism. But in the text it is clear that the extraction of vague and obscure truths and their reformulation in clear and distinct terms is its own end. It would not be necessary to stop to criticize the kind of activity he recommended if it were not as widely held as it is.

The objection to extracting vague and obscure truths from literature in order to give them philosophical respectability is that the critic who engages in the act shows no respect for literature. This lack of respect is probably based on the failure to distinguish "the residential function" of art—the function art performs as art—from its non-residential functions; and this failure no doubt arises from the failure to recognize that there are totally different ways of reading the same text; this in turn is probably related to the obscure and vague ideas that critics and even aestheticians have about the sort of activities and products that in the market place are called art, literature, knowledge and truth. But whatever the reason, the man who holds this belief is not aware of the fact that when a work functions as art its organic wholeness controls the reader's attention, thus leading him to enter into a unique relationship with it. I am led to say this because a critic of repute has made an attack on the theory of art as organic. The attack is worthless unless one shows that the idea of literature considered as literature is nonsensical. It may be, but to prove it it must be shown that in principle it is not possible to focus attention on a work for what is found in it and not outside it. And I say in principle, for the fact that few readers are able to read literature as literature and those few seldom succeed in doing so does not imperil at all the fact that literature can be read as literature.

For aesthetics, it is not a question as to whether the turning of the vague and obscure truths that are said to be contained in literature into philosophically acceptable ones is more or less valuable than the reading of literature as literature. This is a moral question. The aethetician can no more decide between the alternatives than he can, as aesthetician, decide that playing chess is more valuable than watching football on television. Having drawn the distinction between the use of literature for its own sake and its instrumental uses, one can observe that morally it is a poor choice to use it instrumentally. For its use as literature there is no substitute. And this holds for all the arts. If I owned a Ming vase I would not use it as a chamber pot. My attitude towards the vase would not be determined primarily by its value in dollars, although it would be stupid to leave this factor altogether out of consideration. But in our world the right of private property is recognized; therefore, although I have no right to dictate to someone else how he should use the Ming vase he owns I do have a right to my opinions and on the subject of the use of a Ming vase I have a strong opinion. A thing of beauty is something to which one owes a kind of reverence.

Be that as it may, when one extracts truths from a work of literature, whatever he may have before him, literature he does not have. A calf—need I say it?—ceases to be a calf when the butcher dismembers it and extracts its commercially valuable components from it. When butchered the calf not only loses its architectonic structure, its force, and its other aesthetic qualities, such as they may be, but it is no longer able to gambol in the field and push its muzzle in eager search for its mother's teat. A butchered calf is not a living animal but a carcass; more valuable commercially it may be than a living calf, but a calf it is not.

But is it necessary to formulate truths that a poet—an Aeschylus, a Sophocles, a Dante, a Shakespeare—is not able to formulate clearly and distinctly? Of course it is. Until the philosophical critic carries out the extractions from the works of these men and tells us what they intended to say but could not, their works remain—well, what do they remain? They remain, of course, interesting because they display aesthetic qualities, because they display architectonic structure and force; but nothing more, absolutely nothing more. As philosophy these works are—well, what are they? Let us put it charitably and say that they cannot compare with the truths the philosophical critic has extracted from them and stated clearly and distinctly in proper philosophical language.

The advantage of this view is that it decreases unemployment by giving the philosophical critic a job. Unless he tackles it the poet (or literary maker, or artist, or whatever you may wish to call him) remains only partially fufilled. Why? Obviously because men like the ones I have mentioned are not competent to express anything but vague and obscure truths. One is reminded at this point of what the French critic, Claude-Edmonde Magny, said of the interpreter of Kafka who provides dialectical constructions for the unfolding of events in the story or novel. Such an effort turns Kafka "into a kind of frustrated philosopher who needs to be explained to himself and others for lack of sufficient power of analysis and abstraction." Miss Magny points out that the act "implies a gratuitous insult."

7

The reverse of this view, frequently encountered, although not found in the book that initiated these animadversions, asserts that the novelist "inserts" (my term) his view into his work by means of a character that functions as his "mouthpiece." One comes across this view even in the work of writers of the sophistication, broad knowledge, clear thinking, and well deserved reputation of an Isaiah Berlin, who in his Romanes Lecture tells us that in one of Turgenev's novels one of the characters is the mouthpiece of the author. To disclose wherein lies the error of this view we have to take up speculative matters of a technical nature that must be treated seriously even at the cost of making the exposition somewhat difficult. Of course, the view is not in error if it is assumed that it is impossible to read literature as literature.

The first step is to make a threefold distinction. I shall refer to Turgenev the person, the man, and the novelist. The man is the Europeanized Russian about whom a great deal is known. We know for instance, that he considered himself a German, as he told Dostoevsky, we know his opinions about the relation of children to parents; we also know that at one time he loaned Dostoevsky money and that he met Henry James in Paris in 1875. It is not necessary to indicate how the term "novelist" will be used. The term "person" is used to refer to the man and the novelist considered as one individual. These stipulations of usage are arbitrary, but the terms refer to substantive distinctions.

It is of course true that in *Fathers And Sons* we find a character who speaks for Turgenev the man. It is also true that Turgenev the person believed that he discovered his characters rather than created them. But he was nevertheless a novelist, a genuinely creative artist, and when the person of Turgenev sat down to write the novelist took over, pushing the man off the chair. This is not an infrequent event; it happened to Dostoevsky who, after learning about the Nechaev affair towards the end of 1869, decided to write a pamphlet and turned out *The Possessed.* It also happened to George Eliot. And something somewhat similar may have happened to Turgenev himself, for he said towards the end of his life that he wrote *Fathers And Sons* without volition. Indeed, this kind of struggle is not rare: a part of the "agony" of creation consists of the struggle for dominance between the novelist and the man.

The views of the man are not kept out of the novel; they enter it along with those components of his experience that the novelist considers relevant to the job at hand. But they are not present in the novel as the man holds them. A mouthpiece may speak in the novel for the man; but he speaks as one voice of the chorus and it is the song that is the mouthpiece of the maker, of the novelist. There may be solos in the song, but they do not derive their character solely from themselves in isolation from the rest of the song. You can ask the soloist to sing his part when the rest of the singers are not present, but what you then hear is not what can be heard when you are listening to the whole ensemble. If I want to know what Turgenev thought I have to ask myself whether I want to know what the man thought or what the novelist thought; if I don't, what I am doing is jumping unwittingly into a mud puddle, confusing the intention of the man with the novel's intention, and missing the fact that the novel expresses more and less than the opinions and attitudes that constitute the man. Why?

The reason, as succinctly as I can express it, is that the man's mind and the novelist's mind are two different organizations of the person's experience. However honest the man may try to be with himself and however earnestly he may perform what in the catechism I was made to learn as a child was called "an examination of conscience," he is never conscious, or at least he is never fully conscious, of the strategies his mind employs in order, let me put it baldly, to keep itself from seeing the whole of himself in its flattering and unflattering fullness. In actual practice this nullifies the Socratic injunction, for no man can know himself. (It would be wonderfully enlarging of our knowledge of the person of Socrates to get a peep at his psychoanalytic dossier). But the strategies that account for the faulty knowledge the man gains of himself are not the sole causes of his ignorance of himself. The most intelligent and consistent of men tries to organize his experience by means of a kit of poor tools—wireclippers that don't cut, plane blades that are dull, poorly sharpened chisels, and nicked screw drivers, with nothing in the kit in good working order. The man arrives at the idea he has of himself by means of conceptual and dramatic terms ready made, clichés and forms provided by his society in terms of role and rank—all factory made clothes, if I may change the image, that don't fit.

Applying this to Turgenev the man, we remember that among the opinions with which his head was stuffed an important one was about the relationship of parents and children. But since Turgenev the person was not a philosopher, intelligent and clear-headed as he no doubt was, the chances are that he did not systematize his opinions in a satisfactory way, which is to say that he did not rear with them a system of philosophy. Actually we know about the person of Turgenev that he felt deficient as an abstract thinker, but whether he was or not—and he may have been totally mistaken about himself in this respect—we can be certain that when he was impelled to seek coherence and harmony about a particular subject—the relation say about parents and children—the coherence he sought was that of the novelist; he achieved an aesthetic coherence and not a philosophical one. But in an aesthetic whole, it hardly needs be said, all kinds of intellectually conflicting notions can be and are indeed found. This is no objection to a work when considered as an aesthetic whole and it may constitute an aspect of its positive value.

When a person is able to go beyond the heterogeneous jumble of ideas and values that are an essential part of himself—and no doubt many men are—he comes close to the frontier, or he may even cross it, and pass into the territory that Santayana called "literary psychology"; by which he did not mean the psychology of novelists, but if I may be permitted the anachronism, the pre—Watson psychology of philosophers and psychologists. For convenience, although imprecisely, let me call the man who crosses the frontier into literary psychology, a philosophical anthropologist, emphasizing that he is only a philosophical anthropologist of sorts. This man is at least potentially able to write his autobiography, emphasizing again that all he is able to write is some sort of account about himself. He has a more veridical picture of himself and of his world than the man in the street. Compared with a full-fledged professional philosophical anthropologist, his picture remains quite faulty. But that does not mean that the philosophical anthropologist has an utterly adequate picture of himself, in the sense that he has achieved a point by point correspondence between the picture and the reality of which it claims to be a picture. The philosophical anthropologist, I must say it even if it offends his vanity, cannot get a vision of the whole. No one can. He is forced to sacrifice a great deal of what is potentially discernible to the methodological, categorial, and systematic exigencies of his craft. All he can do, all anyone can do, is compare his picture of human reality or of himself with other pictures. The inadequacies which he must learn to live with are his down-payment for the key to his room in The Mansion of Philosophy.

This holds for the novelist no less than for the ordinary man and for the philosophical anthropologist. He too must make sacrifices to his craft. Whether he is able to dive deeper than the philosopher we, or at least I, cannot ask, for I know of no means for sounding the depths or for comparing the result. All we can be sure of is that the novelist dives in a different area of the mind. What he comes up with, I am confident, he grasps concretely in immeditely dramatic terms; he does not dramatize concepts, he grasps drama, concrete action and character, directly. The matter for the novel is a heap of pieces of base metal that the creative alchemy of the maker turns into a shaped jewel of gold.

Here it is necessary to qualify a statement made above. I wrote that the novelist pushes the man off the chair when the person sits down to write. It should be added that the man is not always defeated, but that one of the conditions of the high success of a novelist is his ability to overcome the man. When he does, the characters and their actions develop, so to speak, their own autonomous will; they utter opinions, perform acts, defend and attack causes with a sort of gleefulness, as if thumbing their noses at the man's chagrin, for impotent, he must watch them frustrate his intentions. Conflicts and inconsistencies that the man cannot accept without distress, the novelist accepts, more often than not, I dare say, unaware; for he is not concerned with unanimity of opinion among his characters, indeed he is interested in their differences, and the larger and deeper the amount of conflict he can in-form into his organic whole, the happier he is. Syllogisms and coherence and harmony of theory are for philosophers and unanimity of opinion for Cultural Commissars.

Two other obervations must be made before closing the topic of the relation of the man's theories to the in-formed substance of the novel. Unless I am radically mistaken, a large number of novelists today tend to take themselves seriously as rivals of sociologists and a large number of critics accept their view. Such novelists and critics are, the lot of them, in error. In one sense of course novels are sociological, since they are symbolic constructions of human beings living in groups, or if living alone as Robinson before he met Friday, they live within a culture. In this sense the novels of Henry James' great period are as sociological as the so-called novels written by American Marxists in the thirties, with the qualification that the so-called Marxist novels may have been great propaganda but novels they were not.

As for the critics who take the novelists' view of themselves as sociologists seriously, their irresponsibility is often incredible. I read recently a statement suggested to a critic by a novel to the effect that "the mood of New York in the early twenties was one of laughter." This is a sociological statement but it is utter nonsense. Had the critic said that in the early twenties a number of people, young and old, who drank and danced and whose women were called flappers, laughed a good deal, and that the men and women who lunched at The Algonquin put a lot of effort into thinking up insults that they took to be witty (When you get home, throw your mother a bone) and at which a few thousand people in New York and points West laughed, there could be no objection to this socio-historical statement. But to say that the mood of New York in the early twenties was one of laughter, that the several million people who lived in New York at the time were possessed of a mood of laughter, is to make a statement that passes for serious criticism but that is nonsense. If it is valuable to have an adequate account of historical reality, an account close to what actually happened, the statement is worse than nonsense. As a statement it belongs in the same logical class with my belief—to which I cling tenaciously—that Frenchmen suffer from bad livers; it belongs in a class of irresponsible and sometimes vicious generalizations.

Since it is the author who speaks authentically, aestheticians who take seriously the organic nature of the work of art often have a good deal of trouble with the distinction between form and content. The terms are misleading. The trouble disappears when one remembers that the work of art apprehended for its own sake in its self-sufficiency is not the cadaver the critic dissects, however indispensable the dissection may be for the full comprehension of the self-sufficient object. This is probably the source, or one of the sources, of Croce's antagonism to genres, and the reason Dewey (following Croce, as one suspects) pointed out that what was from one point of view form was from another content. For this reason it is desirable to discard the terms "form" and "content"; it is difficult when we use them not to reify them and to suppose that they are as separable as water and the bucket that contains it.

8

To the extent that the novelist uses his creative imagination, the search for proto-types used by him as matter for the novel can yield only more or less vague similarities between the sitter and the portrait; but however close the similarities may be, they are irrelevant to the reading of the novel as novel. In *Women in Love* there is a picture of a dry baronet of fifty who was always making witticisms and laughing at them heartily in a harsh horse laugh. In the novel the baronet is said to be a sociologist; but we know that the man Lawrence was ridiculing was already, at the time the novel was supposed to be taking place, a well-known philosopher. A great deal is known about other people that Lawrence used as matter for his novel. But I do not believe that light is thrown on the novel as novel by knowledge of the use Lawrence made of his acquaintances. Indeed this kind of knowledge often turns us away from the reading of the novel as novel. It is as valuable to know who sat for the portrait of Hermione as it is to know whether or not Ottoline Morel owned a lapis lazuli paperweight. This kind of knowledge is pursued eagerly by persons who call themselves humanists. They fail to make a distinction between interest in gossip and literary criticism. But let it be clear that the objection is not to the interest in gossip these people display; in our world, which is neither Russia nor China, *Gott sei Dank,* men can pursue any interest they want to so long as they have the means to do so or can get institutions of so-called higher learning to pay them to pursue their interests. Much less is it an objection to biography, an undeniably important activity, of course. The objection is to the confusion of one activity with the other; the reason for the objection is that the confusion does great harm to the proper cultivation of the humanities. Let me add that since my early twenties I have been interested in both Lawrence's novels and in Lawrence the man, and I have picked up with relish every bit of gossip I came across about Lawrence when I was not busy with more important tasks. But while I am the last man to object to interest in gossip, I yield first place to no one who objects to the confusion of gossip wih literary criticism.

But is there nothing that can be said in favor of knowing what the novelist does with his sitters? As biography it is a perfectly legitimate activity. I'll even grant as a possibility that such knowledge may throw light on the novel considered as novel. But the validity of this hypothesis can only be established by an examination of at least one case in the concrete. If and when biographical details about the artist and what he does with his proto-types is shown to throw light on the novel, then that knowledge is a legitimate tool of criticism. But it is the novel the serious critic is interested in. Biographical information remains, for him, forever instrumental.

9

As one would expect, the critic who believes that he can "extract" truths from literature went to the same school as the one who believes that novelists sometimes use mouthpieces, and both were classmates of the man who believes that Kafka's work mirrors the world in which we actually live. The latter is one of those critical clichés that people do not seem to dare to challenge because it is uttered by high authority. But it is utterly false. If the picture to be found in Kafka's novels is claimed to be a picture of the world we actually live in, it must be retorted that Kafka's mirror, on the contrary, was irregularly warped and poorly silvered. To put it literally, the picture he put into his novels was produced by an extremely neurotic mind which, as Kafka sat down to write, seems to have concentrated on those aspects of his experience that generated the actual anxieties, fears, psychic discomforts, and accumulated remorse from which he suffered, these were so extreme as to be different in kind from the miseries through which men of only average neurotic constitution see the world. I shall not draw in detail a contrast between the extreme neurotic features of the picture of the world we find in Kafka's work and the features of the world as we middling neurotics see it. Our picture—the picture of us men in the street, us average people—if we are reflective and keep our eyes open, is not altogether devoid of features that make life, if only intermittently, desirable. If our picture of the world leaves out evil, malice, gratuitous cruelty, pain inflicted arbitrarily by those in power, and some of it as it seems, just for the hell of it, and similar features, our picture is false to our ordinary experience. But if it leaves out love, friendship, goodness, the capacity for self-sacrifice that some otherwise pretty ordinary men and women give evidence of, it is equally false.

How do I know? I have abundant evidence, I'll give you a small piece of it: Read *The Reader's Digest* for a couple of months. I am not suggesting that the blacks and whites that satisfy the millions of middle-brows who read this magazine all over the world give a true picture of the world. All I am saying is that this magazine, with its sugary optimism and its thoroughly bourgeoise picture of present reality will furnish you with evidence that the symbolic presentations found in Kafka's novels altogether lack. Nor am I saying that the picture of the world us middling neurotics have is a true picture of it. Before I could make such an assertion I would have to be sure that my picture of the world is the world as it is in itself and by itself. But this is impossible; all I can do is compare pictures. That is all anyone can do. But it is enough to enable me to point out that the symbolic presentations we find in Kafka's fiction do not mirror the world we actually live in as we see it.

This judgment does not impugn in the least the very high value we ought to put on Kafka's fiction, for its value does not reside in its being a picture of the actual world, but quite the contrary. If I may spoil Oscar Wilde's epigram, Kafka's art does not imitate the world we live in; it's the world we live in that imitates Kafka's art. And this is where the high value of his art resides: It offers us a group of constitutive symbols by means of which we can discern aspects of the world in which we live that, had we not seen them first in Kafka's novels, we would miss in our world—as we see it, of course, always. The thesis that literature mirrors the world was disposed of long ago by Eratosthenes of Cyrene who laid it down that "we may find out where Odysseus travelled when we find the cobbler who sewed the bag of winds."

The theory of imitation that I am quite certain is inadmissible is the Aristotelian version of it, not the Platonic. This erroneous theory finds expression in a multitude of ways. One formulation was advanced some thirty years ago by a well-known critic who told us that the world of art is the actual world and the discourse that tries systematically to record this world is art. Because the record is systematic and objective it gives us knowledge of the actual world. Therefore what is needed is an "ontological" critic. Let's not panic at the big word "ontological." Taken at his word, what the writer is calling for is a critic of *ontos*, of Being. Such a call is silly. What he means is that what is needed is a critic of—well, of what? Of life outside literature which he calls "actual life"? But to criticize life outside literature no literature is needed; editorial writers do it all the time without reference to literary artists.

Let us turn rather to the claim that the artist gives us knowledge. If he gives us knowledge his product must be testable. How is this knowledge tested and by whom? It can only be the reader who does the testing and he tests it by comparing the knowledge offered him by the artist with his own knowledge. It is the reader or the critic he trusts who decides that the picture of the world offered by an Aeschylus, a Dante, a Shakespeare, is true or false. He can apply the test because he has as much acuity, experience, penetration into the texture of human action, grasp of the dubieties and certainties, the felicities and miseries which make up life as the makers I have mentioned. If the critic is a professional American critic today, we know how vast a hoard of knowledge he possesses. The chances are that he spends most of his life in the academic world or in and out of newspaper and magazine offices and cocktail parties in New York—with summers in Vermont. It is this vast hoard of knowledge thus acquired that he brings to the test of the work of the men I have mentioned above and others of equal stature.

But what does "systematic" mean in view of the chaotic and mutually incompataible heterogeneity that literature gives us? The world of Jane Austen may be systematically compatible with that of Céline, but since this does not seem to be the case at first glance, even when we allow for the difference in time and culture, it is necessary, if the assertion is to be taken seriously, to show that *Emma* and *Journey To The End of The Night* constitute a system and are compatible with the rest of available literature. *Emma, Journey To The End of The Night, Agamemnon, King Lear, The Possessed,* the *Divina Commedia*— it may be possible to fit these worlds into a system, which is to say that there is no incoherence among them, but before we believe that it can be done we want to see it done.

10

Another variant of the same error has been advanced by a critic who tells us that literature can be read contextually but that contextual reading can lead back to history and existence. Of course it can; who can keep a reader, unless he is a bully, from going anywhere he wants to go? The question is not whether contextual reading can keep us from, or lead us back to, "history" and "existence"—the theoretical sanction for moving from the text to experience outside of it is given clearly by the distinction between the referential function of art and the proper way of realizing it and the non-referential functions. But this is not all there is to say about the assertion. When one considers what is required to read, whether literature for its own sake or a newspaper for the sake of the information about the events it relates, one realizes how shallow the statement is. For one remembers the utterly obvious fact that in order to be able to read anything in any way at all, one must have knowledge of the language in which the writing is written, and one cannot have this knowledge by distilling from it the history of the people who created it. And the better one knows a language, the more dense and heavy is the historical freight it carries with it. A person who learnt English not at his mother's knees but in his teens can testify with confidence that the basic attitudes and sensibilities that came to him with his second language are not the same as those that came to him with his mother tongue. Those who speak English and write it live in the English language: they can no more live outside it than a man can live outside the atmosphere, whether natural or artificial. We do not carry the language we speak as we carry a package of cigarettes that we can forget to take with us when we leave home. We escape the language in which we live, perhaps, only in our deepest sleep and when we die. But if one lives in the language one cannot be taken back to history since one has never left it. Man lives in history, which is recorded for him whether he is aware of it or not, in the changes the language constantly undergoes. I am not forgetting the culture of which the language is an inextricable component.

Historical inquiry (if I may be permitted the pleonasm) can throw light on the devices employed by the maker to achieve his effects and it can thus lead us to a clearer and more comprehensive grasp of a work of literature. It can do much more still, such as placing a work in its historical lineage. But the man interested in literature and not in something else takes the results of inquiry to be strictly propaedeutic to his reading of the work. When a man interested in literature turns back to the whole, at the completion of a historical excursus, he returns with an enriched mind and he grasps the whole more fully and more deeply than before; but he is still grasping the whole as a self-sufficient whole—if indeed it is, for it may be flawed. When the reader finds it necessary to remove away from the whole, as he may in order to inquire how a device he does not clearly understand functions, he has for the moment become a critic.

Historical inquiry must always precede the apprehension of the whole since no critic is born with innate knowledge of the artistic traditions of his culture. But if all a critic is interested in is to figure out what are the devices that make up a work of art and how they work, and is not concerned with the grasp of the whole, all he is is a critic and not, if I may use the term honorifically, an amateur of literature. But more important yet, if he is not interested in the whole for its own sake, how can he be a successful critic? For only by a reference to the whole can he discern how its components function in relation to one another and to the whole. This point deserves an elaboration that would call for thousands of words to do it justice; here I can only lay it down as an assertion. Let me finish with the statement that adverse criticism of the organismic theory, I have reasons I cannot go into here to believe, arises from lack of interest in the whole. The critic tends to substitute interest in analysis for its own sake for interest in the work. Strange as it may seem, it really is only one instance of which there are an indefinite number in all areas of activity, of the substitution of means for end. But considered from a different standpoint, it really isn't strange, when one remembers that about the whole all the critic can say is: "Once you have grasped how it has been put together, behold it."

Let me ask why is it desirable to go back to "existence"? The desire arises from the acceptance of the dichotomy (alas, I have no lighter word for it) betwen art and "real" life or "existence." Interest in art as art, it is assumed, permits or condemns writers and readers—depending on one's point of view—to live exclusively in a world of pure aesthetic experience but prevents that experience from having any effect on his "real" life. An English critic recently formulated the dichotomy with great clarity. He writes that in the real world we all inhabit personal relationships lead to moral decisions, and the individual life depends on the life of society; reflection on that world leads men to moral philosophy, to politics, to theories of history and sociology. Critics can study literature in a strictly literary way, confining themselves to the quality of the aesthetic experience it offers; they are then "formalists " but since it is the real world that is expressed by poets and novelists, they can work their way *through* literature to moral philosophy or social theory, trying to show what view of man, what theory of ethics, what class attitude or what assumptions about history are implied in this or that novel. We are admonished that the critic should not go through literature by ignoring but by interpreting the form of the work he studies. I have followed the writer fairly closely but not verbatim; the italics of the "through" above are his.

Glance in passing at our old friend imitation; note the familiarity with which it enters without knocking and without making itself heard. The dichotomy depends on it; the work of literature is one thing and "the real world" is another, hence the need to go through literature to the real world.

I shall keep the term "formalist" for the man interested in literature and not in something else, in order to facilitate the discussion, although it grants the non-formalist an initial advantage since it is difficult to drain the pejorative bilge it carries with it. The rejection of formalism is inadmissible because the formalist in literature does not ignore substance any more than the non-formalist can ignore form. Formalists who ignore the substance in-formed in a work of fiction are justifiably open to the reproaches of the non-formalists. Are there any critics who disregard the substance? There are. I once heard a paper by a Frenchwoman on Céline who accounted for his first novel entirely in terms of its form, since she said nothing about its substance. If she had said that this was an important yet partial way of approaching Céline, there would be no ground for adverse criticism. But she did not, thus leaving the listener with the impression that the account covered adequately what was found in the book. But what the formalist—or at least one of them—has to say is that the in-formed substance that is the work of art is self-sufficient and that art when approached as art does not refer beyond itself. This is the reason for objecting to calling such a critic a formalist. But such a critic adds that it is during the period of intransitive attention to the work that it becomes art and that for this reason during this period its non-residential functions are in abeyance. He does not deny, but on the contrary he insists, that the after-effects of an intransitive apprehension of an object are many and that the most important of these is the way in which the work of art works as a constitutive symbol. What the man who approaches literature as literature seeks is as comprehensive and firm a grasp of the presentation as he is capable of gaining. We are thus entitled to conclude that the dichotomy between pure aesthetic experience interpreted as empty of substance and experience of literature that leads us through itself to real life is false. A third alternative, namely the recognition of two moments of our intercourse with literature, the residential and the non-residential, does more than show that the non-formalist's argument is simplistic; it invalidates it utterly.

But what can be said about "pure aesthetic experience"? Nothing until the ambiguity of the term "experience" is resolved. If by experience is meant the inward, purely idiotic, side of one's reaction to an object, all that can be said about the aesthetic experience is that it is an act of intransitive attention that is of high value because of its intensity, because it heightens the sense of life in the person who undergoes it, because it floods one with a surge of throbbing energy. In this sense, for those who have it it is living at its best. But this is not given as a description of the experience of intransitive attention in its idiotic sense, for like all sujective experience it is ineffable. But on this sense of the term "experience" its value is no greater than the value of living intensely in any form. In this sense the aesthetic experience has many rivals.

But if the term "experience" refers to the relational complex of an object that gives rise to a subjective state, then the nature of the in-formed substance that is the sitmulus eliciting and capturing attention upon it can be analyzed. But the formalist claims that the analysis of the in-formed substance is an operation on symbolized meanings and values that in an object functioning as a work of art have no external referential meaning. This is only puzzling to the person who assumes that meaning obtains only when signs refer to something external to them. If that were the case, mathematics and music would always have to be about the world and the idea of pure mathematics would be as odious as the idea of pure music seems to be to many amateurs.

But the dichotomy between literature and life is also false

because the experience of literature as literature is as much a part of real life, for those seriously interested in it, as anything they or man can do: as making love, going to a party, attending with a heavy heart a funeral service for a friend, reacting with repressed irritation at the *niaisseries* of a political speech, as voting or writing to one's senator. It must be said, harsh as it is to say it, that the exclusion of art from real life is the expression of a philistine contempt for literature as deep as it is unconscious. One who is seriously interested in literature as literature, places this interest high in the order of rank of his interests; he does not consider himself to be out of history or existence when he is reading a novel seriously, but on the contrary, he considers activities that keep him from his intercourse with literature as he considers going to the barber; they are not a distraction from real life but something to be endured.

Moreover the critic who is interested in going through literature to moral philosophy, political thought, social theory, or the rest, is a man the seriousness of whose interest in any of these disciplines can be questioned. As a moral philosopher, no novelist or literary critic can tie Kant's shoes or those of Bishop Butler; I know of no novelist or literary critic who as a political thinker can hold a candle to Edmund Burke or Michael Oakeshott, or who as a sociologist can rival Karl Marx or Max Weber. A literary critic who thinks he can go through literature to a well established discipline cultivated by the men I have mentioned or others even of lesser stature is a dilettante in the pejorative sense of this term. He can't take his drink at the bar and take it straight; he sits in a booth and sweetens his bourbon with ginger-ale or, God forgive him, with coca cola.

11

If the views I have examined are erroneous, why have they been held for so long and why are they held almost universally? The error originated with the Greeks, who believed that inspiration was the possession of the maker by an otherworldly agency. Socrates, who seemed really to have believed in his daimon, probably took this notion of inspiration more or less seriously, and his great disciple, who understood the role myths can play in carrying us farther than positive knowledge can carry us, seems to have accepted the notion of inspiration to account for the power of the maker. But Aristotle was too sober to give the myth of inspiration a place in his poetics and we are still suffering from his sobriety; his realistic epistemology could not recognize the constitutive part played by mind in the activity of knowing, either as elementary awareness or as knowledge of a higher kind, hence he did not have the barest inkling of the important part played by creativity in the making of art—*pace* Gilson, with whom I disagree with reluctance. In Aristotle this failure led him to misconceive the function of art, and his misconception is as powerfully active today as it was among the ancients. They did not suspect the part that art plays in constituting our picture of the world. If you remember, besides, that Greek art was realistic and that the highest praise Greeks could pay a painter was to say that he could paint grapes so real that birds pecked at them, you can't fail to see how easy it was for them to ignore the part the creative activity plays in the making of art. It was quite natural for a Greek audience to assume that the maker of tragedies reported events that had happened or might happen. Aristotle's advice to the poet to use likely impossibilities instead of unconvincing possibilities and his theory of the relation of poetry to history were not seen, indeed they are not yet seen, for the crippling errors they are in his poetics. It was not until the trail Kant began to cut reached, with Cassirer, the recognition that the human mind is fundamentally a maker of "symbols" rather than the "signs" that it also uses, and that the world which is independent of the mind is only one of the factors of our picture of it, that we were in a position to see how radical was the error of the theory of imitation. Today our understanding of the nature of the error is deepened by Jung's conception of symbol and by the Sapir-Whorf theory of the part played by language in the formation of our picture of the world. But it would be over-optimistic to expect the disappearance of realistic epistemology before the next leap-year. Endemic and pandemic errors of thought cannot be done away with by means of the fumigations of reason; they will hang on, although the argument that music imitates the emotions was shown up a few years ago for the nonsense it is and no one has yet undertaken to tell us what architecture imitates: does it imitate bird nests, ant-heaps, or caves?

But there is still another reason for the hold these theories have had and still have on criticism and aesthetics. Our Western education has been for the most part intellectualistic and the triumph of modern science has merely strengthened the basic notion on which education is grounded, the belief, namely, that concepts are prior in the order of logic and in the order of experience to any form of awareness. The critic assumes that the thinking of the artist is not essentially different from that of the philosopher or the man of action. It is easy to make the assumption because makers of literature are not burdened with the task of theorizing responsibly about their work; for the most part what they do is to pick up from critics and aestheticians what the latter say about art. In addition morality—a completely false morality in this respect—strengthens the idea that conceptual thought is higher than the products of the creative imagination; our earnest bourgeoise ancestors taught us to distrust the novel as trivial when not downright immoral. We believe that the maker must have something to say, and if he has he must be able to say it—in conceptual terms of course. What he does is to dramatize concepts that it is the business of the critic to de-dramatize, as if the intention of work were to conceal thought. If the critic happens to espouse a contextualist view of literature he feels inhibited by it and invents something he calls "thematics." He is now free to theorize. Whatever thematics is, about the use to which it can be put there need be no doubt.

12

A few words in conclusion. It was not the purpose of this essay to expound my views of the way in which literature can be read as literature and the part that, when so read, it plays in the creation of culture. What I have to say on these subjects has been in print for some time. The preceding pages do not contain, except in passing if they do at all, and as mere assertions without argument to back them, positive doctrine; they are intended as negative criticism of doctrines I take to be erroneous that one runs into in current criticism; these erroneous doctrines are widespread and therefore harmful to the cultivation of the humanities. But there is no obligation of any kind, let me reiterate, moral, religious, political, or aesthetic, to read literature as literature, and the illusion that the views I have criticized as erroneous will disappear and that what I take to be the confusion that reigns in criticism will give way to clarity—this is not an illusion to which I surrender.

Mr. Leavis on D. H. Lawrence*

Nothing will be gained by beating about the bush. To my astonishment, I found Mr. Leavis's book on D. H. Lawrence both difficult to read and unsatisfactory in several fundamental respects. At its best, Mr. Leavis's study of Lawrence is as good as, or better than, his essays in *The Great Tradition* or in *The Common Pursuit.* But one of the factors that account for its excellence, the author's strong emotional ties to his subject, tends to make him see virtues that are not there, and to overlook flaws that should have been discerned with the aid of the critical tools he employs. I also found myself unexpectedly aware of serious defects in the tools he employs, that I had not perceived on reading his pieces of essay length. For this reason, the burden of this review will be negative. Readers of *Sewanee* do not need to hear praise of one of its distinguished contributors. But they may welcome a preliminary examination of one of Mr. Leavis's major efforts. In advance, however, I would like to correct the impression that my emphasis may convey. Mr. Leavis's study has high, positive value. It will remain one of the indispensable contributions to the proper appreciation of some aspects of Lawrence's art. In his best chapters, those on *The Rainbow* and *Women in Love,* and throughout, and frequently, the reader will come upon the subtle and precise discriminations that he is accustomed to expect from our distinguished critic.

About two thirds of the book, counting roughly, consists of essays previously published. But the essays, as they appeared throughout a period of about five years, did not prepare the reader for the impact of the book. We knew that Mr. Leavis admired Lawrence enormously. But the cumulative effect of the sustained, and at times, abandoned, praise that is heaped on Law-

---

D. H. Lawrence: Novelist. By F. R. Leavis. Alfred A. Knopf. 1956. $4.75.

rence in this book, could not have been anticipated by those who read the published chapters. Let me quote or paraphrase a few of the claims made for Lawrence. He is "incomparably the greatest writer in English of his time." He is "one of the great masters of comedy." He is "a great social historian." He has important truths, insight, and wisdom, about human experience, that are urgently relevant to us. His art represents a "power for life at present wasted."

The excessive claims made for Lawrence would not interfere seriously with the reading of the book, were Mr. Leavis's effort intended simply as an act of justice that he takes to be long overdue. But in seeking "to enforce," as he puts it, his claims for Lawrence's greatness, our critic also finds it necessary to engage, with rancorous implacability, in a warfare against those who have criticized Lawrence adversely, and to reduce the prestige of established novelists. The result is a book that is not pleasant to read.

Mr. Leavis's reverential attitude towards Lawrence seems to account for the fact that on several occasions he finds excellences where in fact none are to be found. Consider, as an instance, his opinion of the short story "The Daughters of the Vicar." In his commentary, Mr. Leavis emphasizes the contrast brought out by Lawrence between the attitudes towards "life" of the two sisters, as expressed by the kind of men they choose. Mary's acceptance of Mr. Massy springs from denial of life, while Louisa's love for Alfred springs from acceptance of life at the cost of security and social position. This is indeed what Lawrence intended to bring out. But Mr. Leavis is fond of reminding his readers of Lawrence's injunction: "Never trust the artist, trust the tale." How could he have failed to notice that the account of the relationship between Mary and Mr. Massy lacks the quality of authenticity that we can find in the account of the love of Louisa for Alfred? The latter is convincing. There is no question, therefore, as to whether the values involved in the relationship are true or false, right or wrong. They are what they are in the situation, and they could only be otherwise had Louisa been a different person. But the picture of Mary and her husband is artificially fabricated, in order to convince us of the superiority of Louisa's values. In a well-known passage of the "Foreword" of *Fantasia of the Unconscious*, Lawrence asserts that his philosophy is deduced from his novels, not the reverse. At his best, the claim is true; his men and women are the result of the kind of organization of living experience which is possible when the creative activity is not bullied by the didactic will or by the autocratic intellect. But frequently, his men and women are dramatized concepts, derived from characters originally conceived dramatically, whose significance has subsequently been grasped in abstract terms.

Mr. Leavis's failure to follow Lawrence's injunction to trust the tale leads him to miss how the didactic will of the writer functions in it. Mr. Leavis writes:

> The courage with which she [Louisa] adheres to this resolute election of love and life affects us as movingly noble and heroic. It is in the fullest sense moral courage that we witness. . . . It is courage to live, and the way in which "life" here. . .gets its concrete definition is illustrated by the contrast between the vicarage and the cottage.

This is of course what, by loading the dice, Lawrence made sure we would not miss. However, had he refrained from loading the dice, it would not have been possible for him to define "life" by the contrast between the vicarage and the cottage. In "art," as distinct from "propaganda," the dramatic clashes of wills and of values do not carry on their face, as Mr. Leavis seems to believe, their own self-certification as to their place in the moral hierarchy. Each has its own "necessity" in the context, as defined by character and situation. It is we, as readers, who make the choice, if we do, that Louisa's values are preferable to her sister's. But ours is a *moral* choice, made possible by our introducing our own criteria into a situation which, if aesthetically revealed, has no dominating moral criterion, or, what is the same, has as many moral criteria as there are constellations of values in conflict. For this reason, "art," when it is genuine and not faked by the autocratic intellect or the willful moral conscience, and "life" itself, as we encounter it in our own experience, are inevitable sources of moral outrage to the moralist. They appear to him, with his narrow choices and exclusive criteria, inherently and ineradicably ambiguous.

Nor can we say, in the context of the story as we have it,

that it takes immense nobility and heroic courage to reject an
unpleasant "little abortion" whose "body was unthinkable,"
and who "lacks the full range of human feelings." But it would
have taken courage, had the security been more attractive, as it
often is, and had social position brought with the genuine advantages that, in many cases, it brings with it. An inwardly dead
man who was superficialy less repulsive would have tested
Louisa's choice and challenged the artist in a manner that the little abortion cannot and does not. The upshot of the test could
not have been an unambiguous moral triumph for the values
Lawrence preferred. But the frustration of the moralist would
have been more than repaid by the success of the artist, who, by
allowing a conflict between two sets of values, each of which
has its own authentic claims, would have given us a tale with
genuine tragic tension and deeper wisdom.

Substantially the same observations can be made of the
chapter on *St. Mawr.* Remembering a mediocre story, the
reader is baffled by our critic's panegyric, and turns back to the
book in search of perfections he missed. Alas, they simply are
not there. *St. Mawr* is second-rate Lawrence. It is not even one
story, but two episodes, loosely connected. The two episodes
have different power and authenticity.

Within the first, the English, episode, we find the same
contrast that we found in "The Daughters of the Vicar" between
an authentic conception and a frabricated one. Lawrence's
hatred of Hermoine and her friends, and of Halliday and his, in
Women in Love, was expressed in dramatic terms. But over the
years, that hatred became conceptualized. *St. Mawr* is not genuine drama. Rico and his friends are mere puppets, fabricated to
be sacrificed to the author's hatred. On the other hand, the
horse, St. Mawr, is a genuinely vital animal. The civilized consciousness, for all its sophistication, does not find Lou's response
to it silly.

In contrast, the American episode is essentially inchoate
and inconclusive. It was tacked on to the English episode because Lawrence had to finish the book somehow. Lawrence
takes Lou to Texas, where she abandons the horse on the pretext
that it found a worthy mare, and removes her to New Mexico.
Here the story becomes thinly disguised autobiography, express-

ing the low condition of Lawrence at the time of writing it. There are, nevertheless, passages of good reporting in the American part of the book. Lawrence was always a good travel book writer.

But by and large the writing of *St. Mawr* is stale and flat. Mr. Leavis tells us that Lawrence wrote this book "out of the full living language, with a flexibility and a creative freedom for which [he] can think of no parallel in our times." It is not possible to examine the prose of the book in detail, to show that the contrary is the case. Let me, however, after quoting a few sentences which seem to me to be representative of the bad writing in the book, comment briefly. Lou and her mother are in Texas, and are impressed by it.

> What a world!

> Mrs. Witt eyed it shrewdly. But she failed to participate. Lou was a bit scared at the emptiness of it all, and the queer, phantasmal self-consciousness. Cowboys just as self-conscious as Rico, far more sentimental, inwardly vague and unreal. Cowboys that went after their cows in black Ford motor-cars: and who self-consciously saw Lady Carrington falling to them, as elegant young ladies from the East fall to the noble cowboy of the films, or in Zane Grey. It was all film-psychology.

And at the bottom of the next page, Lou asks herself:

> What, in Heaven's name, was one to make of it all?

These are not the only two of-it-alls in the book, and some of them are not uttered by the characters, but are expressions used by Lawrence in his own person. Faced with them, one remembers Lawrence's own admonition to Edward March, in a letter of 1913: One should not say "of it all," any more than one should say, "I know not why." It is as meaningless as "yours truly" at the end of a letter.

We cannot trace, however, all the defects of Mr. Leavis's book to his reverence for Lawrence. We must go to his critical method, if we are to gain an adequate understanding of them.

Some readers may take the reference to Mr. Leavis's method to be preposterous. They remember his distrust of theory and his explicitly stated fear that interest in aesthetics, or in "philosophy," as he calls it, may blunt a critic's sensibility and power of discrimination. Is not his criticism unencumbered with theoretical impedimenta? It is true that, like an ancient sailor, Mr. Leavis hugs the coast line. And it is also true that in a strict sense of the word, there is not even much *analysis* in the book. What we have are extensive paraphrases accompanied by frequent and long quotations, with indications of values to be discerned: "Astonishing original art," "the whole thing is an astonishing feat of imagination," or "an intuition of life conveyed with power;" a scene or dialogue gives evidence "of great creativeness," or is done with great economy. We can characterize succintly Mr. Leavis's critical practice by saying that it consists of extended exhortations, whose formula can be expressed in two imperatives: "Look at that, see how well it is done," and "Look at that, that is not well done."

We can go to Mr. Leavis for a confirmation of this statement of the intention of his criticism. In his "Reply" to Professor Wellek (*Scrutiny*, Vol. VI, No. 1, reprinted in *The Importance of Scrutiny*, pp. 30-40) he writes:

> . . .The business of the literary critic is to attain a peculiar completeness of response and to observe a peculiarly strict relevance in developing his response into commentary. . . . His first concern is to enter into possession of the given poem (let us say) in its concrete fullness and his constant concern is never to lose his completeness of possession, but rather to increase it. In making value judgements (and judgements as to significance), implicitly or explicitly, he does so out of that completeness of possession and with that fullness of response.

That completeness of possession and fullness of response are the "first" concerns of the critic, I doubt whether any one would deny, if by "first" be meant "most important." But without such a specification, the word may beg an important issue. For there are radical differences of opinion as to that which we respond to when we respond to a work of art. When one literary critic is centrally concerned with literary structure or form and another with irony; when one is intent on coming into possession of the presentments of life and the health-giving virtue of literary works and another on tracing the clusters of images and their imports; when still another analogizes literature to myth and another to ritual—whether he knows it or not, each is falling back on aesthetic theory. And each aesthetic, if I may be allowed the incongruity, serves both as blinkers and as searchlight.

In a limited sense, this is not denied by Mr. Leavis, who is his "Reply" tells us that a critic's efforts to possess a work of art involve, as he matures, a growing stability and coherence of response. But when he goes on to say that out of the stability and the coherence, principles can be elicited and abstract norms can be formulated, one cavils. For one senses in the statement a radical nominalistic empiricism. Mr. Leavis seems to believe that a man endowed with the proper sensibility and power of discrimination, even if he is a theoretically unfertilized virgin, can be a successful critic. On this view, a critic's discriminations spring untutored and unprincipled, by a miracle of parthenogenesis, from the virginal sensibility. But this is, clearly, not the case. His very first choice developed from two cooperating factors: from a pristine germ of theory, however primitive, which is genetically prior to his earliest discrimination and from the reaction, made possible by the sensibility, to the perceived value, which theory enables him to recognize for the value it is.

That theory blunts the sensibility is a scrap of obscurantist theory to which two kinds of critics are addicted: those who do not understand the relation of theory to practice, and those who, probably for temperamental reasons, are inveterate misologists. But let that be as it may. That theory serves as blinkers may be a misfortune, but it is one that must be borne stoically, since it cannot be avoided. A theory of criticism formulates *the method* employed by the critic. And method means, let us remember, way. A way takes us somewhere, and by taking us there, prevents us from going elsewhere. While a critic must aim at fullness of response and completeness of possession, he would be deceiving himself if he overlooked the fact that these are achievements possible only within the limitations of a theory of criticism. The critic can avoid theory only by giving up being a critic. The critic who tries to avoid theory, with its advantages and limiting disadvantages, ends up with many theories, and the upshot cannot but be incoherence. My main dissatisfaction with Mr. Leavis's study has its source in my inability to see how the several scraps of aesthetic theory presupposed in his criticism can be made to go together without incoherence.

If we try to formulate the principles that guide Mr. Leavis's criticism—the categories he employs, the types of excellence he discriminates, and the notions as to the function of the novel as art that are operative in his criticism—we are startled by what we find. The dramatic embodiment of "life" in the story or novel is successful, according to him, when Lawrence, as he frequently does, achieves "marvelous reality" of "evocation" or, more frequently, of "presentment." His "types" are perfectly observed; he renders life in a faithful way. There are (as we have already seen) highly valuable "truths" and "insights" to be found in his art, and these derive from his own experience and observation. Because he renders "life" faithfully, his work has inestimable value as a "recorder of essential English history." But Lawrence is more than a social historian: Possessing a deep reverence for "life," he is a force for health. It is to his reverence, no doubt, that we must trace those "truths" and "insights" that are urgently needed by us. And I suspect that it is also reverence for life that gives his work its "diagnostic value." Some of the novels fulfill another function: they serve as an imaginative self-exploration, by means of which their writer enacts a kind of experiment, a testing and exploring of conclusions he has reached or is trying to reach.

What is astonishing about Mr. Leavis's critical theory is that, however sound it may be, it is anything but novel. It is also clear that his guiding preoccupation is moral. He is interested in discovering whether art ministers to life directly, or whether it does so indirectly, as a means of exploring imaginatively the consequences of actions. When we ask how, on Mr. Leavis's view, the artist achieves the presentment of life or reality, he gives us this answer: By observing faithfully and by recording truthfully what he observes. But beyond this, Mr. Leavis does not go. He does not show interest in the exploration of executive techniques and devices whose discovery is the major contribution of contemporary criticism. Thus, we find only one or two fleeting and inadequate references to an important device employed by Lawrence to express the substance of his art—the use of the *constitutive* symbol, the symbol that cannot be exhausted by paraphrase, because its "meaning" does not exist external to it and independent of it. Mr. Leavis notices some of these "symbols" and realizes clearly that what they symbolize cannot be apprehended independently of them. He is, for this reason, averse to calling them "symbols." With his verbal scruples one cannot but sympathize. Using the term, which is about as polysemic as any in the language of criticism, in the way stipulated by scientific semiosis, he realizes that these devices of Lawrence work "from profounder levels and in more complex ways." But he does not say anything else about these levels or the way in which they work. And as a result, he overlooks the important role that these constitutive symbols play in Lawrence's art. This is not intended as adverse criticism of the quality of his work. His method, like any method, let me reiterate, involves inevitable limitations. It is merely stated "to place" him, as he would put it, in relation to the work of other critics of his day, and to help define the range of his purview. What does constitute a criticism, and in my opinion a serious one, is the observation that our critic leaves us in the dark as to the means employed by Lawrence to achieve his moral end while remaining an artist. I am not demanding, of course, a theoretical discussion of the relation of art to morality—we know he eschews such inquiries. But he could have given us an answer in concrete terms. The point of the criticism is that he by-passes this difficult problem altogether. And as a result, he fails adequately to distinguish those stories and novels of Lawrence which are defective because they are infested with propagandistic intentions, from those that are excellent because they are, if the adjective be allowed, "pure" art, or, at least, more or less "pure" art.

This is not the only difficulty by-passed by Mr. Leavis. Let us turn to another which seems to me to be the source of radical incoherence. He offers, as an explanation of the manner in which Lawrence embodies reality, his peculiar impersonalizing intelligence. This power, frequently referred to, seems to be something so complex that it requires a tortuous syntax to convey it:

> . . .*The Rainbow* exemplifies in a special way the peculiar Lawrentian genius: the extraordinary power of the impersonalizing intelligence to maintain, while the artist, in an intensely personal ex-

ploratory way, is actually living the experience that goes into the
art, the conditions that make creative impersonality possible.

Two observations are elicited by this quotation. The first
is that Mr. Leavis points to a quality of Lawrence's art objectively discernible in it, its impersonality, and he seems to give us a
genetic account of it, namely that it is produced by the power of
Lawrence's impersonalizing intelligence. But the explanation is
specious. We know no more about the production of the effect
by reference to the power, than was known by the student of
Montpellier, in Molière. What we need to know, if we are seeking
to explain certain objective qualities genetically, are the specific
processes by which the artist brings them about.

But perhaps Mr. Leavis is not at all trying to explain the
cause of the impersonality of Lawrence's art. Perhaps all he is
doing is referring to a phenomenon that he can no more explain
than anyone else. Let us, in the teeth of the evidence, assume
this is the case. Still, we must ask whether the power of the impersonalizing intelligence is peculiar to Lawrence. The answer
is that it is not. Under a multitude of aliases, this "power" and
its objective effects have long been known to aestheticians and
critics. They are thought of, and righty so, as defining marks of
the artist and his work. Indeed, what really seems peculiar to
Lawrence is the sharp contrast between the relative infrequency
with which he achieves the impersonalizing feat, and the high
frequency with which he fails to achieve it. Mr. Leavis calls attention several times to works in which Lawrence intrudes on the
tale to its disadvantage. Had he not so rigorously restricted the
number of works of Lawrence he chose to examine thoroughly,
he would have had to indicate failure much more often than he
did.

It is usually acknowledged that one of the means by which
the artist achieves the feat of impersonalizing the matter of his
experience is to be traced to the devices he uses to imprison the
reader in the enclosed self-sufficiency of the work of art, to the
devices he employs to achieve unity. And one of the difficulties
that the reader of Lawrence's best novels has to overcome, in
order to enter into possession of them, is that of grasping them as
organic wholes. This seems to me to be more true of Lawrence's best novel, *Women in Love,* than of any other. I still

vividly remember how baffled I was by it when I finished reading it for the first time in the spring of 1923. What light does Mr. Leavis throw on the principles of organization operative in the novel? We are told:

> The problem of discussing *Women in Love* is that the organization is so rich and close. From the moment the Brangwen girls begin their conversation about marriage, the dramatic poem unfolds—or builds up—with an astonishing fertility of life. This life, so much of which commands the imagination at the first encounter, is all significant life; not a scene, episode, image, or touch but forwards the organized development of the themes. To discuss this development point by point as the dramatic action advances would take a volume. One can only hope to do some sufficiently representative illustrating that will convey the nature of the themes and of the whole organization.

Thus, Mr. Leavis clearly sees the need to give us the key to the organization of the novel. The fifty-eight pages that follow this passage constitute, in many ways, an admirable essay on *Women in Love*. But they do not give us the key. Nor could Mr. Leavis, with his method of citing representative illustrations, have achieved this end. The nature of the themes can be conveyed in this manner. But the organization of the whole cannot be so conveyed. You will not see the forest, if all you are shown are representative specimens of the kinds of trees that make it up.

A similar criticism applies to Mr. Leavis's treatment of the organization of *The Rainbow*. He tells us that a certain page of Chapter IV of the novel gives an episode that, related to an earlier passage, replaces, in Lawrence, "the familiar kinds of organization (plot, fable, climax-and-resolution, and so on)." This episode "has its part in defining the complex rhythm organizing the book—the movement that, by recurrence along with newness, brings continually a significant recall of what has gone before." But nothing further is said about the rhythm involved, or about the components that make up the movement of recurrence and newness, or how these actually organize the novel.

Serious, however, as is the failure to give us the key to the organization of the books that Mr. Leavis chooses to discuss, a more serious defect of the study must be considered.

We have already noticed a term Mr. Leavis frequently employs in his commentary: "presentment." It takes no acuity to perceive the importance of the term and the fact that it plays a technical role in Mr. Leavis's criticism. Since his way of approach to the critical task precludes the definition of terms in an abstract manner, one becomes curious as to exactly what the term does mean in the study. The search, alas, is all too rewarding, for a superficial comparison of texts reveals that the term performs heavy duty in Mr. Leavis's criticism. I shall confine my discussion to only three important meanings in which the term is employed. But I beg permission to preface the discussion with a remark: From his "Reply" to Professor Wellek, we gather that Mr. Leavis is not unmindful of the importance of coherence for the critic. The following observations cannot, therefore, be brushed off, as sometimes this kind of criticism is, by literary men, on the ground that it is mere logical hair-splitting to which professors of philosophy are addicted.

One obvious meaning of the word "presentment" refers to the manner in which Lawrence establishes by dramatic means as an actual presence before the reader's mind, his themes or incident or situation. As synonyms, sometimes Mr. Leavis employs the terms "evoke," "convey," and "render." Thus the term refers both to the substance presented and to the manner in which it is presented. Lawrence's presentments have "marvelous reality," because Lawrence possesses great skill as a writer. Obviously what we have here is the theory of imitation. The writer holds the mirror up to nature, and in it the reader sees vividly the object of imitation. That this is the correct interpretation can be inferred from the fact that Mr. Leavis often praises Lawrence for his correctness of observation. And it is, I imagine, on this basis that Mr. Leavis calls attention to Lawrence's preeminence as social historian.

But we find a second usage of the term "presentment." In this usage, Lawrence is praised because his presentments are *creative.* The difficulty is obvious. How can the presentments be both perfect observations—which is to say, faithful imitations —and creative? And if they are creative, how can they be *social history?* It is, of course, possible that Lawrence was both a social historian and a creative writer, for some of his novels or some aspects of them, may not be novels in the strict sense, but rather extensions of the history which, in 1921, he published under the pseudonym of Lawrence H. Davis, while other of his books may be novels in the proper or strict sense. Or it may even be possible that in his novels he was a creative writer whose presentments portray not "ordinary" reality, but some other kind of reality, or dimension of being, which can be discovered only by the creative act. There may be, in short, no conflict in the polysemic employment of the term " presentment." But without clarification of this difficult problem, the reader is left radically bewildered.

These are not the only senses of "presentment" we discover in the text. We are frequently told, also, that Lawrence's presentments are "diagnostic." The expression, we gather, refers to the fact that Lawrence exposes the illness of our world. This claim brings with it a difficulty. For the diagnostic activity is possible only by a comparison of a faithful picture of the state of the world with a standard of health. The comparison can be accomplished either by the writer explicitly or by the reader when the picture of the diseased state is suggestively presented, in conjunction with a standard. In either case, the writer must make a faithful presentment of the illness—not a creative one—and define with adequate clarity the standard by comparison with which the present state of society is found to be diseased.

The standard, it would seem, is, for Mr. Leavis and for Lawrence, "life." Commenting on one of Lawrence's short stories, our critic tells us that the artist was "preoccupied. . .with defining the nature of a true moral sense--one that shall minister to life." This is a representative quotation. And the defect to which I would call attention shows clearly in it. Carrion ministers to life—the life of the maggots that feed on it. Genocide ministered to life—the life of the Nazi sadists who carried it out. Mr. Leavis cannot, and does not, mean that the moral sense ministers to unqualified life, even if that were what Lawrence himself meant. The moral sense in that which ministers to the *good* life. But in order to convince his readers that Lawrence had a valid conception of the good life, Mr. Leavis had to do more than paraphrase the novels and stories, and assert his belief that the values that Lawrence espoused are better than those he rejected. The burden of proof, or demonstration, was on him, for several reasons. We have already seen that the novels themselves, when not propaganda, are ineradicably and inherently ambiguous. Again, it was Lawrence who was the innovator. He may have been right and our society may be as wrong as he thought it was. But it is no more self evident that an established society, because it is established, is wrong, than that it is right. The burden of proof is all the more on Mr. Leavis since it is not difficult to see that the alternatives Lawrence suggested, if institutionalized, would be conducive to chaos.

But let us assume that Lawrence's values are unquestionably superior to those on which our society is grounded. We still have to ask, What is the relation between the moral insights, the wisdom, the urgently needed sense of life Lawrence offers us and the specific social and individual exigencies of our actual life? One would expect that a critic who is convinced of the wisdom of his subject, would seek to arrive at the uttermost lucidity and precision on this important point. Mr. Leavis disappoints our expectation.

In the "Introduction" to his book, Mr. Leavis tells us that he is seeking to win clear recognition for the nature of Lawrence's greatness, because "any great creative writer who has not had his due is a power for life wasted." This is an emphatic announcement of his intention: Lawrence, the artist, is relevant to our practical needs. One could fill more than a page with quotations to the same effect. Let only one do. He writes:

> There, in the novels, the treatment of the theme has for a major part of its implicit moral this further insistence: except between "fulfilled" individuals—individuals, that is, who are really themselves, recognizing their separateness or otherness, and accepting the responsibility of that—there can be no personal relations that are lasting and satisfactory.

I shall not examine in detail the truth of the moral. It is one of those vacuous generalizations to which moral vitalists are given, that seem true, but, on examination, turn out to be colossal oversimplifications, overlooking the radical and complex differences that exist among diverse types of human beings, the effect of the different operative moral codes by which they seek to guide their conduct, and the complexity of the needs of different persons as they conceive those needs and as they really are. But let that be. I cite the statement to show thar Mr. Leavis seems to think that Lawrence has a wise and true moral code, from the adoption of which we could benefit. But at one point he seems to hesitate. And this single hesitation throws into question the claim made for Lawrence throughout the study. Speaking of the "moral" *St. Mawr* "enforces," he writes:

> To derive, however, from such peceptions and insights as are registered in "St. Mawr," and so many of the best tales, normative conclusions about the relation of the man and the woman in marriage, is obviously a delicate matter.

Of course it is a delicate matter. But it is a matter that a critic who claims his author is a power for life must elucidate. For the success of his case does not only depend on his showing that there are insights in his author. He must also show that these insights can actually be used by the reader and how they can be used. How does Mr. Leavis handle this question? He does not handle it at all.

There is much else that needs to be said about Mr. Leavis's study. I have said nothing specifically about its great virtues. The value of the book lies in the effort to demonstrate that Lawrence is an artist. For this reason, in the bibliography on Lawrence, it has a place among a small number of books. The claims made for Lawrence by Mr. Leavis are excessive. But their excesses can be discounted. Mr. Leavis has done us a favor by his insistence that Lawrence belongs to "the great tradition." His exact place in it will remain, for our lifetime at least, a controversial question.

PART THREE

Criticism

Kafka's Distorted Mask

One need not read very far into *The Kafka Problem*[1] to see how grievously Kafka has suffered at the hands of some of his critics. Mr. Flores has thrown together, unembarrassed by any controlling criterion, a large number of articles, reviews and appreciations of Kafka, of diverse value and gathered from many European languages. A few essays, like that of the French critic Miss Claude-Edmonde Magny, are penetrating studies worthy of their subject. But the problem which most of these pieces raise is as to why the editor should have wanted to rescue them from discreet obscurity. Fortunately, if you want to check for yourself the validity of the various interpretations which have been foisted on Kafka, you are no longer obstructed by the difficulty which has confronted his slowly growing public during the last four or five years. For in the last few months both his German publishers, now established in this country, and his various American publishers, have reprinted—although sometimes at fantastic prices—books of Kafka which it has been hitherto impossible to find. The latest of these publications is the indispensable biography by Max Brod which has just been translated into English.[2]

If one may judge by Flores' volume and by a few other essays which for some reason were left out of this democratic collection, "the Kafka problem" arises from the confused demands made by the readers and not from any unusual difficulty inherent in Kafka's work. This is most clearly seen in those egregious compounds of home-made psychoanalysis and facile sociology of art of a purely speculative nature, which without any inductive evidence to support them find Kafka's meaning in his psychological or political history and in so doing explain it utterly away. The sociological critic takes Kafka's fables to be the expression of the social conditions which allegedly motivated them. For him the question is not, What does the author say? but rather, Why does he say what he does? The psychoanalytic critic shares with the sociological the assumption that the content of Kafka's vision of the world is of no importance, but differs in that what he considers of importance is the way in which the work of art expresses an allegedly pathological condition of the author. Neither sociologist nor psychoanalyst finds the answer by reading the objective, public content of the work; they find it by applying to it a theory devised prior to the reading of it, regarding the relation said to hold between either social or psychological conditions and artistic expression. Now even granting that this kind of genetic analysis of art is valid, and that artistic symbols may indeed point to psychic conditions or to social determinants, it is nevertheless at least possible that the objective traits to which they refer are of interest to the reader as they are without doubt to the artist (or the latter would not have struggled as he did with the problem of choosing them and organizing them into the artistic work). This does not deny the therapist's right to use the work of art as diagnostic evidence. Psychoanalytic criticism is, however, seldom practised by properly trained therapists for their purposes; it is as a rule written by amateur psychoanalysts whose insensibility to the aesthetic values and indifference to the philosophic content of the work is hardly camouflaged by their pseudo-scientific interest in it.

The reader who considers that the critic's most urgent task is to lead attention to those aspects of the world which are expressed by his subject is justified in passing by these highly speculative psychologistic or pseudo-sociological constructions. He must devote his efforts to exhibiting his subject's objective contribution and to essaying an evaluation of it. Inadequately supported speculations about the causes of the complicated difficulties which Kafka had with his father or his women or his job must necessarily be relegated to a relatively unimportant place until the work of objective criticism is finished and a working consensus obtains as to what is to be found in Kafka's fables. But when at last we turn our attention to psychogenetic questions we should do so with a greater respect than the majority of these fanciful speculations show for the demands of inductive verification. The biographical data that we have on Kafka is inadequate because Brod, who was its chief gatherer, interprets Kafka in his own terms and seems incapable of distinguishing his own personal interest in his gifted friend and his interest in the objective meaning of his friend's fables. Brod's book does not enable us to check our fanciful psychoanalytic constructions against reliable and sufficient facts. But even if it did, it would still leave us with the chief problems of Kafka on hand, with the question of Kafka's aesthetic achievement and of the objective meaning and validity of his vision of the world. We have Freud's word, although we do not need it, for the insight that the analysis of aesthetic values is not within the reach of his analytic method. But psychological and sociological criticism—and Freud's own is to be included in it—systematically rides the genetic fallacy when it assumes that the discovery of the complete psychological or social sources of the artist's experience invalidate the objective meaning which is expressed by his art.

Although a large number of Kafka's critics avoid the fanciful constructions of his psychological or his sociological interpreters, they share with these the inability simply to take Kafka seriously as an artist at the objective level. Aware that art performs a very important function in elucidating objective experience but not clear as to how it does it, they have in one of two ways assumed that the key to his work is to be found, not within it, but beyond it. Some find it in some ready-made philosophical conception of the world, usually in Kierkegaard, as if all the artist had to do was to dress up in a dramatic costume a philosophic skeleton. Others, taking Kafka to be merely an allegorical writer, consider the task of criticism accomplished when the more or less superstructural allegorical features of his fables are translated into that for which they stand—or, as I shall call it, employing I. A. Richard's convenient terminology, into the "tenor" of the extended metaphor that is the allegory. The objective of these critics becomes then the translation of what Kafka meant by the Castle, or the Court, or by an advocate conveniently called "Grace," or by the Chinese emperor and his wall, or by the elaborate burrow built by the digger obsessed with a need to seek safe refuge from a predatory world. Although the difference in practice between these two modes of interpretation is important enough to notice, in principle they share the same assumption, namely, that the meaning of Kafka's work is to be found beyond the fables themselves and can therefore be better expressed in other terms than those which Kafka himself used.

Sharing the same assumption, these two modes of extrinsic

interpretation also share a basic error consisting of a misconception of what the artist does and how he does it. The philosophic interpreters ignore the fact that the creative process involves a complete digestion of all the material on which the artist feeds so that what he finally produces is essentially different from what went into its make-up. They also ignore the fact that the poet, in the measure in which he is indeed a maker, does not seek to "imitate" or "represent" a reality which, independently of his poetic activity, possesses already a formal structure which anyone can discover. If this is true, it should be easy to see why the assumption that Kafka's meaning is to be found in a ready-made system of philosophy such as Kierkegaard's or anyone else's even in a more or less sytematic set of abstract ideas of his own, is a disparagement of his achievement. Artistically Kafka failed to a considerable extent. But his was the failure of a man who was an artist of major pretensions. His meaning is something not to be better stated abstractly in terms of ideas and concepts, to be found beyond the fable, but within it, at the dramatic level, in the interrelationships thus revealed to exist among the characters and between them and the universe. The fallacy of finding his meaning in abstract ideas inverts the relationship between philosophy and art, for it is the philosopher who must go to art for the subject-matter which the poet has organized at the dramatic level, in order to abstract from it the systematic relationships which it is his business to formulate.

The allegorical interpreter fails for a similar reason. He translates the allegory into its "tenor" by supplying, not Kafka's own grasp of reality in dramatic terms, but a more or less commonplace version of it in abstract terms, and one which does not possess any of those traits which, in the fable, we discern to be the most distinctively Kafkan. But if Kafka had a contribution to make it was not to be found in the ingenuity of his allegorical "vehicle" (again in Richards' terminology) nor even in a version of a cock-eyed world whose absurdity at the human level had its source in the unqualified irrationality of transcending factors lying beyond human reach and beyond human comprehension. These conceptions of existence had already been expressed in one way or another in literature and in philosophy. What Kafka had to say was something else involving as much freshness and originality as one has a right to expect in literature. It is something which, so far as I know, he could not have borrowed from philosophy, for no thinker one hears of in standard histories of philosophy has ever viewed the world in quite the way in which Kafka viewed it. There are, undeniably, allegorical features in Kafka's vision of the world but they are obvious and relatively unimportant. What is important is the concrete dramatic world exhibited in his fables under the allegorical "vehicles" which he uses to capture it. Kafka, as Brod points out, even when trying to think conceptually, thinks in images and not in conceptual structures. But his vision has a coherence and meaningful inter-relatedness lacked by the vision of the non-artistic mind, since the latter is distracted by the multifarious demands made on it and it is not driven by the need to organize and unify its experi-ence. The picture of the world as it presented itself to Kafka was a mythopoetical one and if it is our business as readers to discover its meaning for us, in our own terms, we cannot do so until we are reasonably clear as to what was its own intrinsic meaning. Miss Magny puts the point so effectively that it is worth transcribing her own words:

> we ought not to. . .provide dialectical constructions for the unfold-ing of events which should be taken as a *real* account. Otherwise Kafka is quickly converted into a kind of frustrated philosopher who needs to be explained to himself and to others for lack of suf-ficient power of analysis and abstraction. . . . That would imply a gratuitous insult.

In spite of her depth and acuity, however, I believe that Miss Magny's interpretation of Kafka's conception of existence can be objectively shown to miss a very essential element. She says:

> the world for Kafka is essentially *turmoil*, something that is not *rational* and whose essence therefore only a fantastic tale can ex-press. . . . Only the gratuitousness of the event itself, of the *con-tingent*, can reveal the essential absurdity of things.

At another place Miss Magny speaks of "Kafka's predilection for the infraconceptual, the infrarational." But Kafka's world was not merely absurd. Indeed what constituted for him the problem which he sought to resolve through his art—and of course the only manner in which an artist resolves his problem is through a statement of it in mythopoetic terms—was that certain transcend-

ing aspects of the universe envisaged through experience and seen
to be those on which normal visible existence depends, blatantly
proclaimed an irrationality which, upon the most casual glimpse,
appeared to be at the same time rational.

But the Magny essay has at least this value, that it poses the
Kafka problem correctly and reveals one aspect of our author
without a grasp of which no understanding of him is possible.
In Kafka, as she puts it, "the irrational. . .the horrible. . .the gro-
tesque. . .are never introduced for the sake of literary effect. . .
but to express a depth of reality." Our problem therefore is to inquire as to what conception of existence is found in Kafka's
fables. The answer must of course be couched in abstract terms,
but it is not to be taken as a translation of Kafka's meaning but
as a means of pointing to it within the fables themselves. The
validity of the interpretation is to be judged by checking to see
whether what I claim to be found in Kafka is indeed there and
whether I do not neglect important factors which are there.
The allegorical features must of course be translated into their
"tenors" but this goes without saying and rather than constituting a difficult task—as in fact it does for critics like Rahv
when they try to translate Kafka into Kierkegaardian philosophy
—it is a relatively easy one.[3] The labor of criticism however begins at that point and what it has to accomplish is a reading of
Kafka. After that one may express one's own opinion as to
whether Kafka's conception of existence is valid or not.

2.

In order to offer inductive evidence in favor of the preceding argument we must turn to an analysis of Kafka's works
in search of his conception of existence. But since an exhaustive
analysis of all of his works is not here possible, I propose that we
turn our attention to *The Trial* and *The Castle* which embody his
most ambitious efforts to integrate his various discoveries about
the world. Let us first turn to *The Trial*.

We must first remember that Joseph K.'s arrest is sudden
and seems to him so unjustified that never between the period
of his arrest and of his execution does he admit his guilt. But

while verbally denying it, unconsciously Joseph K. betrays his sense of guilt from the very first day of his arrest in numerous small ways. Let only one instance suffice: During the preliminary examination that took place the morning of his arrest Joseph K. said to the Inspector in anger and seemingly irrelevantly, "But this is not the capital charge yet." In a more important way Joseph K. gives evidence of his sense of guilt: the outward circumstances of his life do not at first change very radically but gradually Joseph K. gets more and more absorbed in his case and finally finds out that his job is suffering from his preoccupation with it. If he truly were convinced of his innocence he would have laughed at the whole absurd business, as he tried to do the first Sunday at the preliminary investigation when he told the Magistrate that his could not be a trail unless he recognized it as such. To the reader it is quite clear that Joseph K. did not want to admit to himself when he made that statement that he had already through action eloquently yielded the recognition that his lips withheld.

Remember next that while Joseph K. realizes that the Court is a formidable organization he insists nevertheless on his belief that its purposes are absurd, and the evidence for that is to be found, as he believes, in all that he discovers about it at the lower level. Thus Joseph K. seems to be justified in his conviction, expressed angrily to the Magistrate, that the organization is interested in condeming innocent victims and doing so while keeping them in ignorance of what action is brought against them. This belief is strengthened by the result of his efforts to gain information about the higher officials of the Court.

But is Joseph K. really justified in his belief that the Court is an utterly aimless, absurd institution? A formidable organization with a code of Law and with such a large number of employees, with traditions and equipment, an organization that will punish its employees on occasion upon the complaint of a man under arrest—such an organization is simply not aimless. Its aim may not be knowable or may not seem to be intelligible to us but the evidence, without denying Joseph K.'s conviction of its absurdity, points, at the very same time, to a rationality all its own. Joseph K. does not want to admit this to himself and insists on judging the organization and its charges against him by his own criterion of rationality. But all his actions proclaim that he is not altogether ignorant of the limitations of his own criterion. In view of his stiff-necked attitude towards the evidence, the counsel which Joseph K. gives himself on the way to the execution has a tremendous ironic force. "The only thing for me to do now. . .is to keep my intelligence calm and discriminating to the end." He therefore resigns himself. But it has been precisely the failure of his discriminating intelligence that led him to the impasse in which he found himself. For it was not resignation that the situation required of him; what it required was admission of his guilt and genuine contrition. This is precisely what the priest tried in vain to tell him in the Cathedral. But Joseph K. was too discriminatingly intellient and too proud of the primacy of his intelligence to listen.

The Castle is a much more complex book than *The Trial.* Indeed it represents the most ambitious effort on Kafak's part to gather together all the important aspects of his vision of the world into one coherent fable. For this reason the unfinished condition in which it was left suggests a radical criticism of the validity of Kafka's conception of existence. In this book his preoccupations are given a different organization from that which he gave them in *The Trial.* A problem with which *The Trial* is concerned only obliquely is here brought forward, namely the problem of man's place in the scheme of things and, as a corollary of this more comprehensive problem, the question as to the nature of the bond between man and his fellow beings. In *The Trial* that bond, after the crisis of the arrest, is somehow unhealthy; for instance, for the noraml relationship between his mistress and himself Joseph K. substitutes the relationship with Huld's maid, Leni, which does not involve either the fulfillment of genuine love or even the gratification which purely sexual relations can yield. In *The Castle* the emphasis seems to change but both the human and the merely sexual relations result in the same vague frustration. Again the question of guilt which is central in *The Trial* is subordinated in *The Castle* by being presented through the episode of Barnabas and his family. But the cause of the guilt, which in *The Trial* is only indirectly and ambiguously suggested, is in the latter explicitly traced to Amalia's refusal of Sortini's invitation to visit him in his room at the Inn; the guilt is caused, that is, by the pride of those who will not serve and is thus connected with the most ancient of guilts, the guilt that led to the fall before man's. The cause is brought out with sufficient clarity by the contrast between Amalia's attitude towards Sortini and the attitude of the Landlady and of Frieda towards Klamm. K. is himself relatively free from a sense of guilt but he is dominated by a need to find a place for himself in the scheme of things. The need, baffled, develops into anxiety as his efforts lead him to discover the nature of the organization that he has to contend with.

From Olga and from the superintendent who receives K. in bed, the Land Surveyor gains important information about the organization of the Castle. K. tries to make his informants admit that the organization is quite absurd and leaves much to be desired. But the superintendent does not admit that the organization lacks order or is subject to error. The apparatus works with great precision; in the Castle nothing is done without thought and the very possibility of error on the part of the Head Bureau must be ruled out. The superintendent admits that he is convinced that in respect to K. an error has been committed. But who can tell what the first Control Officials will say and the second and third and the rest? However, if there has been one, the error is not established by the evidence K. has from Klamm, for Klamm's letter to K. is not official, and as to the telephone calls, these mean nothing. If Huld in *The Trial* is an advocate without legal standing, Klamm in *The Castle* is a protector seemingly·helpless to protect his man—that is, if there is a Klamm and if it is K. and not someone else in whom Klamm is interested.

I have purposely said in a vague way that K. was trying "to find his place in the scheme of things" because I do not find that K. is anxious about obtaining a livelihood or solving any other purely secular problem but only about finding a place in the village which would give him status not only in respect to the village itself but, more importantly even, in respect to the inaccessible powers of the Castle. K. wants an unambiguous statement of his position before the authorities of the Castle. This involves documents, proofs, something to which he could refer that could not be gainsaid, like the letters from Klamm, but containing of course an official appointment and a definition of his place. He starts with large demands and ends up by offering to take anything that will be given him so long as it brings him the needed nod of recognition for which he craves. But his efforts to get into direct touch with the officials of the Castle are no less pathetically useless than those of Barnabas' father who wants his crime defined. No one can be certain of anything beyond the elementary fact that there must be a Castle which is visible above the village and from which officials and servants constantly come and go. One also suspects that it must have its method, no matter how absurd that method may seem and how deeply it may outrage the feeling of what we take to be fitness or justice or rationality. But beyond that all is doubt and incertitude.

Between *The Trial* and *The Castle* there are important differences, but to me none seems as important as the fact that Joseph K. never learns anything whatever about the invisible Judges, while K. knows the name of the Lord of the Castle, Count West-west, and receives indications, however unsatisfactory, that between the Castle and himself there is some sort of nexus. He first tries to get into touch with the Count, then with the Castellan and, when he sees the impossibility of his ambition, he tries to reach Klamm. K.'s relations with Klamm are more baffling than those of Joseph K. with his Judges in *The Trial* because there is more teasing evidence of Klamm's existence and therefore the evidence is more unintelligible. K. thinks he once saw Klamm but it turns out later that that is very doubtful. Was it Klamm who wrote the letter to K.? The signature is illegible and Olga later tells K. that the letters that her brother Barnabas has brought him were not received from Klamm but from a clerk. Even if they were from Klamm it is doubtful whether Klamm is well enough posted on K. really to be his patron or protector as the second letter that K. receives from Klamm clearly shows. The question is even more difficult since, if you press it, it turns out that there are all kinds of contradictory reports about Klamm, and some people go so far as to say that Momus, the Secretary, is Klamm. Who then is Klamm? Some sort of fluctuating image of him has been constructed but, as Olga tells K., perhaps it does not fluctuate as much as Klamm's real appearance does. However, in *The Trial* not even such a deceptive hope ever urges Joseph K. on and he conducts his defense in a state of unrelieved and increasing enervation.

It is not necessary to demonstrate in detail that the various aspects of the conception of existence that were integrated in these two novels are separately expressed in a large number of his stories and sketches: in *Investigations of a Dog, The Great Wall of China, The Burrow* and *The Giant Mole,* for instance, as well as in some of his shorter pieces like *The Problem of Our Laws.* But it is necessary to state frankly that there are a number of more or less important stories which could not be susceptible of this interpretation, for example, *Josephine the Song-stress, Blumfeld, An Elderly Bachelor, The Penal Colony* and *The Judgment.* In some of these what Kafka was trying to do is not difficult to guess. He was exploring psychological reality strictly at the human level. The result of Kafka's psychological exploration, it seems to me, contradicts the purely hedonic conception of man which is found deeply imbedded in the liberal, secularistic tradition of our western world and which is true only of what Kierkegaard called the "aesthetic stage" of human development. Kafka's discoveries ally him with the tradition which Freud himself joined as a result of his metapsychological speculations and to which Dostoievsky and Kierkegaard belong—men who repudiate the shallow optimism which controls the conception of human destiny at the "aesthetic stage." For Kafka's psychological conceptions we must go to stories like *Metamorphosis, The Judgment* and *The Penal Colony.* With some diffidence I venture the opinion that an analysis of his contributions to the understanding of the purely psychological problems of contemporary men would hardly be worth the trouble it would involve.

Amerika, begun only a few months before *The Trial,* seems to represent, as I read it, an unsuccessful experiment of Kafka's, for in it he views his problem as imbedded in a purely social context. *Amerika* seems therefore to constitute very little more than social criticism of his temporal world and we find in it only faint and incomplete indications of the insights into the transcending aspects of experience which we identify as Kafka's central focus of interest and the elucidation of which constitutes his contribution.

3.

We are now able to put together Kafka's conception of

existence. Note first that what Kafka undertook was a stubborn-ly empirical exploration of experience, beyond which he discovered a constellation of factors for which evidence is found within the texture of experience itself. For this reason allegory must be employed to point to these factors not directly revealed. But the "tenor" of the allegory, being itself beyond direct grasp, must be expressed in mythopoetic terms drawn from ordinary life. Kafka, with whom Brod read Plato in his university days, could have invoked Plato as precedent for his use of myth, for the Greek used it to elucidate the structure which he glimpsed as lying beyond experience through evidence found within it. Kafka's discovery involves an ordered process which we can more or less adequately capture in the following formula: a crisis leads either to a sense of guilt or to a condition of alienation. In either case the crisis generates a struggle which expresses itself, among other ways, in the arrogant demands made by the hero. As he begins to feel the effects of the crisis the hero gradually trims his demands but he never altogether ceases to press them. The reduction of demands results from the hero's gradual discovery of a transcending organization which seems beyond his power either to look into, control or understand. His discovery is based not upon unwarranted assumptions or gratuitous hypotheses but on more or less direct empirical evidence, and although what is discovered seems unintelligible to him, the evidence is ambivalent and points not only to the irrationality of the organization but to its rationality as well. The anguished doubt into which the victim of the crisis is plunged is the result of the fact that the antinomy he faces cannot be resolved since it does not occur to him to transcend his perspective or go beyond his empirical method. But what other method is there? For Kafka's heroes there seems to be no other.

It is of the utmost importance, however, to note that Kafka's "empiricism" differs radically from that which is fashionable today—that which constitutes the foundations of scientific naturalism—since the latter has been devised in order to deny the evidence which experience presents of its lack of self-sufficiency while Kafka through an empirical examination of human existence is led to assert its dependence on transcending factors.

We do not find in Kafka an assertion of a world made up of two aspects such as we find in the traditional dualism of Western philosophy; for in these the two terms, the visible and the transcending, are said to bear certain intelligible relations towards one another and in the major tradition the transcending term is taken as the ground of the rationality of the other. Nor do we have in Kafka a dramatized version of Schopenhauerian dualism in which a pure irrational factor is taken to be the ground of our world of experience. What we find is something quite different, something to a large degree fresh and original, expressing in challenging terms the novel conditions and predicaments of modern man. These predicaments generate anguish. But unlike Kierkegaard, who mastered his "sterile anguish" through faith, or Dostoievsky, who suggested that it could be mastered through faith and love in the way in which the Russian monk, Father Zossima, mastered it, Kafka's man never succeeds in surpassing human anguish. Face to face with what many of his critics recognize as a metaphysical problem—in a vague sense of this conveniently ambiguous word—Kafka tried to solve it empirically. But what he was up against was the problem of theodicy and not in the Leibnizian sense but in the fuller, in the Cartesian sense. The problem that Kafka faced was not primarily the conventional need to find a satisfactory human account of evil once it has been discovered that its roots lie beyond the human level. Neither was it the problem of discovering what attitudes we may be expected to take towards an invisible agent on which we depend and which we know to be infinite—this was the Kierkegaardian problem. Rather it was the problem of discovering the ground of rationality. He went so far as to grasp clearly that that ground transcends human experience. But he could not go beyond this relatively elementary discovery because the stubborn empirical attitude which he assumed is helpless before questions of the magnitude he was raising.

This is not to say, however, that personally Kafka resigned himself to the monstrous predicament into which his discoveries plunged him. And least of all is it to say that the reader must himself be plunged into a pessimistic attitude by contemplating Kafka's picture of the world. Those readers who find him merely depressing have not read him carefully. Brod quotes a trenchant statement in his *Biography* which suggests the precise way in which Kafka himself avoided a purely enervating pessimism and in which the reader may also avoid it. "Our art," it reads, "consists of being dazzled by Truth. The light which rests on the distorted mask as it shrinks from it is true, nothing else is." The light is Truth but the mask on which it shines, the artifact of the maker, is "distorted"—and the rich contextual ambiguities of the statement are precisely what gives it density of suggestive meaning and confirms the reader's hunch that in the ambiguities which Kafka systematically exploits is to be found the comic dimension of his picture of the world and the means of purging oneself from effects generated by its arbitrariness and irrationality. Kafka's artistry makes this comic feature compatible with the sense of anguish and even of terror that is the defining quality of existence in it. But it is not merged with or sacrificed to the latter. And in the reader its perception generates enough detachment to enable him to assimilate all the absurdity and pervasive anguish presented without surrendering to it.

The comical quality of Kafka's world is expressed in the way in which he treats the antinomous nature of existence. Generally speaking, a comic grasp of the world rests on the perception by the writer of a moral duality which elicits from the reader a "comic" response as the only means of freeing himself from the conflict towards values to which he is attached and yet towards which he cannot justify his attachment satisfactorily. It is not merely a moral duality but, if you will allow it, a cosmological duality that we find in Kafka's world, and its perception involves a disparagement of the means which reveal it, a disparagement of the mind as a rational tool of analysis. There is no gaiety in Kafka's irony as there is in Rabelais' satire; nor a deep sense of moral outrage and the bitter laughter arising from the fact that at least you know you cannot be fooled which we find in Swift. But there is nevertheless the essential element of the comic in Kafka: the transparent error involved in any statement that can be made of the world. Such a world, a world about which nothing can be said that cannot in the same breath be as plausibly contradicted, is a quintessentially comic world. You cannot of course expect its victims to find it so but you cannot, either, be expected by them to take them at their own asking value and in your mind you are ready with a discount. A world toward which one cannot develop any kind of attachment, however ideal and prospective, is a world in which the pain it creates, the terror it inspires, the cruelty it shows is not utterly crushing pain or terror or cruelty, because it crushes with its absurdity the piety it generates. The only response to it therefore is the ironic.

In the light of the foregoing it is not difficult to see in concrete terms that the differences between Kierkegaard and Kafka are essential and the affinities superficial. For the one thing one could not impute to Kierkegaard is the empirical attitude. He starts with it but he soon soars away into a region where intuition and faith, free from the demands of empirical evidence, allow him to ignore the insoluble problems which for the thorough-going empiricist stand in the way of accepting a historical or even a personal religious view of man and the world. Kierkegaard is therefore not at all baffled by the nature of those elements which he found to transcend experience. He does not claim that he is able to "know" them; but the proper response towards them is not for him that of the pure knower, the abstract ratiocinator in search of verified "truth." The existentialist is a man of flesh and bones—as Unamuno put it—who disregarding the artificial limitations and restrictions of the pure knower, makes a total human decision and wills the act of belief; and not in the pragmatic sense of William James, either, but in a passionate, affirmative, plenary manner. For this reason Kierkegaard would have pooh-poohed the parallelism which has been found to exist between himself and Kafka. A man who tries to reach plenary conviction as to the transcending structure that subtends human experience by "cognitive" means places himself at the very opposite pole of Kierkegaardian existentialism. Furthermore, because for Kierkegaard the object of faith was infinite, man must be in the wrong and as a result must endure anguish. But this is his highest condition. By contrast, the anguish that at times almost chokes Kafka's characters —the stagnant, the oppressive atmosphere of Barnabas' home or the claustrophobiac closedness of Tintorelli's room, the terrifying searches, the endless corridors—is the result of insecurity which arises from lack of knowledge. In Kafka anguish issues from doubt, in Kierkegaard from certitude.

There is, however, a modicum of justification for the coupling of the Danish philosopher with the Jewish novelist, since the reading of the former does make us aware of the importance of anguish, of the crisis and of absolute disjunctions in human experience. Without a full appreciation of these factors as inherent in the human situation, the effort to understand Kafka turns into a diagnostic hunt for signs of neuroses. It is important to keep in mind however the different way in which these factors function in philosopher and poet although it is impossible to undertake here specifications of the differences.

4.

There is need to make explicit some hints I have given about what I take to be the validity of Kafka's conception of existence. Let us disregard the fact of his failure to bring any of his major works to completion, although such a failure may legitimately be taken as the basis for the most devastating criticism that may be leveled against Kafka's version of reality. Still it must be noted that Kafka's conception of existence is defective because it is inherently unstable. It seems to me that Kafka's picture constitutes a decided advance over that given us by contemporary naturalism, for Kafka has no desire to deny the evidence of experience which points to dimensions of existence which transcend it. But he could not or would not surrender his method to the demands of rationality and left us with a vision of the world which both artistically and philosophically represents an impasse. The change of attitude generated by the crisis opens to the subject large ranges of hitherto unsuspected possibilities as to the nature of existence. But these cannot be realized unless the new attitudes brought about by the crisis are accepted as revealing factors which experience itself cannot explore, but in which one must believe nevertheless even without a basis that those who have not gone through the crisis would be willing to accept as adequate evidence. And this is what the empiricist will not, cannot do. I believe it would be relatively easy to prove from his work that Kafka saw clearly the root of the difficulty. But his intellectual grasp of his perplexity was useless since his difficulty arose precisely from his insistence on the use of the intelligence beyond its legitimate range.

There is therefore a profound justification to Kafka's own remark that he expressed the negative tendencies of his age. Note however that he does so in the sense that he grasped clearly the meaning of certain phenomena as constitutive of normal human development in its break from what Kierkegaard called the "aesthetic" stage.   But he was not able to concede what is demanded in order to reach the "ethico-religious" stage. Having been thrust from the aesthetic his heroes stop before they reach the next stage. And they stop because they refuse—or are unable to bring themselves—to solve their problems by the only means that such problems can be solved; in the manner in which Plato solved his, through the recognition of the valid claims of religious intuition in certain ranges of experience; or in the manner in which Kant did, by supplying the terms required to complete a rational picture of the world as postulates made necessary by the objective demands of practical reason. It is this leap, taken by the greatest number of the major philosophers of our West, that Kafka, faithful to the limitations of his empiricism, will not take. In that refusal Kafka is at one with the negative tendencies of his age and remains impaled on the horns of a brutal antinomy.

NOTES

[1] *The Kafka Problem.* Edited by Angel Flores. New Directions. $5.00

[2] *Metamorphosis.* By Franz Kafka. Vanguard Press. $2.75
  The Great Wall of China. By Franz Kafka. Schocken Books. $3.00
  Franz Kafka. By Max Brod. Schocken Books. $3.00
  A Kafka Miscellany. Revised, Englarged Second Edition. Twice a Year Press. $3.50
  A complete German edition of Kafka's work is in process of publication by Schocken Books, New York.

[3] In his notes to *The Great Wall of China.* Rahv has also published psychoanalytic and sociological interpretations of Kafka in the *Kenyon* and *Southern Reviews.*

Dreiser, An Inconsistent Mechanist

1

It has become the fashion among the youngest intellectuals to dismiss Dreiser in a lofty and condescending manner. The man, we are informed, is essentially confused. Hence he is not worth reading. He is passé. All the more so since, lacking style, he cannot even be superficially enjoyed. Of course if style is defined in terms of cadence and euphony, in terms of choice of the impeccable image and the inevitable word, Dreiser has no style. But if style is more than this, then he cannot be denied style. For he has architectonic genius. In his lumbering, slow, painful, clumsy way he builds up a story. And when the story is built, the manner fits the matter even to clichés and all. Again, there is no doubt that in an important sense Dreiser is a confused man. But to dismiss him without further qualification is to ignore his depth and his range.

Dreiser's philosophy may be naïve, as his critics have so often pointed out, but it should not be forgotten that naïve is a very relative term. In comparison with the views of professional philosophers his ideas are no doubt unacceptable. But they are not foolish or unworthy of consideration. They were held, and not in an essentially different form, by some of the best minds of the last half of the nineteenth century; and essentially in the very form in which he holds them, they are still held by some thinkers whom we can not easily dismiss. But even if we could be sure that these ideas deserve no consideration whatever as systematic philosophy, it cannot be denied that their essential insight, that life has no transcending meaning that we can discover, is still valid and held by the very best of our modern minds. In any case, whether naïve or not, Dreiser's philosophy is still of high importance, for if he is not a philosopher he is certainly a novelist. As a novelist we can ignore him, but we cannot dismiss him. He has a deep sense of the dramatic movement of human life and a knowledge of its dark urges and baffled quality. He also has a wide range of vision and a deep sense of the relation of man to the cosmos. He is not only an American novelist but a universal novelist in a very literal sense of the word. The mystery of the universe, the puzzle of destiny, haunts him; and he, more than any of his contemporaries, has responded to the need to relate the haunting sense of puzzlement and mystery to the human drama. No other American novelist of his generation has so persistently endeavored to look at men under the form of eternity. It is then the surest sign of immaturity and naïveté to dismiss Dreiser on the counts of being naïve and lacking style. His prose is indeed fussy, his language a string of clichés; his thought is indeed naïve in many respects. But his prose is the man; his architectonic is superb; and his vision is turned towards horizons the existence of which novelists seldom suspect. But if all these claims can be asserted consistently the need arises to explain how a man guided by a naïve and unacceptable philosophy can be said to occupy the position he does—can be said to have the depth of insight he possesses.

2

Early in his youth Dreiser read and accepted the then popular materialistic mechanism. The picture of the world which Dreiser gained from his youthful reading must have been grasped by him with a deep sense of relief. He hated for deep personal reasons anything remotely allied with religion. Mechanism had the sanction of science. And the theory of evolution, with its emphasis on the ruthlessness of the struggle for survival, was merely an extension on a larger scale of what he himself had observed in Indiana, in Chicago, and in New York. He was untrained in the ways of rigorous analysis; and the materialism he accepted on affective rather than logical grounds was reduced by him to the notion of "chemisms," a word which had no doubt on him a strong and subtle emotive power. Through "chemism" he thinks he explains adequately all phenomena, organic no less than inorganic. Life is chemism, personality is chemism, the emotions are chemisms. There can really be no difference between the urge of the lower animals, human sex desire, and any sentiment that we have agreed to call higher. The animal in the darkness of the forest, Casanova, Dante, and Petrarch, as well as the Marquis de Sade or an Indiana young couple on a swing under an apple tree—they are all examples of chemism, and are fundamentally but the same thing. On his conception of chemism Dreiser grounds an individualistic philosophy. He tells us, not in these terms but to the same effect, that society is a mechanical addition of atomic individuals, each an independent package of force, each a self-contained monad, each determined somehow by chemical forces, each pushing or yielding, as it comes into contact with forces larger or smaller than its own. Thus society is but an additive compounding of mechanical forces, dynamically seeking a harmony which is constantly disrupted by the addition of new forces or by the disappearance of old ones. The individuals who additively make up society have each their own urges and their own strength. One seeks power, one peace, one the realization of an artist, the other security. Each encounters obstacles which baffle him or meets with helping currents which aid him toward his goal. The strong ones forge ahead, and the weak ones submit and are the tools of their betters. This is Darwinism at its starkest. When powerful individuals like Cowperwood appear, they disrupt the previously struck balance. The giants who have already arrived, and whose power is threatened by the appearance of a new one, gang up against the newcomver, use the pigmies for their purposes, the conflict quickens, and at the end, whatever the result, a new balance is struck.

In such a pitiless Darwinian world, where might is ultimate lord, he tells us that it is not morality but the appearance of it that counts. The hearty acceptance of ethical principles puts a handicap on the individual in the struggle. But pretense is a useful and invaluable aid. Society is a masked ball—that beauty, dancing so gaily with that man, is an old woman, has false teeth, suffers from arteriosclerosis, and has a bad breath in the morning; and the gallant leading her may be a beggar, or a horse thief, or a rat catcher, or a clever rogue, so cleverly disguised that he can deceive even himself. There you can see a great idealist preaching democracy and the supreme worth of each human personality; everybody wonders at his kindness and admires his gentleness. But we are all easily deceived. He is really a small man with a mean soul; he preaches equality because he hates and fears excellence; and he is a mirror of kindness because he achieves through it the sense of power which big-souled men achieve directly and frankly. He hates selfishness, because it interferes with his own selfishness; and hates self-assertion, because he can not tolerate his claims being crossed. He hates men who are arrogant, and loves modest men. But if we only look we can see he is himself the very essence of arrogance. And so with the others. Society is a masked ball. But there is one crime for which there is no forgiveness, no absolution—no man must appear in public without a mask. And a crime still greater, no man must ever tear a mask from another and leave him uncovered.

But this is not the whole picture, for Dreiser tells us that human society is made up of a number of subsocieties arranged hierarchically in terms of power and wealth, and in each one of these subdivisions the same pattern repeats itself. Within each group there are honors to be gained, privileges to be conquered, and relative ease and security to be enjoyed. And in each one, low or high, these are come by in the same way—through cunning, pitilessness, and luck.

In such a pitiless Darwinian world what can morality really mean? Morality is a technique of control, a means of keeping in check those men whose powerful and strong drives would wreck the balance struck by the group; it is in short a conspiracy of some of the masters and the slaves to keep the parvenu from running amuck. But of course truly strong men disregard the mythical sanctions which may deceive the weak but cannot deceive them. And for that reason no moral code ever fits the facts. One of his characters, obviously speaking for Dreiser himself—for he has expressed the same idea in the first person—was "always thinking in his private conscience that life was somehow bigger and subtler, and darker than any given theory or order of living." And for this reason, "life is to be learned from life, and the professional moralist is at best but the manufacturer of shoddy wares." These wares, shoddy and gratuitous for the strong, have another purpose—they are the sole consolation of the weak and the oppressed. And they may even have an aesthetic value, like the ephemeral rainbows one often catches sight of on the spray over an angry wave; but, like them, though they may be beautiful, they are utterly ineffective for controlling the danger of the sea.

In such a world, what meaning can life have? None, of course. In a world which is the product of blind forces, in a world of chemic determinations and mechanical resolutions, how can one expect that life have meaning?

> Privately his mind was a maelstrom of contradictions and doubts, feelings and emotions. Always of a philosophic turn of mind, this peculiar faculty of reasoning deeply and feeling emotionally were now turned upon himself and his own condition and, as in all such cases where we peer too closely into the subtleties of creation, confusion was the result. . .the world knew nothing. Neither in religion, philosophy nor science was there any answer to the riddle of existence. Above and below the little scintillating plane of man's thought was—what? Beyond the optic strength of the greatest telescope—far out upon the dim horizon of space— were clouds of stars. What were they doing out there? Who governed them? When were their sidereal motions calculated? He figured life as a grim dark mystery, a sad semi-conscious activity turning aimlessly in the dark. No one knew anything. God knew nothing—least of all himself. Malevolence, life living on death, plain violence—these were the chief characteristics of existence. If one failed in strength in any way, if life were not kind in its bestowal of gifts, if one were not born to fortune's pampering care— the rest was misery. In the days of his strength and prosperity the spectacle of existence had been sad enough: in the hours of threatened delay and defeat it seemed terrible. . . . (In the end, what one has, is death.) The abyss of death! When he looked into that after all of life and hope, how it shocked him, how it hurt. Here was life and happiness and love in health—there was death and nothingness—aeons and aeons of nothingness. . . .

His own life, a life of arduous labor and the most scrupulous artistic sincerity, has no more meaning than that of anyone else. And this is what he says of it in the *Bookman,* September, 1928, in a statement of his beliefs:

> I can make no comment on my work or my life that holds either interest or import for me. Nor can I imagine any explanation or interpretation of any life, my own included, that would be either true—or important, if true. Life is to me too much a welter and play of inscrutable forces to permit, in my case at least, any significant comment. One may paint for one's own entertainment,

and that of others—perhaps. As I see him the utterly infinitesimal individual weaves among the mysteries a floss-like and wholly meaningless course—if course it be. In short I catch no meaning from all I have seen, and pass quite as I came, confused and dismayed.

3

In its most important details this is the picture of man and the universe which Dreiser seems to believe he has discovered in his experiences and expressed in his novels. But fortunately for his greatness as a novelist, his explicit intellectual vision of the world is not point by point congruous with his vision as a novelist. And the philosophy which he has given us in essays and intercalated in the form of editorial comments in the movement of his dramas is not always true to the record. For there is more to his own concrete dramatic picture of men and society than he finds room for in his mechanistic philosophy. And if we miss this more, we miss, I am afraid, what is truly significant in Dreiser. His mechanism is indeed inadequate, but his dramatic vision of the world is fully ripe and mature. His characters are alive and real, moving and acting and brooding with all the urge and hesitation, passion and fear, doubts and contradictions, of fully real human beings. Few contemporary novelists have built up characters as solid, as three dimensional, as fully bodied, as Dreiser. And the reason why he has succeeded where others have failed is that in spite of his mechanism, few novelists respond to human beings as sensitively as he does. He admires or pities all kinds of men—the forceful money makers; the weak ones who are born to fail and suffer; the brilliant women who walk in and conquer; the respectable men and the disreputable ones; the masters and the slaves; the happy ones and the victims of meaningless forces who are condemned to live a life of pain, frustration, and denial.

Dreiser not only responds to human beings in a very immediate and sympathetic manner, but what is more important, he understands them. And his understanding goes far beyond the chemisms through which he thinks he explains them. For what does it mean to understand a man? Does it not mean to discover some order, some underlying direction, some permanent tendency by reference to which we as observers are able to organize what we know of him, and to decide what is important or relevant and what is not? And this is the reason why we read Dreiser and read him with profit, because in spite of his chemisms, and in spite of his poor taste in words and phrases, in spite of his fuzzy prose, and his addiction to unimportant realistic detail—which is never really as unimportant as we in our impatience think it is—we discover in his books insights about human beings we did not have before.

But what is most important of all, his dramatic picture of society and of morality do not corroborate the theories which he has put forth, and which have caused such violent reaction from conservative critics. His picture of men is not a picture of the hard atomic entities which his individualistic mechanism tells him they are. Nor does he really see society as a mere collection of atomic individuals. His characters are often a-social forces, working for ends destructive of the social equilibrium. But never completely so. Nor is society a mechanical addition of forces. Cowperwood, his reckless Robber Baron, is propelled by a strong will directed to the conquest of power and reckless of the claims of society in its search for satisfaction. But even Cowperwood is not utterly destructive, and his genius, in the pursuit of its own arbitrary ends, has a constructive side to it in quite an objective social sense. Nor is that will utterly arbitrary, nor is he utterly free and a-moral. Less so is Kalvin, a powerful but respectable and conservative business man, and Wittla, the genius. We need not go any farther. The personalities and characters of his big men as well as of his small are socially determined, and this in turn means really that it is society that furnishes the shark-man with the precise mold through which his power expresses itself and sets the limits to how far that will shall express itself unchallenged. We do not need to read this into his picture of society; it is there for us to see. Some of his Titans may even be utterly devoid, as he thinks, of ordinary human ties; this is never entirely the case, but grant it. Still in any case these Titans are what they are only in terms of the forces that shaped them, and thus it is that only in the society in which they were reared could they find the necessary outward resistance in terms of which their will can express itself. Grant this, and one has to grant that the ties one has with society are integral and internal and the relations that exist not external to the individuals which make up society. Thus from his own picture he could have seen that society is an organic pattern and as such makes the individual possible as the individual makes it possible. Morality then is not a club with which the individual is struck down and kept in line. It is, properly conceived, the molds in which the activities of individuals express themselves. There can be no matter without form, no activity without style. And the morality of any society is but the style or manner in which the individuals which are organic parts of it act.

Thus conceived, morality is larger than the codes through which men say they rule their actions, and life larger than any of its codes and rules, as Dreiser claims. But it cannot be larger than the forms and manners in which it expresses itself. "Life is larger than morality," only if morality is a set of rules, a code, which is fixed once for all and is too rigid to give way. And of course the moralist's wares are then shoddy wares. But it is coextensive with living if it is conceived as the manner life finds in which to express itself and through which it channels its forces. The mechanistic, atomistic conception of society and the belief that the individual is prior to it in both a logical and existential sense make this notion of morality incomprehensible. But a more acceptable conception of society would urge as part of it the dependences, the interconnections, and the often deep bonds which underly many of the stresses under normal circumstances, and even under abnormal ones. Even in overt conflict interdependences exist and rules of behavior obtain. Men never can live in utter and complete chaos. There are laws of war as well as of peace. Men simply have to trust others and depend on them mutually; nor are we free, even the least sentimental of us, from loyalties and sympathies and deep-rooted interests. Factors such as these, bonds, ties, forces, deep interconnections, are always found. And they make up society as much as the will of the strong and the yielding of the weak. And they do so as much in Dreiser's pictures as they do in actuality.

Why does he not see this? The phenomenon is common. It is simply a failure to readjust theory to facts. Dreiser does not find the moral code in which he was brought up by a narrow and intense father anywhere operative in the world into which, ill equipped but sensitive, he was thrust. But emotionally he has never ceased to demand that morality be what he was taught it was—a rigid code, where idealism is always unmistakably good, and selfishness distinctly an unalloyed evil. His characters are capable of pity and courage and idealism as often as of ruthlessness and strength and indifference to their fellows. But a man's idealism must needs adjust itself to other forces, is but a need among many, and needs be intelligent and enlightened; nor is there guaranty that it will be even then unconditionally successful.

Essentially the same considerations apply to Dreiser's discovery that life has no meaning. Nowhere in the cold ranges of the sky and in the wonders of submicroscopic space can we find a direction, a purpose, to guide us and give our activity as assurance of transcending significance. Hence his perplexity, his sense of futility, his monotonous refrain regarding the vanity of effort in such a sorry world. But would he think that life was without meaning if it were not for the fact that though he is a mechanist, he insists nevertheless on a transcendent meaning? His characters and his own life never lacked drive, never lacked purpose, never lacked meaning. One of his characters finds the meaning to his activity in success, another finds it in power, another in love, and one in dedication to a Benevolent Deity. Dreiser himself, an artist, finds it in the sincere and uncompromising expression of his vision of life. What meaning can it have besides that? Obviously what has happened to Dreiser is that he never outgrew his childhood training, and though intellectually he knows better, emotionally he still hankers for transcendent support. He *knows*, that is, that the universe is a purposeless affair, but he never learned a lesson Spinoza might have taught him, namely that it couldn't but be, since purpose and therefore value, are relative human affairs. What are they then? Where do they spring from? From within, of course, from drives and wants and needs. Given an organism which has urges and seeks their satisfaction in a social environment, and value and purpose appear, at the level of intelligence, in terms of plans, directions, and campaigns.

Dreiser is a bigger and more faithful artist than his philosophy permits him to be. As editor, he is always telling us that the picture he paints is meaningless. But within his novels his men and women always find life has a driving significance which overpowers them. Sometimes the meaning it has is sinister; some-

times pathetic; sometimes tragic.   But meaning it always has.
And if life's meaning is sometimes sad or tragic, in Dreiser we
find, in his enormous pity and in his sympathy, a vision of life
not altogether impossible to realize in which some at least of
the darkness he records could be eliminated.

Dostoevsky: Philosopher or Novelist?*

It is Professor Wasiolek's explicit intention to go beyond the available works of criticism of Dostoevsky's novels. Much work on the Russian, he tells us, appears year after year: biographies, source studies, editions of letters, and bibliographical aids. But "time has frayed away much that once seemed useful both in Russia and in the West." The work of older as well as more recent critics is cited only to be dismissed as useless for one reason or another, but chiefly because it does not explain the actions of Dostoevsky's characters. In order to achieve an understanding of the strange behavior of the characters we want not only an understanding of the technique used by Dostoevsky in his novels "but we also want all the ideas we can understand, and we want neither as an end in itself. . . . The wedding of both procedures that unique logic that characterizes the work of every great novelist." It is the exposition and analysis of that "logic" that Professor Wasiolek undertakes to give us. And with the aim, stated in general terms, no one can quarrel. The trouble may begin when we ask ourselves what our critic means by "ideas," by "wedding," and by the manner in which "ideas" and "technique" are "wedded" to produce the "logic" of Dostoevsky's work.

In the very useful bibliography that Professor Wasiolek offers us at the end of his book, he characterizes George Steiner's *Tolstoy or Dostoevsky* as "a brilliant 'bad' book." I hope it will not be considered a case of boiling the kid in the milk of its mother if I imitate Professor Wasiolek and say that he has written a useful, a learned, a welcome, but nevertheless a "bad" book. It is not a book to be dismissed as inconsequential or shallow. It is not a bad book *tout court*. It accomplishes some of the aims that the author sets out to accomplish. But it suffers, in the opinion of the reviewer, from a serious defect that puts it in the class in which its author puts Steiner's book.

---

*Dostoevsky: The Major Fiction. By Edward Wasiolek. Massachusetts Institute of Technology Press, 1965.

The book's virtues are many and some of them deserve high acclaim. Professor Wasiolek reads Dostoevsky seriously in the light of Russian thought of Dostoevsky's own day and ours; he knows Russian literature and philosophy—or at least, he so impresses one who does not. Nor is his erudition confined to Russian letters. Again, his commentaries on the novels he has chosen for detailed analysis—the major ones—are often illuminating, they are never dull, and on the whole they contribute a great deal of information of the kind that will enable the reader to return to novels he may be acquainted with and find in them values— meanings, significances, relationships—he had not suspected, or that will lead him to discover in themes he was fully familiar with depths he might not have adequately probed, nuances he might not have noticed before. But above all, Professor Wasiolek is not repelled by Dostoevsky's commitment to God, to Russia, and to the Czar. Many critics who consider Dostoevsky a profound psychologist have been embarrassed by his religious and political commitments. Freud's characterization is typical. It will be remembered that Freud puts Dostoevsky next to Shakespeare as an artist and deplores that a genius who might have employed his talent to liberate mankind employed it to keep it in chains. Our own liberal critics have reacted, as one would expect, in very much the same manner. That Dostoevsky might not have been the psychologist he was had he continued to develop his pre-Siberian attitudes—his shallow socialism, his struthonian belief in the perfectability of man, his myopic dogoodism, his pro-enlightenment optimism, his pro-European attitudes—this is something that no believer in the perfectability of man and the rest of the syndrome of shallow liberal errors can, of course, face. But Professor Wasiolek, without approving explicitly or even by indirection Dostoevsky's politics, grabs hold, if I may be allowed the expression, of the bristling porcupine that is Dostoevsky, without fear, evasion, or crippling selectivity to fit the prejudices of our regnant liberal ethos. On Professor Wasiolek's interpretation Dostoevsky comes out a great novelist who is a profound psychologist—and, alas, a deep Christian and a great philosopher.

It is in respect to the last claim that I must disagree with Professor Wasiolek. I doubt whether Dostoevsky's novels are Christian in any acceptable sense of the term. I do not doubt that Dostoevsky himself was, or more exactly, that he tried desperately to be, a Christian. But I stick to D. H. Lawrence's dictum:

> Oh give me the novel. Let me hear what the novel says.
> As for the novelist, he's usually a dribbling liar.

It is the novels, and not the novelist, that do not seem to me to be Christian. However, I do not want to argue this point. I want to examine the claim that Dostoevsky's concern over his "ideas," as Professor Wasiolek understands that concern, is to be taken seriously by us. But before I put my criticism of Professor Wasiolek on record I would like to iterate something already acknowledged above in passing: If the matter were to be decided in terms of knowledge of the available scholarship on Dostoevsky I would not allow myself the luxury of an opinion for or against this book. For I simply do not possess the broad acquaintance with the relevant literature that Professor Wasiolek obviously has.

Why then do I dare to disagree with Professor Wasiolek? I do so because the disagreement is fundamentally not about two incompatible interpretations of Dostoevsky's novels—interpretations that might depend on the correct reading of texts; the disagreement goes deeper; it is about what a novelist, any novelist writing in any language, attempts to do. And this is not a question of scholarship on Dostoevsky or any other novelist; it is a question of aesthetics. Not only does Professor Wasiolek claim that Dostoevsky is seriously concerned with his "ideas"—which in one sense the great Russian unquestionably was—but he would have it—and he states it in so many words, in several places, and in diverse contexts—that Dostoevsky first thought out his problems in the way in which philosophers think theirs and then "dramatized" his thought. And this—I must put it bluntly—seems to me to be a radical misunderstanding of the nature of the novelist's creative process; or, what is the very same thing, a misunderstanding of what a novel attempts to say, and when successful, does indeed say. The upshot is that Professor Wasiolek's view is not only inadmissible as aesthetics but that it results in leading him to attribute to Dostoevsky the intention to defend in his novels a great many ideas—conceptual structures, hypotheses, opinions, doctrines—that are sheer nonsense. If Dostoevsky is putting forth, in the manner in which Professor

Wasiolek would have it, the views attributed to him, our critical problem would not be to state and explain the obviously silly nonsense Dostoevsky is said to defend, it would be to explain how and why a man who holds such nonsense has gained a powerful grip on some of the best minds of our culture since he first came to their attention.

I cannot go into the kind of analysis that the problem calls for in order properly to elucidate it. For the sake of succinctness I shall have to put my argument in specific terms. The issue is, however, a complex one, and one to which we cannot do justice in terms of the examples that I shall offer for consideration. Kindly note, therefore, that the examples serve merely to define the issue, not to establish my thesis.

Professor Wasiolek tells us that Dostoevsky holds, among many other philosophical hypotheses, the tenet that the laws of nature do not exist because reason itself as an objective entity does not exist. He continues: "There is no 'reason' in Dostoevsky's world, only reasoners. . . . There are no 'ideas' in Dostoevsky's world apart from the men who carry them." And indulging in an irritating, fingerwagging, schoolmasterish habit he has of alerting the reader when he is about to pronounce what he takes to be an important conclusion, Professor Wasiolek italicizes the following statement: "*Every act of reason for Dostoevsky is a covert act of will.*" Earlier he had told us that for Dostoevsky the *will* (italics his) is an unqualified first premise of existence. And toward the end of chapter 4, from which I derive these views, he tells us:

> The problem that Dostoevsky faces after writing the *Notes* [*from the Underground*] is how to preserve the freedom [of the will] and restrain its destructive implications. In the next novel, *Crime and Punishment,* he attempts to dramatize a way out of this. . . .

Let us look into these statements. First, if any man were to tell us today, or even had told us in the middle of the last century, that "the laws of nature do not exist," we would simply shrug our shoulders and wonder how this paleolithic Papuan managed to disguise himself and learn the language of contemporary men. Since Newton, since Galileo, even earlier, such obscurantistic nonsense has not deserved refutation. That the laws of nature "exist" is a claim that would have to be examined with greater care than Professor Wasiolek's Dostoevsky would have been capable of putting into it. Exactly what is the mode of existence of a law of nature? The verb "to exist" and other related grammatical forms bring with them difficult technical problems on which philosophers do not agree and will not agree till kingdom come. But that the laws of nature do not hold for reality—or at least for that aspect of reality called "nature," to which man to some extent belongs, for there may be an aspect or level of reality for which they do not hold—this is a belief that only a madman or a paleolithic mentality could seriously maintain. The laws of nature can be established as the tenet of the freedom of the will cannot be. I believe in the freedom of the will—if I am allowed to define the terms. But the argument that can be advanced in favor of this belief cannot claim the evidential strength that a scientist's proof brings in support of any law of nature. This is so obvious that in these post-Carnapian days of our misery one is ashamed to have to state it. But in view of the seriousness with which Professor Wasiolek seems to take Dostoevsky's ideas, or his "ideas," the obvious must be asserted. If Dostoevsky really believed that the laws of nature do not exist he was mad, or paleolithic, or both, and to take his ideas seriously is, today, for an educated man, impossible.

Furthermore, according to Professor Wasiolek, Dostoevsky holds that the laws of nature do not exist because reason does not exist. What can this statement mean? And above all, what could it mean to a man who, like Dostoevsky, believed or rather tried to believe in God? For if God exists then reason has some sort of objective reality in the sense that reasoning or reason is part of God's nature. Let us take another step. Surely the laws of nature "existed" before man was on earth and human reason discovered them. How could one deny this? To do so would be to believe that nature is pure chaos, and were it the case, we would not be discussing the question. Or did Professor Wasiolek's Dostoevsky mean that it is man's reasoning that creates the invariant relations formulated in the laws of nature? Or perhaps that it is man's reasoning that created nature itself? A view something like this one has been held in all earnestness by some philosophers; but the statement, as we find it in Professor Wasiolek's book, is too vague to identify, or analogize, with any responsible philosophical doctrine.

Professor Wasiolek tells us, further, that there is no "reason" in Dostoevsky's world, only reasoners. With this view behaviorists today would be in hearty agreement. And I, who am not a behaviorist in the philosophical sense, am also in hearty agreement with it. If by "reason" be meant an immaterial organ, something like a mental liver or lung, a hypostatized mentalistic affair, Dostoevsky is utterly right in denying the existence of "reason." But why then does he hypostatize the will? To be consistent, Professor Wasiolek's Dostoevsky should have said, "Every act of reasoning is a covert act of willing." But had he said that, he would have to say that it is not the will but willing, pure willing, that is the unqualified first premise of existence; and this is a harder thesis to maintain, since it involves the denial of substance, material and spiritual, and this denial entails the denial of immortality. That every act of reasoning is an act of will or willing is a patently false statement in one sense, but in another it may be turned into tenable doctrine, though I would want to know more than Professor Wasiolek tells us about the will and much else before I would accept or reject the doctrine or would modify it in order to be able to entertain it.

As a philosopher, let it be put as plainly as it can be, Dostoevsky has no claim whatever on our serious attention. He was a superstitious, credulous, obscurantist mind, darkened by radical incoherences, and bent on hanging on to beliefs that were the sheerest drivel. And for this harsh judgment there is more than sufficient evidence from Dostoevsky himself. But note that the discussion has been carried on in Professor Wasiolek's terms; on the assumption, that is, that Dostoevsky thought in the way in which a philosopher thinks, and then proceeded to dramatize his thought. If he had done that, his novels, a sample of which I have just examined, would be a large puddle of nonsense and utterly unworthy of the serious attention of serious readers. But a novelist is not a philosopher nor is a philosopher a novelist. There may have been novelists who were philosophers and philosophers who were novelists. If I remember correctly, May Sinclair was one of them, and I have been told that Iris Murdock used to be one of them too. I only report the rumor as to Miss Murdock, for I have not read any of her novels and I have been told that she gave up "doing philosophy," as the members of her

Club call it, some time ago. But if there have been successful schizophrenics of this kind, writers who were not hybrids but truly schizoid and who therefore did not look like a cross between a borzoi and a dachshund, Dostoevsky was not one of them. He was strictly a novelist and it is as a novelist that we must honor and cherish him. That he showed concern for ideas in his notebooks, in his letters and newspaper articles, as Professor Wasiolek points out, no one would wish to deny. But what we must consider first (and as far as I am concerned, last) is what is to be found in his novels. Some scholars may be interested in Dostoevsky's philosophy. We have already seen a sample of what they will turn up when they begin to investigate it. But for what Dostoevsky the novelist thought and how he thought it, we must go to the whole novel. When we do we see the error of confusing the philosopher and the novelist.

That his novels are "philosophical novels" no one would care to deny. But what this statement means is not easy to explain and I do not intend to expound it here. Let me merely suggest that the informed substance of a philosophical novel possesses a dimension that the most successful stories of Hemingway altogether lack. But whatever it means, it does not mean that a philosophical novel is one in which "ideas" are "wedded" to "technique" remain separate from the technique after the wedding, even if they happen to share legally and sacramentally the same bed; for no priest or judge can fuse two bodies and turn them into one organism. Russian biologists claim to have attached an extra head to a dog, and the pictures show what they have accomplished aesthetically. In art it simply does not work. Often "ideas" "wedded" to "technique" try to act as if they were one organism. But the effort is futile, and the neighbors can hear the squabbling even before the wedding night is over. To write a novel one must think dramatically and technically at one and the same time and from the start. What one thinks about depends on oneself. At one pole we have Hemingway thinking about fishing and bulls and at the other Dostoevsky thinking about the agonizing puzzles of man's life. But it should be borne in mind that as fiction writers they think alike, novelistically, dramatically. From fishing and bulls the philosopher is not able to abstract—to take out—the ideas he takes out of the novelist's dramatic grasp of the agonies of man's life. But to organize human puzzles dramatically, so that they can be gathered

by the mind as presentations, and to take out of them ideas, are
two totally different acts.

Note that I am not saying that a novelist does not think.
Of course he does. And Dostoevsky the novelist thought profoundly. Moreover, as a novelist he thought ever so much better
than as a philosopher. My guess, for what it may be worth, as to
the reason for the enormous difference between the novelistic
and the philosophical thought of Dostoevsky is not only that he
thought concretely and not abstractly, but that he could organize
the cataclysmic contradictions that wracked his soul in terms of
dramatic agonists although he could not resolve them conceptually. He could pit the Karamazovs against Father Zossima;
but he could not build a coherent system out of the *aporiai* he
discerned at the heart of being. For it was from the heart of
being whence flowed the *aporiai* that wracked him. Most philosophers could easily have done it. A few passes of their verbal
wands and being turns out to be altogether good, altogether holy
and beautiful and true. Dostoevsky saw too deeply and too
clearly and his vision was too honest to try such tricks.

In any case, the notion that the only kind of thinking that
goes on, goes on in the skull and by means of concepts, proposi-
tions, judgments, is a notion worthy of some philosophers, but
hardly worthy of a man whose business is to examine the work
of poets. The true novelist thinks dramatically as the dancer
thinks with her whole body in movement, and as the composer
thinks with the notes and scales and the conventions of his art,
and as the painter thinks with his eye and hand or arm and his
passion for color and line or whatever he puts on the flat surface
he seeks to cover. The dancer's body, of course, includes a brain
—often of considerable volume. But a dancer's "ideas" do not
call for words or anything that can be expressed in words. A
novelistic or a dramatic "idea" is not a philosophic idea. And the
relation between a dramatic situation or idea and an idea in the
philosopher's sense of the word is not one of skeleton to fleshed
or dressed up skeleton. It is inadmissible intellectualism to hold
that a genuine novelist poses a problem to himself and then
dramatizes its solution in conceptual terms.

Your true novelist—and Dostoevsky was the truest of the
true—thinks dramatically, in terms of scenes, in which the per-

sons of the drama are related in affinities and oppositions of diverse kinds—love and hate, desire and rejection or acceptance, contempt or admiration, the call of duty and the flight from it or its acceptance. But these are abstractions about a situation which for the novelist comes first and for the philosopher comes last, if it comes at all. A philosophic idea is a hypothesis or a set of hypotheses. A "dramatic 'idea' " (and there is no reason why we should seek to avoid the term) is a scene such as the great scene in the Elder's cell with which, after the preliminary exposition, as Professor Wasiolek rightly asserts, Dostoevsky begins his last great novel. One of the abstractions of the "dramatic 'ideas' " may be an idea in the philosophic sense: the idea, for instance about whether everything is permitted if there is no immortality. But this abstraction is only a part of the dramatic idea or scene, and if taken outside the scene it must be tested not by its dramatic function but by its truth, thus quartering the novel and turning part of it into a compendium of the kind of irresponsible notions about the will and the laws of nature that we are told Dostoevsky held. He may have held the pack of nonsense that he is said to have held. If he did, no one who takes philosophy seriously need waste a minute's time examining Dostoevsky's philosophy.

Professor Wasiolek sometimes writes as if he accepted the doctrine from which my criticism has been launched. Thus in his Preface he writes: "But what is major in Dostoevsky is his vision and his grasp of the human situation. . . ." Aside from the fact that "the human situation" should be carted off, in company with "the image of man" "in our time" to the village dump of clichés, this is a statement that it is a pity Professor Wasiolek did not use to control his examination of Dostoevsky's fiction. It is Dostoevsky the man, not the novelist, who writes the well-known statement that Professor Wasiolek uses as the first epigraph of his book:

> Even if it were proved to me that Christ was outside the truth, and it was really so that the truth were outside of Christ, then I would prefer to stay with Christ rather than the truth.

A man who writes this is asseverating a conviction that he is having a hard time hanging on to.

Professor Wasiolek tells us that it was characteristic of Dostoevsky that, as he matured, he came "to grant so much that the antagonists are almost unanswerable." There is a truth here, but the formulation hardly does it justice because the writer assumes that in the novel Dostoevsky is on one side of the conflict and some of his characters are on the other. This is probably the case with Dostoevsky the man; but it is not at all the case with Dostoevsky the novelist. Even if a person called Fyodor Dostoevsky were one of the characters of the novel, *The Brothers Karamazov,* he could not speak for Dostoevsky the novelist. The belief that he could, or that some of the characters of the novel— Father Zossima, say—speak for his views, while others speak for the views he is opposed to, follows from the inadmissible belief that the writer of fiction first thinks through a problem in the way in which a philosopher does and then dramatizes his thought. What happens in Dostoevsky's novels is that as the novelist matures and comes to grasp more firmly the "logic" of the demonic agonists of his dreams, he succeeds the better in giving them an authenticity that he could not have given them earlier. I use the word "logic" as Professor Wasiolek intends it— or as I believe he does. But I would prefer another expression; however, the use of it would call for a more extended exposition of the aesthetic that controls my criticism than I could give it here. Be that as it may, as Dostoevsky matures and digests his experience, he sees more deeply into the murky depths of the human soul, and what he glimpses is the demonic element in man. But being a novelist he does not see it in man generically but in individuals: Ivan, and earlier, Stavrogin and the others. What he sees is not simple. And among the complexities, he grasps the chaos and despair from which Ivan's anxiety wells up when he confronts evil and faces the consequences of atheism.

Call the novelist the poet, as I prefer to call him because he is a maker. The more deeply the poet's vision penetrates into the depths of the human soul, the less the philosopher is able to fit the poet's vision into the neat, systematic, selvage-edged fabric of his thought. What has happened is that the philosopher has been given the lie by the poet. This has been happening from time immemorial and helps to account, incidentally, for the animus, concealed as contempt, that the philosopher displays toward the poet. In any case, as the poet's vision goes deeper, it discovers, as Dostoevsky the poet did, that the demonic aspect of man is considerably more attractive, more forceful, more irrepressible, more truly real, than the religious man or philosophic God-believer would like it to be. Dostoevsky the poet is not embarked on the hopeless task of answering Ivan. It was the man who wrote the letter from which Professor Wasiolek obtained his epigraph who tried—in vain—to answer. How can a man be answered, even if he is a fictive man, particularly when that man is the imaginative creation of one of the greatest—to my mind the greatest—novelists that our Western civilization has produced? You can shoot a man and you may even disprove his hypothesis. You may be able to brainwash him. But answer *him*? A man, an honest man such as Ivan—a man whose mendacity was too deep for us to throw it in his face—cannot be answered.

Novelists who dramatize conceptual problems do not write novels; they write bad philosophy in novelistic garb. This is what Dostoevsky the man would have liked to have written to disprove Ivan. But he could not do it. It takes less talent than he had to succeed at that kind of prostitution. These novelistic call-girls try but their dramatized ideas—their hypotheses, their doctrines, their notions—never achieve the luminous self-sufficiency of a person. Dostoevsky wrote good novels; no one ever wrote better ones. When we try to squeeze "ideas" from them what we get is nonsense—nonsense about the laws of nature, about the freedom of the will, about all sorts of other topics. Unfortunately to do more than state this, to elucidate it convincingly, as it deserves to be elucidated, is, as I have already pointed out, more than I can undertake here. It would take a long essay or a number of essays. And in any case these essays are already in print.

We must be grateful to Professor Wasiolek for his effort to take Dostoevsky the philosophical novelist seriously. But we must also recognize that to turn Dostoevsky into a philosopher is to do him and ourselves serious disservice—as serious a disservice, I would say, as is done to him and to themselves by the liberal critics who accept his "psychology" and reject the rest of his vision of the world.

Dostoyevsky, "Poet" in Spite of Himself

I am an old "Nechaievetz" myself.
Feodor Dostoyevsky[1]

1.

Very few critics of Dostoyevsky have pointed out why one of the greatest "poets" of the West—using the word in its extended meaning—failed almost entirely to do what he intended. A few have been aware that he spoke with many voices; but we have not been told why. It is assumed that in his major novels he defended doctrines he professed and attacked successfully those he rejected; and he gave his critics reasons for doing so. To a friend he wrote about one of his great novels, *The Possessed:* "I am anxious to express certain ideas, even if it ruins my novel as a work of art. . . . Let it turn out to be only a pamphlet. But I shall say everything to the last word."

The majority of his critics have taken him at his word. Some of them write seriously of him as a philosopher; a professor—Teutonic, of course—has expounded his thought "systematically." I shall attempt to show why such interpretations of the Russian are incorrect.

To establish this thesis satisfactorily is a job for a book consisting of two parts: one an exposition of the theory on which the criticism is based, the other the application of that theory to the texts. In an essay all one can do is outline a sketchy defense of it. After suggesting briefly the theoretical assumptions I bring to my reading of *The Brothers Karamazov,* I shall sketchily discuss the novel as a whole in very general terms; and I shall finally detach from the novel a part that can be read separately without serious impairment to it, in order to show that when properly read this part contains something quite different from the propaganda that is usually found in it and something that is considerably more valuable than that propaganda.

Such a detachable section is Ivan's famous poem or legend, "The Grand Inquisitor." A Russian critic, writing in 1891 and recently translated into English, asserts twice in his book that the connection of "The Grand Inquisitor" with the plot of the novel "is so slight that it can be regarded as a separate work," although he contradictorily qualifies and writes that it can be regarded as the heart of the whole work. I take no such view. The novel is an organic unit; it is no more the loosely connected episodes Dostoyevsky originally planned than one of the baggy monsters or fluid puddings that Henry James took Dostoyevsky's works to be. What the novel says cannot be understood by regarding the poem or legend as slightly connected with it; but I am convinced that the poem, together with the two chapters preceding it—with which it is inseparably tied up—can be separately analyzed if we remember that in so doing we are not saying anything about the whole novel.

To read Dostoyevsky's novels as poetry it is necessary to distinguish between Dostoyevsky the man and Dostoyevsky the poet. The man I shall call Feodor Mikhailovitch, or occasionally plain Feodor or the man, when the designation is clear. The poet I shall call Dostoyevsky. And the man and poet I shall arbitrarily call the person, whom I think of as Feodor Mikhailovitch Dostoyevsky.

We know the views that Feodor Mikhailovitch entertained because we have his letters, *The Diary of a Writer,* and other reports of his opinions, such as his wife's. Here we find Feodor's beliefs outside the novels. Why can't we say that when we find these opinions stated in the novels they are what Dostoyevsky intended to say? They certainly are the opinions Feodor Mikhailovitch intended to express, but not what Dostoyevsky actually expressed, what the novels expressed. We make the distinction because we can show in general terms that writers do not always do what they set out to do and in the case of the person Feodor Mikhailovitch Dostoyevsky that the novels expressed dramatically profound conflicts, each side of which had equal value in the novels considered as novels. On these conflicts Feodor Mikhailovitch took sides but the artist clearly did not. Indeed, some critics have argued that the side Feodor rejected occasionally gained the upper hand in Dostoyevsky's novels. For instance, it has been said that Dostoyevsky "does not answer Ivan." A close look into the novels will show that Dostoyevsky was too much of a poet to do what the man set out to do, to write propaganda.

We find that the psychological-philosophical chaos that was Feodor Mikhailovitch Dostoyevsky, the person, was brought to order in two distinct ways: the poet brought the chaos to order by aesthetic presentation of it; the man by the exercise of a powerful fiat of faith, choosing one side and repudiating the other. But the conflicts that Feodor Mikhailovitch tried to do away with willfully outside his poetry are found in the novels, fully organized aesthetically and presented as dramatic conflicts among the characters or within them. This is old hat—or should be. But the conclusion that must be drawn from this fact is just what partisan critics, for or against the opinions of Feodor Mikhailovitch, would like to deny or ignore; namely, that the novels do not defend the tenets espoused by the man. Feodor Mikhailovitch sought to strangle with the iron fist of a willful faith the nonreligious or antireligious other—as I am forced to call him, inappropriately, to avoid an extended characterization—while upholding the Christian, conservative man. But one set of values is as truly the poet's as the other and both are completely authentic. To say that one comes from his hand while he rejects the other is to undertake a selection by means of a criterion that is external to the novel, based on an assumption that, when carefully considered—as I cannot consider it in this essay—must be rejected.

Let me dwell on this point, for it is the keystone of my argument, although I cannot defend it satisfactorily here. If the critic should say, "We can easily detect in the novels the views that Dostoyevsky wanted to defend and attack," I ask, "Which of the two individuals that make up the person do you have in mind?" For the critic making this assertion has failed to distinguish between the man and the poet and seems to assume that the Feodor Mikhailovitch is more authentic than Dostoyevsky. I hold that what Dostoyevsky has to say comes from the whole person's hand and therefore expresses more completely, much more authentically, what the whole person has to say than what Feodor Mikhailovitch has to say. Feodor, the Christian, lover of the Russian peasant, hater of the Crystal Palace, compulsive gambler, anti-Semite and the rest, a man who gave evidence of admirable and also of contemptible traits of character, was constituted by a crust of customs, habits, values, dogmas, loyalties and profound repudiations, sympathies and aversions, brought into being by both external and internal exigencies. It is necessary to sketch hastily both the external and internal pressures that made Feodor Mikhailovitch.

The external ones include first, the impact of his Siberian experience on his socialist illusions. He went to Siberia believing in reason, progress, the Pelagian notion of man that is at the basis of socialism, and everything else that he later turned against and packed into the image of the Crystal Palace. In the house of the dead he was confronted with appalling human types that challenged profoundly his Pelagian faith in human perfectibility and aroused to a high tension his psychological talent; he read the Gospels during the whole sojourn (he was not allowed to read anything else). Many other factors contributed to his conversion. The result was profound remorse and his turning fiercely against his earlier convictions in an attempt to uproot them. The Feodor Mikhailovitch to whom I have been referring is the post-Siberian man. Feodor tightened the powerful fingers of his new faith on the throat of his old beliefs and let go with relief when he thought that they were no longer breathing; but it is not easy if at all possible to do the past in. Feodor Mikhailovitch left us evidence outside the novels that with his penetrating acuity the fact did not escape him, at least at times, that he had not killed his old beliefs. In a letter written after he left prison to the woman who gave him the copy of the Gospels on the way to prison, he wrote: "I will tell you regarding myself that I am a child of the age, a child of nonbelief and doubt, up to now and even (I know it) until my coffin closes." The paragraph ends with the much quoted statement that if someone were to prove to him that Christ is outside the truth he would prefer Christ. In *The Diary of a Writer*, much later, he tells us: "I am an old 'Nechaievetz' myself." If a man saw clearly the double, it was Dostoyevsky, and his sight came from self-knowledge.

The distinction between man and poet must be qualified, however, in one important respect. Occasionally, Feodor Mikhailovitch manages to intrude himself into Dostoyevsky's work. The narrator who tells the story of *The Brothers* breaks into his account with what I call "editorial remarks;" one of these will be noted below. Exactly how these editorial remarks can be handled without impairing the distinction between man and poet is a question I cannot go into here, suffice it to assert that when they are reckoned with the distinction nevertheless remains.

To justify the distinction between the man and the poet we have to consider the nature of the creative act. Feodor Mikhailovitch is thinking about writing a novel with full intention of defending his post-Siberian beliefs and refuting his earlier socialist errors. A number of years before he finally sits down to write the novel he conceives a vague theme, the life of a great sinner. The theme serves various purposes: it serves as a mnemonic device and a sort of North Star; it also serves as a means of grouping roughly what he slowly discovers he wants to say, which John Dewey calls "the matter for" the novel. (I use Dewey's terminology, although awkward, rather than the language employed by A. C. Bradley in his famous inaugural, "Poetry for Poetry's Sake," because Bradley, brilliant and substantively clear as he is, does not employ fixed terminology.) As he gathers this "matter for" he stores it in a notebook.[2]

When does the poet emerge? He does not come out all at once, as the chick out of the shell, ready to peck. Gradually, as he works with the matter for the novel, slowly or rapidly informing it, the in-forming process transubstantiates the matter. Slowly, the poet is emerging, finally to rise triumphantly when the job is finished. We know something about the actual making of *The Brothers Karamazov,* it did not occur exactly like this. But this is what, ideally, could have occurred. It follows that to the extent that the in-formed substance is like the matter the poet used for the novel, to that extent the creative act has failed.

The matter for the novel is utterly heterogeneous; it consists of dramatic sketches not yet fully drawn, images, recollections of discussions with friends, of books Feodor once read, of individuals and situations that intrigue him, fears and hopes, it may even consist of cadences—in short everything that comes to mind that seems more or less relevant to Feodor Mikhailovitch's theme.   But his job does not merely consist of trimming and fitting pieces that existed before he began his work.   As Dostoyevsky proceeds, he brings to the job his previous experience— a sense of form, a habit of working, the way to make what he does not clearly know as yet he wants to say, which he slowly discovers as he makes.   As he seeks to in-form the matter for the novel he adds to the object in the making, from the absolute spontaneity of his mind, notions that float mysteriously to the surface of consciousness from a depth that is beyond introspection, where the genuinely creative work is going on.   The result, the finished novel, is a genuine synthesis.

As he makes, Dostoyevsky gradually comes into more and more firm control of his job; but that control remains limited to the end.   Remember how often we have been told by poets that they could not make their characters behave as the maker wanted his characters to behave.   We know the way George Eliot's characters wrestled with her till they pinned her shoulders to the mat, got up victoriously, and went their way doing as they pleased, while helpless Miss Evans looked on puzzled and resigned. George Eliot's characters had their way while the artist had the grace, or was forced, to yield.   Arnold Bennett has told us that he was no man to let his characters gain the whip hand over him. Well, this is one of the reasons George Eliot was George Eliot and Arnold Bennett was—alas, only Arnold Bennett.

In *The Notebooks for the Brothers Karamazov* Feodor Mikhailovitch writes, for instance, "All is permitted."   This is a reminder of a conceptual or ideational, nondramatic bit that jostled in his mind with other components he was thinking of for his novel, some conceptual, some of other kinds, such as snatches of memory difficult to classify because of their hybrid nature, phrases, pictures, and perhaps even wordless cadences. He thinks of a boy lying down on the tracks as a train goes over him and wants to make sure that it can be done; he wants to know about monks and visits a monastery—he is researching.   As he works, the mixture loses its initial heterogeneity and becomes the substance of the novel, but it is not yet fully transubstantiated from the "matter for" and not yet fully in-formed.

2.

What, then, can we find in *The Brothers Karamazov?* A vast universe enclosed in a "little town," as Dostoyevsky called it, named Skotoprigonevsk or Cattle Pen, in Richard Peace's translation. I once distinguished in print two dimensions of reality in the novel, the natural and the metaphysical; but within the first, several could be distinguished with profit. For instance, the psychological, the social, and that aspect of the religious that is a distinct expression of man's efforts to respond to the divine through man-made institutions and is therefore endowed with all the defects we may expect to find in the work of human hands. The metaphysical domain is the domain of Father Zossima and one which ends up by impinging on the lives of some important characters who dwell at the start in a totally secular, naturalistic universe.

Can this vast universe be apprehended as a unity? The difficulty in apprehending it as an organic unity arises not merely from its vastness, its many dimensions and the very large number of fully-realized characters who move in it and whom we have to keep in mind, but also from the fact that the grasp of the whole in-formed substance calls for our viewing it from two different standpoints and bearing in mind that we are looking at the same object. We have then two different groupings of the same characters and two themes which I shall speak of as two "worlds" making up the universe of the novel.

The first world, and the most prominent, is the world of the "Karamazovs" and "Father Zossima," taking each name to stand for a group of people of somewhat similar beliefs, in opposition to each other. This is to say that I use the names eponymically, for I include in this world the whole population of the little town and even the visitors from the outside such as the Poles and the experts—the doctor and the lawyers. These people express diverse forces and espouse conflicting values; they are all Russians except the Poles and Doctor Herzenstube, who has resided in the town for a long time. The Poles are a sorry three, as contemptible as they could be without being altogether incredible caricatures, which would have damaged our response to Grushenka.

Shifting the standpoint, we look on another world, some-what recessive, in which the same characters are grouped in a different opposition and which I call the world of "Russia" and "Europe." The label does not make much difference; I could have called the contrasting groups of this second world "Russia" and the "Crystal Palace" or "Russia" and "the ant heap of the Grand Inquisitor." One of the groups consists of Father Zossima and his faithful monks, the peasant woman who has faith, and Mme Hohlakov, a woman of little faith. The other group is made up of Pyotor Alexander Miüsov, Rakitin, and Smerdyakov, men clearly oriented toward Europe, who repudiate Russia, fail to understand its worth, and wish to leave it as Miüsov does and Smerdyakov intended to do until his last days. Ivan, until his breakdown, belongs to "Europe."

I cannot, without modulation, place each one of the inhabi-tants of the town in one group or another of either of these two worlds, even if I accept the device of indicating that some of them straddle the groups. Dostoyevsky is drawing complex, well-rounded personalities who cannot be classified by means of a simple label, and more than any other poet he has a sharp eye for the duplicities of the human psyche. If we look for "Russians" or "Europeans" in the novel we find a number of characters who are both, as for instance Ivan, and others who are essentially Russian or not completely Europeanized: the character who comes closest to being a full European is Miüsov; the quintes-sential Russian is Zossima after his conversion. If we look into the first world, the Karamazov-Zossima world, we find that some characters defy classification. For instance, on first thought it would seem that Alyosha belongs in his Elder's group *tout court;* but the allocation would overlook his solemn words to Lise: "And perhaps I don't even believe in God." Alyosha is a deeply religious soul and a good youth, but he is also a full-blooded Karamazov although the son of an exceptionally meek and sub-missive woman, as we are told. As regards this attractive youth, it is well to take a hint from the epigraph of the novel: during the action Alyosha has not yet fallen into the ground and died; he has not undergone the experience that transformed the Elder into a saintly man. It is idle to speculate about what would have happened to him had the novelist had time to finish his trilogy.

Although these two worlds are different, they embody the poet's fundamental theme and connect the poet with the man. I have had to distinguish them, although the distinction at times comes close to violating Leibniz's principle of the indiscernibles. But they are different worlds, although easily taken to be the same. If I burden the reader with distinctions that may seem too fine, I can only plead that if *The Brothers Karamazov* is worth reading seriously, it is worth the effort to find out all that it contains.

Feodor Mikhailovitch thought that all he had to do in order to show the superiority of that aspect of the world he approved of over the other was to contrast one with the other: to contrast the Zossima component of the Karamazov-Zossima world with the Karamazov component. The latter component was founded on rebellion, sin, excess, and the satisfaction of desire, while the other component was based on piety, submission to the will of God, self-denial, and devotion to God and country as Feodor took it to be then constituted. It is more precise to say that he hoped that the contrast was all that was required, for he expressed passing fears as to the success of his intention. It seems to me that his fears were well-founded, for neither as poetry nor as exposition and defense of Feodor Mikhailovitch's views does the novel show that the Zossima component of this first world was superior to the Karamazov component, or that the Russian side of the second was superior to the European side.

Consider the novel as exposition and defense of theory first. So to take it is to read it as a treatise. Is there in it an argument such as one might find in a sociological or historical analysis of the qualities of contrasting cultures or subcultures? I put in print in 1965 an opinion that I had been presenting to my classes for many years previously, that Dostoyevsky was no philosopher; he didn't have the "instinct," if I may be allowed to put it in this way, for argument that a theoretical thinker, whatever his interests, has. He did not employ an appropriate categorial scheme, he did not order his thought, he did not go about the job as a philosopher goes about it—and by a philosopher I do not mean a professor of philosophy, for serious philosophers have worked in the world without the benefit of academic institutions or professional instrumentalities. It is easy enough to find a systematic body of thought in Dostoyevsky's poetry; as noted, it has been done. To find it, all one has to do is to look for it selectively by ignoring much of what his novels contain; and one does not have to be a German professor to perform the feat with great success; others still are doing it. It is just as much a misreading of Dostoyevsky's poetry to find two bodies of thought as to find one. If one wants to be instructed in the elements of a theistic, metaphysic, or naturalistic or purely secularistic vision of the world, there are serious sources where responsible readers can find that for which they are looking. Dostoyevsky's works are not substitutes for serious philosophy.

This is not to deny that Dostoyevsky read philosophy. One remembers the urgent request to his brother, immediately after leaving the house of the dead, for Kant and Hegel. It is to say that Dostoyevsky was a novelist, a poet—in the wide sense in which I use the term—and not a man who thought the way, say, Kant or Hegel thought. Eminent men, immense figures in their own bailiwicks, these great thinkers totally lacked a drop of poetic talent in their makeup—as I shall declare by fiat, in the teeth of Hegelians who will argue with great plausibility that Hegel was an essentially dramatic thinker. Berdyaev, who should have know better, said that Dostoyevsky was the greatest metaphysician Russia had produced. The statement is puzzling coming from a philosopher until one remembers not only how few philosophers but how few men, learned, sophisticated scholars, not mere academic pedants, have ever had the intellectual seriousness to ask themselves how the various disciplines and the distinct activities of the human spirit can be distinguished one from the other. Nor is it to say that Feodor Mikhailovitch did not possess a philosophical mind of great amplitude and finesse. But a philosophical mind and a philosopher's mind are two distinct things. Genuine philosophers—a Plato, a Kant, a Hegel—could not have been the giants they were had they lacked a philosophical mind. Some so-called philosophers utterly lacked philosophical minds while making contributions to philosophy. And some philosophers had philosophical minds and were also endowed with poetic vision: Heraclitus, if we can judge by his dark fragments, Plato, and in their tortured way, Kierkegaard and Nietzsche. The human zoo contains many interesting specimens and the "races" are not pure. But the man who seriously calls Dostoyevsky a philosopher does not know what philosophy is or, if a Berdyaev, does not know how to read poetry.

Let us consider next the novel, as it is often taken to be, as an imitation of the real world. This sort of document is not a poem in the highly restrictive sense in which I have been using the term. I shall call it a novel to avoid being charged with a crime against Webster III, but a novel in the narrow sense it is not. As an imitation, the novel is dramatic, not poetry-for-the-theater, but a referential account of a crowded world whose fidelity to that which it imitates cannot be adequately checked either by us or by our contemporary Russians or by Dostoyevsky's own Russian contemporaries. When critics say of a novel that it is true to life, they do not mean the same as is meant of a piece of physical investigation, that it is true to the facts to which it refers. Literary critics seem to mean that the poem feels to them as life feels—which opens a nest of problems which it would be profitable to explore, but which I shall have to pass by in order to pursue my objective and ask whether *The Brothers,* considered as a referential document, defends views the writer favored and disposes of those he rejected.

I do not think it does because what we find in it is a dramatic contrast between the components of the two worlds now considered as more or less congruous with some real world—congruous with the actual world, let us say, in which Feodor Mikhailovitch lived in the seventies of the last century. If one asserts that the novel defends Zossima's conception of human destiny and attacks the mode of living of the Karamazov component, he can only say it by applying his own external criteria to the Karamazov-Zossima world. That the life of the father, Feodor Pavlovitch Karamazov, is unsavory, I imagine all readers would agree, and the poet took the trouble to tell us editorially what an unpleasant-looking buffoon and unpleasant person he was. But the Karamazov component of the Karamazov-Zossima world was not made up of Feodor Pavlovitch alone, any more than the Zossima component was solely made up of the saintly Elder. The fact is that even considered as a referential account of Skotoprigonevsk, the novel presents us with a world the two components of which are both made up of a large number of

persons of widely different characters; the moral worth of these
people is not self-evident. I remember saying in class years ago
that I found Kolya a rather likeable boy, in spite of those qualities that make one want to give him a spanking. A girl in class
objected in an intensely angry way; she said Kolya was impossible and she would like to beat him within an inch of his life.
Whatever the sources of her reaction and however wrong I may
be about Kolya (about whom I have not changed my mind), the
fact remains that it is quite easy to judge Kolya in a number of
different ways. This holds for the others: for the Poles, two de-
spicable men; for Rakitin, who is, I guess, contemptible, but
who could be admired by people I have known although he is
an unprincipled pander, *arriviste,* and corrupter of youngsters
because of his utterly unscrupulous capacity to achieve his ends.
But there is still more; considered referentially, the reader can
defend the view that while the Karamazov side was, if you like,
made up by just a varied group of human beings, no better and
no worse than most groups the world over, the Zossima side was
not much better. Which is to say that Feodor Mikhailovitch did
not succeed in doing what he set out to do.

        Considered as poetry the novel neither defends nor attacks,
proves nor disproves, the validity of one of the ways of life in
either of the two worlds I have distinguished above. It merely
presents. Note that the term "presents" is a technical term; it
seeks to convey the idea that what is figured forth in words is
not propaganda, although, of course, since no object can be apprehended in itself and by itself, we must expect that presentations can never be absolutely free from angling. Renoir's visual
presentations are not free from angling; nor are Céline's verbal
presentations. But there is a difference between caricature and
satire and poetry in the narrow sense in which I have been using
the term. Because poetry as poetry is a presentation, the novel
when approached as poetry, is ineffaceably ineradicably and indefeasibly ambiguous. But I am not going to argue in favor of
this doctrine, since much of my work for more than the last
quarter century has been aimed at its explication and validation
and at the drawing of its many implications—carrying the thesis
as close to its logical conclusion as I could.

Considered as a presentation, considered, that is, as an aesthetic object, the conflict between the Karamazov and the Zossima components of the first world—as many critics have pointed out—fails to make the Zossima side as aesthetically attractive as the poet makes the Karamazov side. The latter is powerfully drawn, full of three-dimensional characters each of whom moves with a dramatic force and vividness that elicits and holds on himself intense attention in a way in which the life of the Elder does not. Father Zossima, saintly, recognized, and venerated as Elder, meeting those who sought him, consoling them and advising them, is listened to with respect and is admired, but the account of his actions as monk is gray when compared with the account of the actions of the denizens of the Karamazov side of this world. The "Conversations and Exhortations of Father Zossima," saved for us by Alyosha, were intended by Feodor Mikhailovitch to show the superiority of the monastic way of life—of the life of prayer and denial of desire over the purely secular life of gratification and sin. They show no such superiority. I am not arguing that the "Conversations and Exhortations of Father Zossima" fail to prove theoretically the superiority of the Elder's religious conception of human destiny over the purely secular, whether the latter accepts or rejects God and immortality; that was already discussed above. I am saying that the Karamazov side of this world has greater aesthetic power than the side with which it is in conflict.

Whatever the reason for the aesthetic superiority of the Karamazov side of the Karamazov-Zossima world, and the relative failure of the other, the fact cannot be denied. A critic whose theory permits him to wander away from the text, as mine does not permit me, could point out what at first sight would seem to be the case—that the saintly life is good matter for hagiography but not for poetry. Were I not afraid of risking the charge of cynicism, I would observe that to the pious all holy things are good and beautiful, but the sinful world has other standards. It may be a sad comment on man or not, depending on your standpoint, but sin is much more interesting to the ordinary run of men than goodness; and a novel about crime makes much better reading than a novel or a biography about a saintly man.

3.

The famous poem or legend "The Grand Inquisitor" has been taken as the central episode of *The Brothers Karamazov*. At least two books based their analysis of Dostoyevsky on the chapter—if we judge by their titles. Feodor Mikhailovitch himself called it "the culminating point of the novel," and even so antagonistic a critic as Freud praised it as "one of the peaks of the literature of the world," adding that it is a composition that can "hardly be valued too highly." Although it is often taken to be self-sufficient, its full significance can only be appreciated, if I may repeat, in the context of the whole novel; but an important part of its meaning can be drawn when read as the sequel to the two preceding chapters, III and IV, "The Brothers Make Friends" and "Rebellion," of Part II Book V. Read without reference to these two chapters the substance of the poem loses much of its philosophical and psychological density and dramatic power; it beclouds the despair that drives Ivan at this point in his career and it leaves you wondering why Feodor did not see that Dostoyevsky "had not answered Ivan."

In Chapter III, "The Brothers Make Friends," Ivan and Alyosha get acquainted in a tavern. As is usually the case in *The Brothers* when Alyosha takes part in the action Dostoyevsky endows it with a charm and "tenderness," if I may be allowed the word, that is difficult to convey abstractly. Ivan expresses his love and respect for his younger brother without condescension, and shows himself during the meeting to be a very charming person—at least when he puts himself out. But the conversation is not about trivialities. Ivan tells Alyosha that he accepts God and His wisdom and His purpose, that he believes in the underlying order and the meaning of life, in the eternal harmony in which we shall one day be blended; but in the final result, he does not accept this world of God's because of its evil, its gratuitous cruelty. From newspapers Ivan has collected instances of gratuitous cruelty inflicted on children that I call "Ivan's dossier against God." He wants justice. But what is the good of casting into hell those who are guilty of cruelty when the children have already been tortured? He tells Alyosha that he chose the instances of cruelty to children to make his case clear, for of the other tears of humanity with which the earth is soaked from crust to crust, he will say nothing. Ivan recounts case after case,

each more outrageous than the preceding one. There is the case
of Richard, the Swiss savage, burnt at the stake in Geneva; the
case of the Russian peasant who beats the horse in the eyes; and
then the cases of the children, culminating in the story of the
eight-year-old child thrown to the savage hounds in front of his
mother for a very slight injury inflicted on the paw of one of
the General's hounds.

> The General orders the child to be undressed; the child is stripped
> naked. He shivers numb with terror, not daring to cry. . . . "Make
> him run," commands the General. "Run, run!" shout the dog-
> boys. The boy runs. "At him!" yells the General, and he sets the
> whole pack of hounds on the child. The hounds catch him and
> tear him to pieces before his mother's eyes.

One sentence completes the story, and it is superbly ironic
in its bathos: "I believe the General was afterwards declared incapable of administering his estates."

It is, of course, impossible to convey to the person who
has not read it, by means of an abstract, the depth and complexity of feeling that the contents of his dossier arouses in Ivan. He
responds with anguish, with deep outrage, and with an intensity
of rejection of its ultimate cause that verges on despair. The response arises from the promise of final harmony when "everything in heaven and earth blends in one hymn of praise and
everything that lives and has lived cries aloud: 'Thou art just, O
Lord, for thy ways are revealed.' " But what sort of harmony is
it that is brought about at the cost of torture to the children? "I
must have justice, or I will destroy myself," he cries. In its intensity, in its powerful presentation of feeling, bewilderment,
outrage at the gratuitous cruelty and the way those who inflict
it get away with it, this chapter is at least as successful as any
other scene in the novel, including even the deservedly successful poem of "The Grand Inquisitor."

We are ready to turn to Ivan's poem. Its fame absolves me
from the impossible job of giving the reader an idea of it; a tele-
graphic reminder of its substance must suffice. The action, Ivan
tells Alyosha, takes place in Seville in the sixteenth century, the
day after there had been a splendid *auto de fé* in which almost
one hundred heretics had been burnt by the Cardinal, the Grand

Inquisitor, *ad majorem gloria Dei.*   Jesus came softly, unob-
served, and yet recognized by everyone.   The people outside the
Cathedral are irresistibly drawn to Him; an old man, blind since
childhood, asks Him to heal him and Jesus does.   A dead child is
resurrected.   The Grand Inquisitor sees what is happening and
orders Jesus arrested and that night visits Him in His cell.   He
upbraids Jesus for returning to hinder the Inquisitor and his co-
workers, who have taken ten centuries to correct His work.   Jesus
would give men freedom, which men do not want, instead of
bread.   The Inquisitor claims that the merit of his Church is that
at last they have vanquished freedom in order to make men happy.   The wise and dread Spirit, the Spirit of self-destruction and
nonexistence, made Jesus three offers—the three temptations—
and Jesus turned them down.   He turned down the offer of
bread, the suggestion that he throw himself from the temple,
and he rejected the worship of the kingdoms and their glory,
for their acceptance entailed the enslavement of man.   Jesus
came to offer man freedom.   But weak man is vicious and rebellious, says the Inquisitor, and finds nothing more insupport-
able than freedom.   Rejecting Jesus' gift, the Inquisitor tells
Jesus that his Church is just on the verge of success and is going
to bring men happiness.   It can be done.   Out of a feeling of pity
for rebellious men, which the Inquisitor does not suffer in a pure
state, but which in his soul is mixed and thickened by an addition of disappointment and betrayed idealism—as we can see
from his disclosure of his motives—he came to the conclusion
that if man was to be saved from himself he had to be enslaved,
as men themselves asked to be.   "Make us your slaves, but feed
us," men cried.   The Inquisitor heard the cry, and at the heavy
sacrifice of accepting lies, for which he had a deep revulsion,
the Inquisitor joined the few who took up the burden of saving
men from themselves.   He did not join his group with a joyful
heart in response to a power drive; his bitterness does not merely
have its source in the fact that Jesus has come back to threaten
the work of his Church on the verge of succeeding; nor does it
have its source in the bitter disappointment he suffered when he
was forced to return from the wilderness to undertake the job of
enslaving men.

     We do a grievous injustice to Ivan's poetic insight and to
ourselves if we overlook the fact that neither the Inquisitor nor
his fellows are conceived by Ivan as men moved by contemptible

motives. The Inquisitor's Church was forced to accept what I suggest we call "theocratic socialism" without joy. If we overlook the Inquisitor's reluctance to turn down Jesus' gift and undertake the enslavement of men through socialism, if we overlook his sincerity, which we have no grounds to suspect, if we read his impassioned indictment of Jesus with post-Hitler or post-Stalin eyes, if we look at him through the categorial concept of a clever animal psychologist who finds low value in freedom and dignity, we not only shrink the gigantic figure of the Inquisitor but reduce the radical nature of Ivan's dilemma and thus fail to understand what Dostoyevsky is telling us. Feodor Mikhailovitch hated the Roman Catholic Church and equated it with socialism, with Europe, with the Crystal Palace; he contrasted these hateful symbols with Holy Russia which he was certain would never allow atheistic socialism to take root in its Christian soil, for as Feodor Mikhailovitch tells us editorially in *The Brothers,* commenting on Alyosha's choice of the monastic life, socialism is not merely the labor question, it is above all things the atheistic question. Feodor intended to show up the monstrous conspiracy that was Roman Catholicism or socialism. No man ever suffered a more praiseworthy defeat than Feodor; no artist a more glorious triumph than Dostoyevsky. What we find in Ivan's poem is a man reluctantly accepting the burden of power. If we confuse the Inquisitor with the monsters who have been the dictators of our age, we merely perform the usual misreading of the poem and the usual missing of its true greatness.

It is essential before proceeding to clear a widespread misunderstanding introduced by Feodor Mikhailovitch about Ivan. Feodor wrote that atheism was expressed by the Russian youth of his day by returning God His ticket, and Ivan has been taken generally for an atheist. When asked in his father's dining room, Ivan himself asserted that he did not believe in God. But the evidence is against Ivan's atheism. First, he tells Alyosha in the tavern that his denial of God in his father's dining room was made to tease his younger brother and he adds now in deep seriousness that it is not God that he does not accept but a world in which final harmony is brought about at the price of torturing children. The whole chapter shows that Feodor Mikhailovitch

and the critics who have followed his lead have not read what
Dostoyevsky wrote in the chapter in which Ivan displays the tales
of his dossier. In any case, Ivan could not have been an atheist
for no atheist can be wracked by "the problem of evil"—as I
shall call it inappropriately for convenience; he cannot be outraged by a world that could not have been created by a God that
does not exist. The atheist may be as sensitive to pain and in-
justice as the theist, he may be torn by the outrage of tortured
children, but the outrage that makes Ivan return God His ticket
and which philosophers—using the term coined by Leibniz—call
the problem of "theodicy," can only trouble a man who, believing in the final harmony or hankering for it, faces the torturing
of the children. I am using my own pale words. Ivan's words
claw deeply at the heart of the reader; it would be foolish to try
to rival their power. "What good can hell do, since those children have already been tortured? And what becomes of harmony if there is hell?" His plea cannot be doubted. "Oh, Alyosha, I am not blaspheming!" A few moments later he exclaims,
"I want to forgive, I want to embrace, I do not want more suffering."

I have said that Ivan is tormented by "the problem of evil."
This is the label that philosophers apply to the contradiction between the patent fact of evil in the world and God's all-goodness,
His omniscience and omnipotence. Philosophers treat it as a philosophical problem, and a "philosophical problem" is something
for which there is or there ought to be a rational solution. Philosophers are not found of *aporiai;* they have tried to solve the
problem in a variety of ways—each and every one of which can
be shown to fail. But for Ivan, strictly speaking, the fact of evil
in a world whose final harmony is promised and hankered for
is no "problem" in the philosopher's sense. If I could allow myself the use of a term that has been kidnapped by partisans for
their purposes, I would write that Ivan experienced the contradiction between evil and the final harmony in an "existential"
way. He is tormented by it; he is not merely puzzled as philosophers have been by the fact that the terms "evil" and "God,"
of the kind he believed in, do not go together. He was not a professor of philosophy.

We must bear in mind when we discuss "The Grand Inquisitor" the circumstances in which Ivan brings up the poem. He has just presented his younger brother with a few choice stories of his dossier and has gotten Alyosha to admit "with flashing eyes" that there is not a being in the whole world who would have a right to forgive the torturers of the children. But, adds Alyosha, "He can forgive everything, all and for all, because he gave His innocent blood for all and everything." Ivan replies that he has not forgotten "the One without sin and His blood." He then adds that he has made a poem which he wants to tell Alyosha. Ivan's mention of the poem immediately after Alyosha's reproach that he has forgotten He who can forgive everything is highly significant, for the poem presents in a powerful constitutive symbol the ineluctability of his dilemma: Jesus came to offer man freedom but he could not offer man happiness. The Grand Inquisitor can give man happiness—at the price of freedom. But let us turn to the poem.

What does "The Grand Inquisitor" say? What it says is not unambiguous. Alyosha pointed out the ambiguity when Ivan finished telling the story. Alyosha's words, we are told by Dostoyevsky, "came out with a rush": "But. . .That's absurd!" he cried, flushing, "your poem is in praise of Jesus, not in blame of Him—as you meant it to be."

Is Alyosha right? Ivan grants that the poem is a fantasy, but he does not reply to Alyosha's remark and if he had we would have to check his judgment against the poem, for this is precisely what the distinction between the man and the poet entails: one or the other or both may be wrong about what the poet actually accomplishes.

We cannot overlook the ambiguity of the poem. Nor can we overlook the fact that it is preceded by the stories taken from Ivan's dossier against God. Nor can we ignore that the dossier was collected by a man who is outraged by the torture of children and who wants to believe in "the final harmony" but cannot. Take the dossier; take Ivan at his word when he tells his brother that he believes in God; take the tone of the poem, particularly the pain, the contempt, and the pity of the Grand Inquisitor for rebellious man; remember that his pity arises from an idealism that has been betrayed by man's rejection of dignity and freedom for the sake of bread—ponder these matters and you will see that readers who believe that Ivan was praising Jesus or the Inquisitor or that Dostoyevsky was trying to answer Ivan are chasing a nonexistent quarry. Feodor Mikhailovitch wanted, desperately we can say, to answer Ivan. Dostoyevsky did not attempt to do it. He had to face his dilemma in aesthetic terms as the conflict between Jesus and the Inquisitor, and the result was Ivan's anguish. Call it catharsis if you will or leave it unexplained; the conflict that is presented to us through the dossier and "The Grand Inqisitor" is a radical dilemma, which is a pleonastic way of emphasizing that for Ivan the poet there was at the time no third alternative: freedom or bread, and either is unacceptable because of its consequences. Freedom means dignity but it also means the General and his hounds, bread avoids the torturing of children, but it means the ant heap, achieved through miracle, mystery, and authority. (The Inquisitor reproaches Jesus for rejecting the use of means needed to rule mankind which his Church has adopted: miracle, mystery, and authority. But upon being recognized by the people of Seville outside the Cathedral, Jesus performs two miracles. Has Dostoyevsky contradicted himself? I do not think so, for Jesus rejects the Dread Spirit's prompting that He perform miracles to prove who He is and thus gain dominion over men; the two miracles He performs in Seville are acts of mercy.) But denizens of an ant heap are not human beings.

4.

Since we have had a hasty glimpse at what is to be found in the vast universe of the little town of Skotoprigonevsk and have also had a hurried look at what Dostoyevsky presented in "The Grand Inquisitor" and its two preceding chapters, we can ask what the novel helps us see in the actual world of Feodor Mikhailovitch and in ours ninety years later. Besides the way in which it increases our psychological acuity and presents a metaphysical dimension our naturalistic vision might have made us blind to, it suggests that we take a philosophical stance toward his age and ours. But first we must remember that what the novel presents is not necessarily found in the actual world of Feodor Mikhailovitch's day or ours. Dostoyevsky might have been utterly mistaken—as a large number of his critics believe he was. How can we ascertain whether what Dostoyevsky saw in the novel was actually to be found in Feodor Mikhailovitch's world? This is not a question the novel can answer, nor can, of course, Feodor Mikhailovitch. How then can we get an answer to this question—on whose importance no one would want to cast doubt? The question asks whether what Dostoyevsky saw in the novel was seen by his contemporaries without the aid of his novel or could be seen by us had we not had his help (and that of other poets, like Nietzsche) and had not Lenin crowned the catastrophe of our day with his work. This question can only be answered in speculative terms that would argue for a conception of the function of art. Here and in a very few words all I can do is to asseverate ex cathedra what I have argued for in my work on aesthetics, that I do not believe we can see without the borrowed eyes of poets.

With Dostoyevsky's eyes we see the struggle in which we ourselves are engaged. That we are engaged in it Dostoyevsky does not, he cannot, prove; we prove it ourselves if we are serious about the matter as we prove that Lenin initiated events that some of us call catastrophic and others a great step forward for mankind. It is at this point that partisanship does its worst. The struggle in Ivan's mind, the larger and more confused struggle in Skotoprigonevsk, through which we see our condition, is a bitter battle in which we are engaged, fighting desperately and not all of us knowing we are fighting, or if we know, not all of us knowing who the enemy is. What is of basic importance about the conflict in which each of us in engaged against each and all the rest is that it is going on also within us. Next in importance is the extent and depth of the struggle. It is historical, it is cataclysmic. It portends the promise or the threat of a new man, a different animal, a different species. Will he be better than us? I do not think so. Neither did Ivan, who could not choose between the ant heap and freedom. But a choice does not enable us to transcend the struggle, since it is within us as well as without. Some of us may be able to transcend the struggle as Father Zossima did, through total abnegation and rejection of the world, but his way cannot be turned into a universal maxim; his alternative is open only to a very few of us and only because the greater part of the world rejects it. Others like Feodor Mikhailovitch, more or less successfully, will to deceive themselves into believing that they have eradicated the enemy from within themselves, that they have drawn out of their souls what I have called "Europe" or the "Crystal Palace." But a man with the probing acuity of Feodor Mikhailovitch cannot deceive himself for long. The factor sooner or later catches up with him: "I am an old 'Nechaievetz' myself."

NOTES

[1] Nechaiev was the author of *The Catechism of a Revolutionary* and the founder of revolutionary groups throughout Russia.

[2] *The Notebooks for the Brothers Karamazov.* Translated and edited by Edward Wasiolek (Chicago, 1971). The notebooks for four other major novels are also available. The non-Russian reader owes a deep debt to Professor Wasiolek for the successful undertaking of a task as useful as its must have been onerous.

PART FOUR

Tragic Vision

Atrabilious Thoughts on a Theory of Tragedy

This paper invites you to consider a theory of tragedy that drains some tragic poems of an important component of their substance. And it advances one that preserves the tragic in tragedy. It is true that the theory it proposes is adequate to only very few tragedies, those I call *unmitigated tragedies.* But only one such tragedy would suffice to make my point.

The thoughts here advanced are atrabilious: this fact is stated, not apologized for. As my acquaintance with theories of tragedy has become broader of recent years, I have become more and more opposed to the efforts of distinguished literary critics to cut down to the comfortable size of a myopic theodicy some of the boldest, most unfettered, most courageous, profoundest, yet darkest products of the human imagination.

The order of exposition to be employed is the following. Considerations will be presented, first, in general terms, and they will then be used to examine the *Oresteia.* This reverses the order of inquiry for the purpose of facilitating the exposition. For the following remarks are not the product of a priori lucu-brations or the gracious gift of infused science; they are the result of an inductive examination of the poems under discussion.

The moralistic interpretation of tragedy goes back at least to the days of Doctor Johnson, for his objection to the ending of *King Lear* was that it outraged his sense of poetic justice. In the nineteenth century it was common, even at the end of the century when other aesthetic currents were beginning to flow. Thus A. E. Haigh, in a very learned book, *The Tragic Drama of the Greeks* (Oxford, 1896), refers frequently to the morality of the work of Aeschylus, Sophocles, and Euripides. In our own century, it finds important defenders; for instance in the work of Harold C. Goddard on *The Meaning of Shakespeare* (Chicago, 1951). But it is not my purpose to review the history of this mode of interpretation. What I shall try to do is to examine the theory. One formulation of the theory has been offered us by a critic for whom I have boundless respect and unstinting admiration. I pick this version of the theory to criticize because I would take nothing less than the best against which to make my point. In *This Great Stage,* a perspicuous analysis of the imagery and structure of *King Lear,* from which, I am confident, even much less ignorant persons than myself have learned a great deal, Robert Heilman writes:

> The Aristotelian definition of the tragic hero as the good man who by some error frailty comes to disaster is the basis for many statements which this essay will make about tragic quality. . . .

> That disaster follows from the hero's tragic flaw implies that the world is a moral organism in which events are morally meaningful. Tragedy is concerned, not with evil fortune that may lead to cynicism or despair, but with evil that is understandable in terms of human character. . . . Tragedy records, eventually, victory rather than defeat; it asserts the authority of the spiritual scheme of things to which man, because of his flaw, does violence.[1]

Limitations of space do not allow me to quote in full the passage from which these lines have been taken. But the quotation is enough to make perfectly clear that the moralistic interpretation of tragedy goes back to that millennial fountainhead of crippling rachitogenic deformations in poetics for which no antibiotic has as yet been discovered—Aristotle. The moralistic interpretation adds to Aristotle's analysis of tragedy a notion that we do not find in the *Poetics.* There is nothing in that text about redemption, about the world being a moral organism, or about the spiritual scheme of things. Overlook the fact that for Aristotle tragedy could have an ending other than catastrophic—Aristotle does not make any reference to a scheme of things beyond the human to which the tragic flaw does violence. In the *Poetics* Aristotle mentions the gods only once, and then to formulate the formidable *niaiserie* that we must suppose that they see everything. It should be remembered that for Aristotle God was a metaphysical gimmick utterly indifferent to man and the rest of the world. He was a Most Perfect Introvert, whose sole occupation was the omphalic contemplation of his own contemplation. In respect to the rest of the world, his function was to get the spheres rolling. But His Perfect Frigidity did not do anything so coarse as to push or to pull them. He was no subway packer. The spheres moved because the silly things were in love with His Perfect Frigidity and yearned for it. The Greek tragedies we know cannot be fitted to the Aristotelian interpretation of tragedy since the gods play important roles in their human world, and of this fact there is no recognition in the *Poetics.* However, Aristotle's philosophy did involve, as any undergraduate knows, a teleological conception of the world. But his view was not anthropotelic. This latter view is an assumption of the moralistic interpretation of tragedy that finds no support in Aristotle. A man's frailty or error, according to the moralistic interpretation, disturbs cosmic harmony, which his catastrophe restores. There is nothing about this disturbance and this restoration in the millennial source of error which is the *Poetics.*

It must be granted without reservation, as above suggested, not only that this interpretation may apply to a large number of tragedies, but also that all tragedies can be interpreted in its terms. We can always fit a giant to the bed of Procrustes. All we need to do is to chop off its legs. The question we need to consider is whether some tragedies—not many, I acknowledge—can be interpreted moralistically without neglect of an important component of their substance.

The defects of the moralistic view of tragedy can be ordered under two headings. Under one, we can group its philosophic (or perhaps its cosmological) defects; under the other, its aesthetic defects. But it is important to bear in mind that the separation of philosophic from aesthetic defects may lead to the damaging assumption that substance and form can be separated from each other.

The first point to be advanced against this view is this: we are asked to believe that unless the catastrophe takes place in a world that is a moral organism we are led to cynicism or despair. On what evidence such a momentous judgment is pronounced is not disclosed. But I do not see why the contemplation of a world which is indifferent to man must lead to cynicism or despair. Contemporary humanists and materialistic revolutionists for the most part hold to the view that the world is morally indifferent or neutral. They seem to draw from this premise the conclusion that since there are no cosmic agencies that can help man, he must help himself.

The second point to be made against the view requires a brief preface. It should be noted that the moralistic view holds— not explicitly but sufficiently clearly for us not to be in doubt about it—that tragedy is somehow representative or imitative of the actual world, of the world external to the tragedy. But its anthropotelic view of the universe is a view that has been put on the defensive, to pick a convenient (although a late) date, since 1859. A naive religious mind can today believe that human action is directly controlled by a spiritual scheme of things; but a sophisticated mind cannot, not simply and without a tremendous philosophical effort. Nor will the *saltimbanqueries* of Leibnizian theodicies help the view in the second half of our century. I myself happen to believe that values have status in being independent of human desire, need, or will. But to believe that man's actions disturb the spiritual scheme of things takes more, considerably more, than can be found in unsophisticated philosophical assertions. It takes a carefully worked out, a thoroughly sophisticated axiological realism. And by a "sophisticated axiological realism," I mean one that takes into consideration what we men of today have learned about the world from the sciences and the philosophies that the sciences inspire. If man's moral reflection is, or should be, an effort to discern what lies behind the veil of more or less immediate appearance and discover behind it the evanescent and hidden structure of value that becomes teasingly evident through that reflection, it is not at all clear that the most honest and most sustained effort to discern the structure puts the maker of the effort in facile possession of certain knowledge of it. Least of all does it put him in possession of the certainty that when this structure is disturbed by man's defect or frailty, that structure responds in any way whatever.

To these philosophical objections I must add a third. This one is also a moral objection. An anthropotelic conception of the universe is today an outrage to the conscience. What have the events of our century taught the religious mind if they have not led it to perceive that the human world is not controlled naively by a spiritual scheme of things? Ivan Karamazov's dossier was a collection of petty misdemeanors compared to what we have to add to it since the sixth decade of the nineteenth century. If Aristotle is to be our crutch, it must be said that, in so far as tragedy claims to be an imitation of a world in which events are morally meaningful, it is a preposterous lie, unless the phrase "morally meaningful" refers to a sequence of events that has nothing to do with our unslaked thirst for justice. Men are moral animals. Think of the worst criminal imaginable, and he has loyalties and fiercely espoused values; think of the worst society, and it espouses a moral scheme. But there is no comfort in this fact for the mind that thirsts for moral harmony. For in Ivan's words, in justification for the tears of humanity with which the earth is soaked from its crust to its center who, in decency, will dare to say anything?

Let us turn to the objections that can be classified as aesthetic. And let us note, first, that it is difficult to see how a diaster that occurs within a poem, an imaginative fabrication, can imply that the actual world, the world outside the poem, is a moral organism in which events are either meaningful or meaningless. A poem can imply that the world of the poem is a moral organism, as another poem can imply that the world of that second poem is an immoral or an amoral organism. And a third poem can imply that there is a conflict between aspects of its world that are moral and other aspects that are amoral or immoral. But only an Aristotelian (whether paleo-Aristotelian or neo-Aristotelian) could discover a relation of implication between a poem and the world outside the poem. Implication, in a rigorous sense, he could never discover; at best he could claim a relation of entailment. But we will have to let that point go, since he is not aware of the distinction. Assume, what I would only grant under torture, that tragedy imitates the world outside of it. Our world is too large, too complex, too confused and confusing, and, from a moral point of view—any moral point of view that is responsible—too incoherent, for a single poem to imply or entail anything about it in one way or another.

A reader for whom tragedy—one or many tragedies—can be the basis of a generalization about the world is sadly in need of a course in logic. But there is more than the fallacy of generalizing from insufficient instances without considering whether these instances constitute a representative sample or not. There is a failure to look at the world, the world of Aristotle or our own world or the world between his day and ours as revealed by history. If we look at it, what we perceive is an utterly mysterious world, about whose ways we know next to nothing. We have witnessed in the last few hundred years an enormous advance in our knowledge of the physical world. And biology, we are told, is today making a prodigious advance. But still, for Newton's little candle, no substitute has yet been found. The gigantic advances in positive knowledge that we have witnessed leave us today as much in the dark about the world—whether physical or moral—as they left the man who held the candle at the edge of the ocean of darkness sometime between 1642 and 1727. We have, indeed, much less reason to clutch at spiritual certainties today than Newton or his contemporaries had. And the diminished reason is not only the result of the advance in knowledge of the physical world but also the result of the historical events we have been forced to witness. It must be said again: a Leibnizian optimism bespeaks today a struthonian attitude.

I know perfectly well that The Philosopher argued that tragedy is more philosophical than history, on the ground that its statements are of the nature of universals, whereas those of history are singulars. But the assertion, although it comes from one of the six or so major philosophers that our Western civilization has produced, seems to me, nevertheless, utter nonsense. And the reason is that poems make no statements, although plenty of diverse statements, often of an utterly contradictory nature, are found in poems. Poems are presentations; they are revelations (not in the Heideggerian, but in the etymological, sense of the word). But let us suppose that they make statements and that the statements they make are of the nature of universals rather than singulars—the post-Carnapian mind today would ask how does the defender of the moralistic interpretation know whether the statement made by a poem in the form of a universal proposition is true or false. We know from *Posterior Analytics* how Aristotle got his first premises. But surely considerably more is required today than a facile appeal to intuition to assert that a poem makes a statement and that the statement it makes is true. We want to know how we distinguish the statement made by the poem from statements found within it; and we want to know how we test the statement made by the poem. Hunches, intuitions, and our preferences for certain truths as against others will not serve as criteria. Let us assume that we can go from the poem to the world in such a manner as to be able to decide that the world is of one sort rather than another. I do not see how such a decision can be taken as anything more than a hypothetical suggestion, to be treated as any hypothetical suggestion should be treated, and treated by the philosopher who subjects the hypothesis to the kind of scrutiny that his methods prescribe before he decides about its truth. The test of the hypothesis that the world is a moral organism is made by the theodicist, a kind of philosopher who today is not held highly in esteem by his fellow philosophers. All a reader of tragedy can affirm, if he is serious about knowledge and is not confusing emotional responses with cognitive claims, is that a given poem seems to assert that the world of the poem is a moral organism. Whether it is an actual representation of the actual world, he is no more in a position to assert than he is to assert or deny the truth of Hoyle's views about the universe.

But there is more. For what can it mean to assert that the world is morally meaningful? Is the phrase "morally meaningful" a univocal phrase to the significance of which we all would agree? We need not refer of course to those who find the doctrine that value has status in being altogether erroneous: men like Hobbes and contemporary naturalists and materialists. With such men there can be no discussion. But let us take the others. Is the universe that is morally meaningful to Augustine meaningful in the same sense to Pelagius? Is the universe morally meaningful to Calvin morally meaningful to Loyola? Is the universe that is morally meaningful to Royce meaningful in the same sense to Scheler or Hartmann? The phrase "the universe is morally meaningful" is certainly a pretty phrase. But before we can take it seriously, before we can assert it of the world, we need to know much more than a tragedy can tell us.

Is is not high time, one is forced to ask in pain and bewilderment, that critics quit treating poetry as if it were sugarcoated philosophy made easy for those who cannot wrestle with the real thing? They tend to make statements about poetry as if poetry were a privileged kind of philosophy that does not have to meet the methodological and probative demands that a man seriously intent on philosophical knowledge voluntarily and rigorously imposes on himself. Confronted with the philosophical irrespon-

sibility of some critics one is forced to ask whether they are interested in knowledge, as they claim to be, and whether they
know what they are doing when they make the statements they
make.

Kindly observe that I do not intend this question as merely
rhetorical, nor would I allow anyone to dismiss it as one of those
questions that philosophers are often accused of entertaining and
that misologists say philosophers entertain because they love
quibbling. It is a very serious question. If we are to speak in
an intelligible sense of a morally meaningful universe and if we
are speaking seriously, we cannot overlook the enormous difficulties involved in making such assertions—and the difficulties
are difficulties of fact and difficulties of language. Once the
objection is stated, it should be obvious that very little has been
said in a significant substantive way about the meaningfulness of
the universe until we go on to make explicit and precise what we
intend by the phrase "the moral meaningfulness of the universe."
Until we do so, we are open to the charge that we are satisfied
with emotive staements when hard and difficult thinking is required.

When we try to apply the moralistic interpretation to the
Oresteia, we encounter a number of difficulties, some of which
are of an insuperable kind. One that the writer encounters but
that not all of his readers come up against is that the only version
of the *Oresteia* he is acquainted with is the English poem published under the signature of Richmond Lattimore. This is a
disadvantage that would be crippling were we concerned with a
total analysis of Aeschylus' tragedies. The next difficulty is that
we know nothing whatever about the philosophical views of
Aeschylus outside the poems we have of his. We have no record
of the doctrines that were espoused by the son of Euphorion,
the Athenian to whose valor the Persian could testify. We do
not know how closely or how fully the professed doctrines of
the citizen came to expression in the plays of the poet, or by
what means they came to expression, or through what mask. If
Aristophanes can be relied on, we can say that Aeschylus took
the function of tragedy to be moral or civic. But that would
leave us with the difficult question whether he held that the

morality he sought to preach could be defended cognitively or not—in other words, whether he would have taken the side of Plato or Aristotle in their conflict about the cognitive value of poetry. Obviously these are not questions we have the means even of broaching.

One of his critics tells us that in one of the plays the chorus expresses the poet's own views, while the views of the actors are not his views but views with which he disagrees. But what evidence could be brought to bear in favor of this comforting thesis? None. Even if he had left us an autobiography, or numerus letters, and nonpoetical documents of some sort, one could not assign to these documents primacy over the plays. Had Aeschylus been asked for his views, it is not likely but it is not altogether nonsense to imagine that he might have answered: "Go to my poetry; there you will find the results of my efforts to inform the matter of my experience. As for my letters, essays, speeches, my interviews, and the autobiography, they do not represent the poet; they represent the man who has been concerned with conceptual coherence, with system, with the exigencies of the philosophic imagination. These conceptual efforts cannot be given primacy over the products of my poetry." But even if Aeschylus had not answered in this way, this is the way we must treat his poetry: it is poetry, not philosophy. And this reply goes for the conceptual doctrines professed by any man who is a poet, in so far as he is a successful poet. We do not, of course, have any such documents as I have had Aeschylus refer to in his reply. All the more reason, then, to be careful not to attribute to him views arbitrarily selected from his plays while assuming that other views, equally arbitrarily selected, are those he rejected.

But whatever the professed conceptual views of Aeschylus, this much we can assert with a modicum of confidence: while the difference between the first two plays of the *Oresteia* and the third is abysmal, we cannot ignore in the trilogy what we happen to disapprove of.

To grasp the difference between the first two plays and the third, consider the gods of Aeschylus. One necessary presupposition of the first two plays of the *Oresteia* is the belief in the inheritance of acquired guilt. The guilt of Thyestes and Atreus

passes on to Aegisthus, Agamemnon, and Orestes. There is no
diminution of the guilt from one generation to the next. On the
contrary, one crime brings on several other crimes, which in turn
bring still others. Nor are these solely the crimes of men suffering from moral defects. They are fully their own crimes, deeds
of morally defective men. But the gods are also involved in
them. And the crimes of the gods are as nefarious as the crimes
of men. Because an eagle kills a hare and her unborn ones, a
maid is sacrificed—and by her father. For all we know, she
might have been an immaculate child. Yes, says the defender of
the moralistic interpretation, but it was no ordinary hare; it was
Artemis' sacred hare. I know. Aeschylus' is a world in which a
sacred animal is more valuable than a human being. So be it.
But this was not the beginning of the bloody cycle. A man had
earlier seduced the wife of a brother, and in revenge the brother
served the seducer his children as food. A wanton woman was
carried off to Troy and Zeus Xenios condemned a generation
of youths, the flower of two cities, to a bloody bath for ten cruel
years. These are years of valor in which deeds are performed
that exalt their doers to heights men seldom reach in any other
activity save war. But is this reason for forgetting that they
were made possible by the sacrifice of a maid, who paid with
her life for a hare—a sacred hare, admitted—and its unborn ones?
The crimes pile up. A city is erased, and its altars are desecrated.
The women and children are taken off to slavery. A seer is
murdered, and a husband. For the murder of her husband, a
woman and her lover fall at the hands of her son. The matricide
is committed at the command of a god, Apollo. And while these
horrible crimes are taking place, the gods not involved in them
look on, indifferent to the monstrously usurious rate of interest
exacted for the original crimes, crimes in which some of the
gods were implicated. Let the claim be made that these two
plays presuppose a universe that is a moral organism in which
events are morally meaningful. Should not the critic advancing
this view make it emphatically explicit that the moral universe
of these two plays is quite different from the moral universe in
which he believes? Or is he content to accept the moral universe
of these two plays? That the first two plays of the *Oresteia* embody a moral universe is not denied. The point is, however,
that unqualified phrases about the world being a moral organism
and about the spiritual scheme of things erase important differences between the first two plays and the third, and between

the first two plays and our moral views—if we can speak of our moral views as if they were systematic and coherent.

At this point, the defender of the moralistic interpretation relaxes confidently. With a smile of triumph playing on his face, he replies: there is the third play, the *Eumenides.* It is in this play that the authority of the spiritual scheme of things is asserted. With this view, if I do not misread him, E. R. Dodds seems to agree, for in a well-known book to which all of his readers must be deeply in debt, *The Greeks and the Irrational* (Berkeley, 1951), and writing of the haunted, oppressive atmosphere in which Aeschylus' characters move and the fact that a German writer asserts that Aeschylus revived the world of the demons, and especially the evil demons, Dodds tells us that Aeschylus did not have to revive the world of the demons; it was the world in which he was born. Dodds goes on to say that Aeschylus' "purpose is not to lead his fellow-countrymen back into that world, but, on the contrary, to lead them through it and out of it." Dodds adds that Aeschylus seeks to do this, "not like Euripides by casting doubt on its reality. . .but by showing it to be capable of a higher interpretation, and, in the *Eumenides,* by showing it transformed through Athena's agency into the new world of rational justice."[2] It is not inappropriate here to remind the reader of a remark made by H. D. F. Kitto to the effect that Athena's reason for voting as she does is frivolous.[3]

Dodds's interpretation of the relation of the first two plays of the *Oresteia* to the third is a plausible one. I do not accept it, but I shall grant it in order to simplify the argument. It is important to note that Dodds's interpretation appeals to a theory of moral evolution. The haunted, oppressive world of evil demons evolves into a world of rational justice. This is progress. But as is usually the case with theories of moral evolution, the cost of achieving the end has been overlooked. The pain, the anguish, the outraged conscience that preceded the settlement with the Furies has been ignored. Let us not reckon in the sum the death of Agamemnon, his wife, and her lover, lest the moralist be ready with the judgment that they fully deserved their deaths. So be it. But what of the dead maid, the murdered seer, the lives of the fallen warriors, the pain and humiliations of the years of slavery of those who survived the massacre, the dese-

crated altars, the choking bitterness of iniquity—can the beneficiaries of the new world of rationality do away with these
pains, once endured? For their benefit, others suffered, and
some of the sufferers, whatever crimes they may have been guilty
of, were innocent of the crimes for which punishment was meted
out to them. Even if the beneficiaries could recall the past and
make sure that in the second run no gratuitous evil visited the
innocent, once undergone, the suffering could not be made to
disappear. Those who at any time choked with the outraged
sense of justice could not, in a second life, do away with the outrage they once suffered. The citizens of the new rational world
brought about by Athena's buying off the Furies will forget the
monstrous crimes that preceded the new rational order. They
must forget for the sake of their own sanity. The Athenian who
had the good fortune to live in the post-Orestes world cannot
continue to brood on the horrendous past. He has his own life
to live. But nothing, nothing whatever, will convince the moral
conscience that the iniquities that once took place did not in
fact take place. What the moral evolutionist seems to imply is
that the end justifies the means. And for him no doubt it does.
For no other interpretation can be put on the cavalier manner
in which he ignores the pain, the outrage, the throbbing anguish,
the choking bitterness that preceded by three generations the
vote of Athena.

Prior to the chiliastic plenum of moral development, men
are condemned to be mere means for the realization of an end
they will not be able to enjoy. And this denies that men prior
to this full development are persons. A materialist has no difficulty on this point. He does not use the term "person" in the
same sense in which one who believes in a spiritual universe must
use it. If this is the morality in which the defender of the moralistic interpretation believes, it behooves him to define it explicitly and with great care. When he does, I shall be first in line re-
spectfully to return their ticket to his monstrous divinities.

This then is what the moralistic interpretation of the
Oresteia adds up to. We are asked to believe that tragedy asserts
the authority of the spiritual scheme of things. But for whom?
Not for the innocent victims. Nor for those who committed
crimes they were fated to commit. It is a serious fault—I would
assert that it is a crippling fault—of the moralistic interpretation

of tragedy—a fault of the theory considered in its own terms, not in terms external to it—that its proponents cannot give us a satisfactory account of the cost innocent victims were made to pay for bringing about the post-Orestes reign of rational justice after Athena buys off the Furies. But we can hardly blame its proponents, since their struthonian optimism prevents them from thinking the matter through.

And it prevents them, in part, because they make a number of mistakes that must be classified as mistakes of aesthetic theory. And the first and most damaging of these is that the moralist must accept the view of the millennial fountainhead of error in poetic theory, the *Poetics,* and must believe that Aeschylus was interested in the character of the hero and in the flaw that brings about the catastrophe. That the *Oresteia* can be read in this way is proved by the fact that it is often read in this way. What I would assert is that properly envisaged, it is not possible to say that the hero brought about a catastrophe because of a flaw of character, since it is not possible to say who is the hero in a play made up of three parts running through more than three generations and involving as agonists both gods and men. Who is the hero of the *Oresteia?* Someone called it a play in three acts. Let's ignore the point and ask, Who is the hero of the *Agamemnon?* Agamemnon himself, of course. And of the *Libation Bearers?* Orestes, of course. And of the *Eumenides?* Orestes, and again, of course. But are we to deny that Zeus and Artemis were just as much involved in the events as Agamemnon and his father and his father's brother? And Apollo, are we to ignore him? The castastrophe is not a catastrophe of two or three men and a woman. In the *Oresteia* are involved three generations of human beings, hundreds, perhaps thousands, of unknown victims, at least three women whom we can name, and numerous wives, sweethearts, and sisters of the vanquished and the victorious. Eliminate from your consideration these human beings, forget the daughter, the seer, the victims, those who died in battle, the vanquished carried off into slavery, eliminate the gods who started the monstrous events, and you have a humanistic tragedy. But this manageable play has been produced by turning the lights off from the cosmic stage, sweeping out of our minds the multitude of victims, focusing a single pencil of light on one man—one among many agonists—who has received a brevet promotion to hero in the field. This humanistic interpretation of the *Oresteia* cuts it down to Aristotle's size. Let us remember here what was said above about the omphalic Introvert, His Perfect Frigidity, Aristotle's God.

But let us assume that each of these plays has a hero, whoever he or she be. Can we assert that the intention of each of these plays is to present to us a character from whose defect catastrophe flows? Such a reading of the plays emphasizes an interest in psychology that is not borne out by the text. Kitto observes that in the *Agamemnon* "there is no revelation of motives."[4] We can add that neither is there a sufficient revelation in the second play. If the interest in these plays were in character and what happens when character is flawed, the playwright would have dwelt on motives at greater length and much more in detail than he does. A great deal has been written on the reason Agamemnon sacrificed his daughter. But whatever we take the reason to be, to fail to recognize that in the *Oresteia* there are two levels of reality is to fail to attend to what the poet offered us to see. The human realities and the human morality involved in the actions are of course presented: crimes committed by men, which lead to other crimes. But there is the divine level: the crimes committed by men not only affect somehow the cosmic order but they are the result of that order, such as it is. But the divine order—if order it can be called—is not one of which it can be asserted without careful qualification, definition, and modulation that it gives evidence of a spiritual scheme of things to which we, today, can give unqualified approval. Back of the deeds of men are the gods, and back of the gods such eternal principles as *anakê, dikê,* The Furies, older than the gods, and more intractable, less susceptible of envisagement in anthropotelic terms. What we are invited to look on is an archaic vision of a world that connects in mythic terms a deeper cosmic ground than the gods themselves with the acts of men. In the human motivations of these acts, the plays give little evidence of being interested. Aeschylus was not writing a novel of character. He was interested in something else.

The moralistic interpretation of tragedy involves another error that can be classified as aesthetic. To disclose it, consider what happens when we concentrate on the hero, his flaw, and the consequences that it is said to bring about. We have seen that the fortunes of those whom Chicago journalists would call "innocent bystanders" are ignored. They do not count. But now comes the Houdini act. Without as much as a "watch your head!" warning, the light is turned away from the stage, the hero and innocent bystanders simply disappear, and the light is turned on—on whom? Why, on us, the spectators who, when the last words are heard, having had our pity and fear evacuated like the dirty oil in an old crank-case, are now fit to go home to a good dinner, assured that a universe in which these frightful iniquities have taken place is a moral organism. Let us not challenge the theory that pity and fear slosh in the soul like dirty liquids until tragedy pulls the plug. A strange theory, but let it pass. Once more I submit. And this time I submit that while we had been witnessing a tragedy that brought catastrophe to the hero and the innocent bystanders, for us it has turned out to be a most valuable visit to the aesthetic leech. For evacuated of our sloshing humors, we are now ready for a dinner we could not have enjoyed prior to their evacuation. Duly purged, we are now ready to assert that the world is a moral organism. How else could it be, when a good dinner is waiting for us? But what happened to the victims of the gods, to the innocent bystanders, prior to the buying off of the Furies? The moralist interpreter tells us nothing about them. I must iterate: the catastrophe was unmerited. Iphigenia, Cassandra, the fallen warriors, the razed city, the women and children sold into slavery, the desecrated altars: it was the gods that initiated this flood of evil. Why? The moralist answers: There was a flaw in the hero's character. Again I submit. And this time I submit that if anyone was ever open to the charge of iniquity, these gods are, who initiated these flagitious deeds and charged monstrously usurious rates of compound interest for acts they initiated.

I do not see how we can argue that a world in which such crimes take place can be called a moral universe. Theories are always susceptible of *ad hoc* tinkering, and words have, as I frequently find myself in the melancholy necessity of pointing out, an almost unlimited co-efficient of elasticity. Can we call this universe a moral one? Why not? The word "morality" cannot be copyrighted by any defender of any one moral scheme, actual or conceivable. But if we call it moral, let me repeat that we should at least observe that it is moral in a very archaic sense of the word, for it is a universe ruled, up to the buying off of the Furies, by a very primitive morality. I shall say nothing about the settlement, except that it is belied by everything that preceded it.

But did not Aeschylus intend us to notice the difference between the first two plays of the *Oresteia* and the third? Of course he did. And is not the difference, as I have granted, abysmal? Of course it is. How then can I account for the difference? Well, I must confess that I am not satisfied with any hypothesis that has been put forward that I have come across and that tries to account for the difference. It may be that the plays intend to put forth a sequence that marks moral progress. And it may further be that the poet noticed the difference between his own more enlightened moral intuitions—if we can allow ourselves to call them that—and the archaic ethos of the older world in which, as Dodds tells us, he was born. A number of other hypotheses are plausible, but I do not think any can satisfactorily explain the transition. We are confronted with two totally different moral universes. The second is incompatible with the first. But however we explain the transition, the third play or act cannot erase what has been presented in the first two. We, or Aeschylus' contemporaries, may be glad that we or they are not living in a world like that of the first two plays. But that world is not improved by the world of the third. Nothing, nothing whatever, can recall the past and make it happen in a way it did not happen.

NOTES

[1] (2d ed.; Seattle, 1963), pp. 30-32.

[2] (Berkeley, 1951), p. 40.

[3] *Greek Tragedy* (2d ed., rev.; London, 1950), p. 91.

[4] *Ibid.*, p. 71.

Tragedy and the Broader Consciousness

1.

Since one could not possibly cover the subject of tragedy in an essay, all I can do in these notes is to broach, I hope not too superficially, a topic that has preoccupied me for some time. I have discussed it previously in print; but I am not satisfied with what I have written on it, and hope that the present effort, in which I treat tragedy from a different standpoint, and treat a somewhat different topic, will yield a more satisfactory result.

I propose to discuss the relation of tragedy, as poetry, to the tragic vision that the reader or spectator discovers to be the informed substance of a tragic poem. Note that I use the term "poetry" as it is most widely accepted and that by a poem viewed as poetry I mean an object that aesthetic or rapt, intransitive attention beholds as self-sufficient and autonomous.

The comments that follow are based on *King Lear,* some aspects of which I shall examine in the later sections of this essay. The reason for the choice is that this play is, in my view, one of the few thoroughly unmitigated tragedies that it is our privilege to be able to witness or read. It was this quality of it that made Doctor Johnson find fault with it and led that other eighteenth-century sage, Nahum Tate, to improve it—as he and God only knows how many of his "enlightened" contemporaries thought. It should be noted that the essay is not offered as an exhaustive interpretation of the play. For that a book is required and several have been written. I shall dwell only on one aspect of the play.

The unmitigated tragedy—as the term suggests—presents an action that, to our sense of equity, reaches the extreme limit of sheer gratuitous or arbitrarily ordained catastrophe, in comparison to which no other set of more appalling events can easily be conceived. But it is a tragedy. And this means, first, that it is an aesthetic object, as I conceive an "aesthetic object." It is not a mere tale of horror, a shocker, or something intended to lead us to moral or political action or to arouse a visceral reaction and little else. That it is a tragedy also means that the catastrophe does not come about by the working of mere chance, as a purely aleatory disaster comes about, an accident that cannot be traced to a man's fault or to what we call "acts of God." This in turn means that the action, in spite of its conclusion, seems to have some sort of rationale. The rationale of the unmitigated tragedy is more difficult to grasp than that of the moralistic or of the psychological tragedy and remains dubious through the whole play. But if the opposite of reason is chaos, sheer unintelligibility, the unmitigated tragedy does not present an altogether chaotic set of events.

Tragedy in general fascinates because the meanings and values that it presents are grasped intransitively as portentous of dread eventualities for the experience of the *dramatis personae*. By contrast an unmitigated tragedy presents for contemplation eventualities whose threat, and whatever sense of inevitability that threat carries with it, has its source beyond man. It directs the mind to a transcendent source of the disasters it presents. If metaphysics is the cognitive effort to go beyond the manifest reality of our daily experience, if it seeks for subsistent structures and submerged foundations, tragedy ought to furnish the metaphysician with an indispensable datum, for it is the poet's effort to present in dramatic terms a symbolic version of the relationship between the manifest reality of the poem and its suspected ground, so to speak, beyond the merely visible. The unmitigated tragedy carries an ingredient in complete solution in the action that gives the play a density that exclusively moral or psychological tragedies—tragedies that present us an ultimately rational universe—do not have. This ingredient adds immensely to the force with which the play captures the mind. And it accounts for the wonder with which we respond to it during its performance and for long afterwards. We may not be able to satisfy or slake the wonder, but we cannot rid ourselves of it. It is impossible to ignore or to still the reverberations that the play sets going in the awed mind.

If I am right, it follows that an unmitigated tragedy cannot have for its stage an exclusively human world. To be totally unmitigated it must somehow involve the universe. A purely human tragedy cannot be unmitigated since that which brings about the catastrophe in such a tragedy is the result of corrigible error, or of agencies for which, since they are human, some sort of an exculpation may be found. The rationale of an unmitigated tragedy, played in a cosmic stage, is by contrast obscure.

If this is true, it follows that the universe that is the stage of an unmitigated tragedy cannot be the value-free universe of contemporary naturalism. This does not mean that a naturalist cannot respond with a modicum of adequacy to an unmitigated tragedy. None of us is fully coherent; we all enjoy the grace of a dash or two of schizophrenia. The naturalist, however, will have a tendency to interpret all tragedy in purely moral terms, ignoring or giving insufficient emphasis to the cosmic ingredients.

It follows that tragedy questions, so to speak, our cosmic piety. Tragedy, of course, does not literally question: what a presentation does, when taken as aesthetic, is to suggest questions to a given mind when the mind is set free from its captivity at the conclusion of the play. The play itself neither accuses nor absolves, neither reproaches nor approves, the informed substance it presents.

If *King Lear* is an unmitigated tragedy and if unmitigated tragedies have for their stage the universe, we must contradict Karl Jaspers who, in *Beyond Tragedy*, asserts that Shakespeare "moves in a purely secular stage." For in the play the various conceptions of nature that the agonists appeal to, and the gods that are synonymous with these conceptions, are an organic, an irremovable part of the action. They have an important, an indispensable role to play in the movement towards the final catastrophe; this role is as important as that played by the actual *dramatis personae* themselves. It is therefore not an exaggeration to say that they must be metaphorically included in the table of *dramatis personae*. Without them, the tragic substance of the play would be considerably mollified.

But while contradicting Jaspers on this point, if this view holds, it reinforces two insights of his. Speaking of Calderón and Racine, Jaspers writes that "the genuinely tragic has become extinguished by Christian Truth." He iterates this statement when he tells us that "seen from the Christian point of view, salvation opposes tragic knowledge." Christian Truth does indeed extinguish genuine tragedy. In the realm of ideas, where solely logical considerations rule the latter is impossible if the former is accepted. But Christian Truth is espoused by men and Christians no less than pagans or atheists are human beings which is to say that they are persons endowed with the saving grace of a touch of schizophrenia.

The other insight of Jaspers that is reinforced by the view of tragedy that I have proposed is one that could be called truly Nietzschean. Jaspers tells us that "Tragedy is not intended to evaluate morally the justice of the doom of a guilty man who never ought to have become guilty. Crime and punishment are a narrower framework submerged in moralism." As I interpret this statement, or misinterpret it and put it into my own jargon, I take it to mean that one of the non-residential functions of a poem, to the extent that it is tragic, is to make us see the parochial nature of the scheme of morality by which we rule or pretend to rule our lives and by means of which we apprehend the world. A human scheme, any human scheme, however broad and catholic, however venerable and wise, is partial. But one is not apt to see its limitaions until one looks at it through the prism of a tragic poem. The universe that serves as the stage in which a tragic poem takes place cannot be conceived as value-free. But its value structure is larger and more ambiguous and less clearly discernible than the schemes by which we rule our conduct and by which we judge men and events. Our moral schemes are less complex and therefore more intelligible, but we pay the price of their virtues: they obscure the limitations of our criterion of equity.

Unmitigated tragedies contradict what William R. Elton, in his overwhelmingly erudite study of the alleged background of *King Lear,* has called "the optimistic Christian interpretation" of this play. The effort to reduce unmitigated tragedies by looking at them as optimistic Christian presentations is a systematic misreading of their texts.

Small in number, unmitigated tragedies are, neverthelss, important documents in the shaping of our culture, for they serve as categorial means by which we see beyond the complacent range of our ordinary experience and are forced to discern the threatening waters on which the frail sanity of our civic life—such as it is—floats. Anyone capable of dwelling in the universe of an unmitigated tragedy will see that it presents evils that, in its universe, must be conceded to be real, gratuitous, invincible, and cosmic in their source. Let me emphasize "in its universe," for I would not wish to suggest, let me say in passing but forcefully, that the universe of the tragedy is an icon or imitation of the world in which we live. To assert that it is so is to confuse the means of seeing with the object we see through these means. To what extent the tragedy enables us to perceive features of the universe we had not perceived before, or not perceived as clearly, is a question that must be answered by techniques of inquiry similar to those by means of which we ascertain whether the objects that any kind of empirical observation claims to disclose are indeed truly disclosed or not.

Let me dwell briefly on the thesis that unmitigated tragedies contradict the optimistic Christian or moralistic interpretation. We can begin by conceding that unmitigated tragedies can, without much ingenuity, be interpreted in such a way that the lack of mitigation is ignored, by reducing them to solely psycho-moral plays. *King Lear*, thus interpreted, hinges on at least two factors that are indeed an indispensable part of the play, but that for the reader who takes it to be an unmitigated tragedy are not those that give the play its essential quality: the total lack of filial piety, including the ingratitude, exhibited by the daughters immediately after the partition of the kingdom takes place; and their lack of respect for the consecrated person of the King. The psycho-moral discussion would emphasize the King's faults, displayed the moment Cordelia arouses his anger, and would dwell on the disastrous error of judgment involved in the confident assumption that he could give up his power and retain the respect that he used to recieve as king. If we should miss the full depth of the error, the Fool, by throwing it up to Lear, appraises us of it. Thus the defects of character, in good Aristotelian fashion, lead to Lear's and Cordelia's deaths.

Gloucester's story can also be interpreted in purely psycho-moral terms. Indeed, a good deal of ink has been used in justifying the view that Gloucester's fate is fully merited. His faults

are many. Coleridge called attention to the way in which he
speaks about his illegitimate son to Kent in the opening lines of
the play. Nor does this exhaust the indictment that we could
draw of Gloucester's character. But since the unmitigated nature
of *King Lear* can be made out without an analysis of the causes
of Gloucester's catastrophe, we can concede this—but solely
for the sake of getting on with our main discussion. Certainly
Edmund's motivations are fully accounted for in psychological
terms. He is a bastard and resents it. His first soliloquy appeals,
in terms of an ancient quarrel in philosophy, to nature against
the plague of custom and the curiosity of nations. His dimensions, he tells himself, are as compact, his mind as generous, and
his shape as true, as honest madam's issue. If the vaulting ambition and the ruthlessness would seem to surpass the cause of it,
there is still a cause that can be said to account for his acts.

2.

What I hope to show about *King Lear* is that the foregoing
interpretation robs the play of its depth and of the density of
its informed substance. In order to show it, let me begin by reminding the reader of something he knows well. It is universally
agreed that *King Lear* is a pagan tragedy. When this is mentioned, it is usually done in order to call attention to such surface matters as the fact that it is the gods, in the plural, who are
invoked or imprecated throughout the play. We have been told
that there is only one reference to God in the singular. But the
pagan quality of the play goes further, for in the context of the
action, the gods, the stars, the heavens, and nature—in the various disparate senses in which the word "nature" is used in the
play—function as synonymous terms. And from this it follows
that even when the gods are conceived to be moral agents, they
do not have the providential quality of the God who would have
an analogous role in a Christian play. A God that can be called
Christian, in any traditional sense whatever, is Father, Redeemer,
and Holy Spirit. But the most benign of the pagan gods, whatever moral demands he may make of us men, lacks the profound,
the intimate, the hope-giving relationship to men that endows
the Christian God with His inexpugnable anthropotelic appeal.

Nature, in *King Lear,* has been a subject of extended and of intensive discussion. There is at least one whole book dedicated to it, and no one can duscuss the play without dedicating a few pages to it. It has been pointed out that in *King Lear* there are at least two general concepts of nature or of its various synonyms (the gods, the heavens, the skies, and the stars above) in opposition to one another. In fact it is well known that there are more than two; were a Lovejoy examining the play, he would find more distinct notions than a critic could possibly handle. For my limited purposes, only two notions are required—with, of course, variations of at least one, called for by the different circumstances in which nature is invoked and in which the person who invokes it finds himself. In a previous note on the play, I grouped one of these concepts under the heading of "providential nature," and the other, alerting the reader to the anachronism, under the heading of "Hobbesian nature." This is true as far as it goes and, as noted, for some purposes it is quite sufficient. But it tends to conceal the depth of the tragedy by softening its unmitigated character. To bring this character out, let us first turn to the nature to which Edmund appeals, in the first soliloquy of Act I, scene 1. This is the nature of some of the Greek sophists, a nature that is, in current academic jargon, value-free, and hence close to Hobbes's conception of nature, since for Hobbes social arrangements were the product of man's design. But the nature of this soliloquy is not clearly a Hobbesian nature, any more than it is, as it has been called, a Machiavellian nature. Edmund is a thorough Machiavellian, as the term was understood in the seventeenth century—or rather, popularly misunderstood—as indeed it is still misunderstood among us today. But Edmund's ruthless immorality did not stem from his belief in a nature that is opposed to the curiosity of nations and the plague of custom. For that notion of nature could be used, and was later, as the basis of a humane appeal against slavery. In any case, the point that calls for emphasis is that Edmund does not express a coherent philosophy. Shakespeare conceived Edmund not only in terms of traits that would be taken as odious by a normally decent person then or today, but he also put in his mind diverse ideas stemming from several sources that he knew his audience would consider not only erroneous but flagitious. This is not an adverse criticism of the poet or of his creation. In the play Edmund is fully there, fully coherent in his intentions and in the execution of his criminal plans; he may be bent on ends that, when we shake ourselves free from the grip in which the play holds us tightly, we cannot approve of. But he is fully motivated, completely coherent, and our approval or disapproval, if it intrudes, is irrelevant during the period when the play holds us in its grip. This is all that in fairness we can ask of him or his creator. Edmund is, furthermore, an attractive man. Kent tells us so in Act I, scene 1, when he replies to Gloucester that he cannot wish the fault undone, the issue being so proper. And Edmund, as we saw, knows it. But if we discount this evidence, we still have the objective evidence of the dog-hearted daughters, both of whom are eager to cuckold their husbands for him. Nevertheless, in dismissing as the excellent foppery of the world his father's belief in astrology, the heart of Edmund's view of nature is better characterized as Hobbesian than as Machiavellian, in spite of the anachronism. This is the concept of nature introduced by Galileo, and in our day holding the educated mind almost universally in its grip in the United States. The contradictory idea of a universe in which value has status in being other than the psychological is held by the uneducated multitude and among us by a few philosophers with whose arguments I am, in general terms, in sympathy.

But while Edmund's notion of nature, as opposed to the plague of custom and the curiosity of nations, would be taken as both odious and erroneous by probably a great number of those spectators in Shakespeare's day who were reflective and had some education, it would be a poor reading of the play to assume that within the play it lacks its own validity in its own terms. One of the major factors giving the tragedy the profound cosmic resonance with which it vibrates is the opposition of diverse and mutually incompatible notions of nature or the gods with which we are confronted.[1] Each of these concepts is, under the circumstances that one of the agonists invokes it or imprecates against it, as valid as the other notions of nature that are appealed to by other characters at other times and under other circumstances. In a note to line 39 of Act III, scene 1, Kittredge tells us in his edition of *King Lear* that Edmund "adapts his story to his father's superstition." What he should have told us is that Edmund adapts his story to what he takes to be his father's superstition. Edmund does not believe in astrology and neither does Kittredge. As to myself, I am not so sure that Gloucester was altogether wrong. It is not eclipses that may portend no good, but other heavenly events—sun spots, for instance. But to take Gloucester's belief that eclipses portend no good to be superstition is to pass an anachronistic judgment on Gloucester's belief that affects our reaction to the informed substance of the play, reduces the objective conflict, weakens the tension, and denies the play much of its tragic quality. Nor is this a question of what was believed in Shakespeare's day, by whom, or by how many, or by what kind of men, as William R. Elton contends.

Those who read the play with care, even if they bring to bear on it only a light briefcase hardly filled with learning and not the vast library of scholarship Elton applies to the play, should see that Elton's interpretation—if you can call it that—fails to give us an idea of what the play is about. As he puts it, *King Lear* "leaves us with a Hamlet-like confusion of values in terms of a chiasma of ethical and religious ideas and consequences." "Confusion" is the word to be taken exception to in this quotation. If Shakespeare had intended to demonstrate a dogma or a philosphical conception of the universe, *King Lear* would leave us in confusion.

What Shakespeare leaves us with is a vision of a world, not ours but that of *King Lear,* the tragedy, in which the ways of nature or the gods as conceived by any one of the agonists are not congruous with any of the views presented by the rest of the *dramatis personae.* Confusion—con-dash-fusion—results when we try to fuse several incompatible hypotheses or visions of reality into a logical whole. And at the worst, such confusions lead to logical incoherences, contradictions. But the non-harmonious views which Elton finds to be a confusing chiasma of ethical ideas and consequences are put forth each in its appropriate place at a point in the development of the action by an individual who finds himself facing or contemplating a man suffering or inflicting pain gratuitously. And the depth and amplitude of the play and its profound cosmic reverberation—I beg leave to iterate it, since their importance cannot be exaggerated—depend precisely on the aesthetic or presentational validity under the circumstances in which each ethical and religious view is expressed, however much it may contradict other views, even of the same person, each in its place claiming full validity. In other words, Elton's judgment is irrelevant. There is no aesthetic confusion. We can demand nothing else. But there is not even philosophical confusion, if we take the references to the diverse notions of nature contextually. Why should the views of different individuals, endowed with different characters, and looking at the events of the tragedy or enduring them from different standpoints, not appeal to different conceptions of nature or of the gods, conceptions that, as the action proceeds, they may modify?

But from your interpretation, I hear the defender of Elton reply, we cannot tell which one of these agonists holds the right view and which others the wrong ones. My reply is that we certainly cannot. For these views are not put forth by the playwright in order to advance the truth of one and deny the truth of the others. And if that were his intention we would be foolish to take him seriously. If we want to know which of the views of nature and the gods found in the play is the right one we have to take them all away from the play, and consider each, not for its own dramatic role in the play, but for its own philosophical validity, for its truth, as this is decided by philosophers when they examine diverse and not satisfactorily coherent views about anything—about the gods, or nature, or immortality, or freedom, or the intelligence of dolphins. From the standpoint of truth most literate people today—outside Hollywood, of course—would call Gloucester's belief in the portentous nature of eclipses superstitious. Many would call Edmund's notion of nature closer to the truth. But the whole question is irrelevant for the reader of the tragic poem. In the play they function, not as truths, but as the views of characters, without the aid of which the drama would be as philosophically shallow as one of those perfect short stories of Hemingway about trout fishing.

3.

When we turn to the providential conceptions of nature that have roles in the tragedy, what we find is a whole family of them, ranging from the bountiful nature of Lear's kingdom (Act I, scene 1):

> With shadowy forests and with champains rich'd,
> With plenteous rivers and wide-skirted meads,

through the unintelligible nature that produces dog-hearted monsters in human shape for daughters, on to the nature whose eclipses portend no good to man, on to the nature or stars, the stars above, that govern our condition, on to the gods to whom we are as flies to wanton boys. It is legitimate to call these gods or natures, with the exception, perhaps, of Gloucester's wanton gods, providential. But Gloucester's gods can also be grouped with the providential gods or natures, since malign gods are no less concerned with man than benign ones. In any case, to take full possession of the play, to fully examine its dark depths, we must consider in extension the diverse, often contradictory presentations of the natures, or the gods, or the stars, or the heavens above. Here I cannot take up each one of these notions in order to show what the character means by it when he imprecates or appeals to it. Nor is this anlaysis necessary, since a number of critics, as already indicated, have undertaken it with full adequacy. It is enough to state in passing that besides Lear and Edmund, Albany, Kent, and inferentialy, Cornwall's servants, refer to nature or the gods.

But it is Lear, when he arrives at the nadir of his sanity, who challenges the belief in the anthropotelic notion of nature with the bitter question he asks just as the mock trial scene comes to a close. Let us consider the storm scene of which the trial is part, the trial itself, and the question. The trial takes place in some sort of shelter to which Lear is led by Gloucester when he finds the King in the open in the storm. The dreadful pudder has been going on for some time. It has been often noted, and rightly, that the heavenly pudder and the storm raging in Lear's breast are two facets of the same event. If they are, are there two storms in correspondence with one another or are they, properly viewed, only one, manifesting itself in the mind of Lear and in the skies? No doubt only one, so that the nature that produces the storm makes the daughters' hard hearts, although we will not be told how it can accomplish the latter feat. One storm only, then, although in Lear's mind the behavior of the skies is distinct from the conduct of his daughters; for he does not tax the elements, as he tells them, with unkindness. But he does call the elements servile ministers that with the two pernicious daughters joined their high-engendered battles against his old and white head. Are there two storms or only one? One only, of course, since the pernicious daughters and the skies not only work towards the same end—Lear's destruction—but much more important, the daughters' hearts are made by the nature that unleashes the storm against him.   But why is the storm against Lear?

> Let the gods,
> That keep this dreadful pudder o'er our heads
> Find out their enemies now.

Lear names some of the enemies of the gods. But he himself is not one of them. He is "a man more sinned against than sinning."

It is in the midst of the storm, then, that we are presented with the constitutive symbol of the trial in which justice itself is arraigned before us, as the daughters are before the preposterous commission.   The scene is an incongruous compound of fantasy and reality.   But the reality is that of the stage in which the King and his commission are meeting the fantasy is that of the King bringing his daughters, one of them a joint stool, before the bar of justice. The King is mad, but he is in possession of a higher sanity that enables him to ask the question to which he receives no answer, but which is one of the keys to the play.

The scene is crucial since it gathers in a powerfully ironic constitutive symbol the events that led Lear to the heath and to madness.   And by showing him to us, after the inconclusive arraignment, going gently to bed, it prepares the mind of the spectator for those events that will follow. It is hard to imagine how any other symbol could have expressed more powerfully, more bitterly, in a more concentrated ironic manner, the King's calamity and his incapacity to understand the agents of it, his daughters.   But the need to understand persists in his madness, and how can one comport oneself properly toward evil except by bringing the evildoers to trial? This is what Lear proceeds to do. "It shall be done," he decides suddenly. "I will arraign them straight." And he appoints the commission: the possessed madman we know to be Edgar, and whom Lear has earlier called a noble philosopher, a learned Theban, is called now a robed man of justice. Some thirty lines later Lear, for all his madness, will see him to be not properly dressed. The Fool is also named to the commission as "a joke fellow of equity." And Kent, a stranger to the King now, is also appointed.

And the accused? Goneril is a joint stool, for the Fool sees truly. And the other one? We do not see her, but she is there for Lear. She is one

> whose war'p looks proclaim
> What stone her heart is made on.

As Lear notices the looks of Regan, Goneril flees. All this, of course, has been taking place, as we know, in Lear's mind, and the fact intensifies the pathos of the scene and proclaims, as nothing else could, his deranged condition and the cause of his derangement. Goneril's flight creates an interruption. Edgar and Kent intervene. But Lear returns to the trial and asks the pregnant question for which there is no immediate answer:

> Then let them anatomize Regan. See what breeds about her heart.
> Is there any cause in nature that makes these hard hearts?

But Lear, not waiting for the answer, turns to Edgar to "entertain" him as one of his hundred and to comment on his Persian attire. The question has been asked: "Is there any cause in nature that makes these hard hearts?"; and although Lear does not receive an answer, it cannot be unsaid. The incongruity of this powerful constitutive scene is all that is needed to set forth the tremendous weight of the question. That the question has not been, that it cannot be, answered now does not matter. For Lear, it expresses pure bewilderment. Yet there must be an answer, for there are the hard hearts to prove that there must be a cause in nature to produce such monstrosities. But what is the cause? The whole play conveys the answer. The bountiful nature of the first scene is also the nature that unleashes the storm, breeds hard hearts, and cracks the mind of a gigantic king to turn him into a fully human man before it kills him. Worse yet, it is this nature that mocks our sense of human equity by killing not only the evil but those who, in context, are relatively innocent.

The scene, with its heartbreaking pathos, its lack of surface continuity, and the intense bitterness of its irony, puts forth for our contemplation the reality of the state of justice of *King Lear*'s universe. But, you say, this is not yet the final scene. It need not be. For the answer given by the whole play will establish, as will be shown, the unmitigated nature of the tragedy.

Did space permit, this would be the point at which to discuss the constitutive symbol through which Shakespeare brings to a climax the subplot, the plucking of Gloucester's eyes. By the obvious interpretation, stated in the play itself by the victim, it is through the loss of his sight that Gloucester learns to see. He stumbled when he saw and now he sees feelingly. There is considerably more to the horrible scene; however, this is all I can say on the subject. I return to the gods.

Gloucester, after his ordeal, in an unforgettable cry frequently quoted, exclaims in anguish and despair:

> As flies to wanton boys are we to th' gods.
> They kill us for their sport.

It will not do, in order to muffle this cry of despair, to gloss it optimistically. To argue that it is the cry of an anguished man, an utterance of pain physical, no less than mental, that he now feels, does not rob the cry of its force. A denial of its force, and in its context, of its validity, would be admissible on the assumption that at moments of unutterable suffering men do not know what they are saying. I would counter with the assertion—one that would require a development I cannot give it here—that it is at such moments that certain aspects of the universe, usually beyond our normal, 20/20 moral myopia, reveal themselves in their unmitigated brutality. It is then, at such moments, that we grasp the mockery of the gods that the Leibnizian theodicy cannot conceal.

May I press the obvious and reiterate that we have been discussing a tragedy and not a thesis in cosmology or metaphysics or anything you like to call a systematic discourse about nature or the gods. This means that Lear's question must be answered in terms of the play itself. It is in the play that Lear, driven to insanity by the cruelty of his daughters, asks the question about their hearts, for which he receives no answer. And it is in the play that Gloucester blasphemes and tells us what his ordeal has revealed to him about the wantonness of the gods. And it is the play, finally, that tests the interpretation I have proposed of this tragedy. True, Gloucester's ordeal does not last forever.

Gloucester finds reconciliation with his fate after his attempt on his own life. And Lear regains his sanity for a moment before his death and grows immensely in his human stature. But the reconciliation with life and the restoration of sanity and the gain in humanity cannot erase the words of blasphemy nor can it do away with the anguish the King suffered. Nothing that happens later can cancel what has already taken place. The blasphemy was justified when uttered in the moment of despair. The words cannot be unsaid. They hang over the roiled soul, a blasphemy that accurately characterizes the moment and what it revealed about the gods. Nothing Gloucester will later undergo can do away with them, nothing. The words are there, hovering timelessly over the anguish; they are there also, timelessly, pointing inexpungably to the order of events, irrefutably true in their context. At the moment they are uttered and about the situation that elicited them, they are a true characterization of what the moment revealed. And of course the same is true of Lear's ordeal. He has a moment of sweet illusion before his daughter's death, when he sees himself united to Cordelia, in prison, where the two will sing like birds in a cage. The sweet dream, with the bitter pathos it has for us, does not last long. Soon we see him return with the dead daughter in his arms. And immediately after, his heart breaks. But the *via crucis* that led to the last pathetic moment with its pain, its choking sense of the unutterable cruelty of hard-hearted daughters—these cannot be undone.

One other consideration tests and rejects the moralistic interpretation of this tragedy: the altogether unmotivated cruelty of the hard hearts of these women. Theirs is an utterly gratuitous evil for which there is no explanation, and for which there cannot be any, in the play. This is the reason Lear's question cannot be answered immediately. In his conception of nature— the nature of Act I, scene 1—how can there be a cause of these hard hearts? Asked about the other villains, the question is not difficult to answer. Consider them: Oswald is intelligible—a knave, rascal, lily-livered whoreson, beggar, coward, pander, and the son and heir of a mongrel bitch—it takes no psychological acuity to account for him. Cornwall's cruelty is not so easily understandable, but I can hear the defenders of the moralistic theory argue that he is the puppet of his wife. Let's waive the issue, although to my mind his evil has the same source and hence is of the same kind, if not of the same degree, as his wife's evil and that of his sister-in-law. The Captain who is sent to kill the King and Cordelia has a good reason for obeying the order. He is promised a reward, and he is a man who holds that if it is man's work, he'll do it. But the evil of the dog-hearted daughters is unintelligible in human terms, and utterly gratuitous—by which I mean that it is not brought forth by anything in the play that could account for it. No sooner have the daughters received their portions than they state their intentions to disregard the conditions on which they accepted their lands. And the arguments they give each other, while plausible, are clearly rationalizations. Everybody has left the stage, and Goneril and Regan alone remain. Immediately they begin their concerted plans.

> GONERIL. . . .Pray you let's hit together. If our father carry authority with such dispositions as he bears, this last surrender of his will but offend us.
>
> REGAN. We shall think further on it.
>
> GONERIL. We must do something, and i' the' heat.

Their subsequent treatment of their father throws light on their patent rationalizations. Evil, so utterly uncalled for, must be traced to a source beyond man and thus gives the lie to an unqualified providential notion of nature. This gratuitous evil (gratuitous, that is, in human terms) relates the human events that take place in *King Lear* to the cosmos—to nature, to the gods: but not to a nature that can confirm an optimistic view that the world of *King Lear* is an organism in which events are morally meaningful and which, therefore, asserts the authority of the spiritual scheme of things. What *King Lear* does is to reveal, which is to say to tear the veil of, moral *aporiai* at the heart of its cosmos. Whether these *aporiai* correspond to similar defects in our universe is not a question we can put to a poet. It is a difficult question; for a serious answer to it we must go to a man who has the technical equipment to tackle it, and he is none other than the philosopher. Is there any cause in nature that makes these hard hearts?—in the nature of the play, let me repeat, not in our nature. And the answer is that on an anthropotelic notion of nature this question cannot be answered. But if nature transcends the neutrality that Hobbes assigns to it and if it makes hard hearts which give evidence that the world is not a moral organism in which events are morally meaningful, the moralistic theory of tragedy does not hold for *King Lear*. The evil of these hard hearts is transcendent evil; it is cosmic in nature. It cannot be accounted for in psychological, which is to say in human, terms. And this fact contradicts those who would turn unmitigated tragedies into treatises on theodicy.

There is another aspect of *King Lear* that the moralistic interpretation of tragedy must account for and does not. And that is utterly gratuitous death of Cordelia. Let us assume for the sake of the argument that Lear has brought on himself his own catastrophe, and that Gloucester merited his. This concession is unjustified, at least insofar as Gloucester is concerned. The sisters, Edmund, and Cornwall were evil people in favor of whom it would be difficult to arouse pity. Lear suffered when he was a king and immediately after from the defect of character that would, on a moralistic interpretation of tragedy, bring about his protracted suffering and death. It would be a harsh justice that exacted from Gloucester his punishment, but let us waive the point. It remains to fit Cordelia to the moralistic theory. Let us draw up the charges against her. She was abrupt, unnecessarily rude, since the provocation of her sister's hypocrisy does not justify her behavior. She lacked understanding of her father's need although she could not have doubted his love for her. She was proud and uncompromising, and were the play a tragedy of character, we would have to inquire into the duality of her nature. In short, she should have acted differently, not for the sake of her portion of the kingdom but for the sake of the father she loved. She certainly could have phrased her reply to his question in different, less provoking terms. But when we add all these faults and double the amount to make certain that we have not underestimated them, we have a perfect right, on the moralistic interpretation of the tragedy, to react to it as Doctor Johnson and Nahum Tate did.

But why should we expect the tragedy to confirm our preconceived ideas of what the world is like? Aside from the worthless aesthetics on which the assumption is based, what the demand does is to lay the play on the procrustean bed of our parochial standards. It will not fit. It did not fit for Doctor Johnson; it cannot fit for us. Doctor Johnson measures the poet's creative vision and rejects it, rather than letting the poet measure his own vision and deepen and broaden it. But it is desirable to let him speak in his own words before commenting. Doctor Johnson has written that the poet has had the opportunity "to impress" the "important moral, that villainy is never at a stop, that crimes lead to crimes and at last terminate in ruin." He continues:

> But though this moral be incidentally enforced, Shakespeare has suffered the virtue of Cordelia to perish in a just cause, contrary to the natural ideas of justice, to the hope of the reader, and, what is yet more strange, to the faith of the chronicles. . . . A play in which the wicked prosper and the virtues miscarry may doubtless be good, because it is a just representation of the common events of human life; but since all reasonable beings naturally love justice, I cannot easily be persuaded that the observation of justice makes a play worse; or that, if other excellences are equal, the audience will not always rise better pleased from the final triumph of persecuted virtue.

Let us forget the chronicles--they were useful to the poet, but we cannot claim any authority for them whatever. Whose natural ideas of justice and whose hopes did Shakespeare fail to meet? Doctor Johnson's, of course. And where did Doctor Johnson get these ideas and hopes? He does not tell us, but it is clear that he brought them to the play, he did not get them from it. Doctor Johnson's *a priori* criteria are in any case better than the poet's and hence good enough to bring the play before the bar of the critic's knowledge and condemn it. This certainly is not the first time, nor was it the last, that poems have been condemned before the bar of the critic's knowledge. The game, as far as our records go, started with Plato. Doctor Johnson played the game openly, he made no effort to cover it up. Today it is not played in this candid way. Critics do not bring a poem before the bar of their knowledge. They read their knowledge into the poem and read it out. The Age of Enlightenment was lit by the flickering candles of its Reason. And in spite of Newton's wise observation that the light did not reach far and there was darkness beyond it, these men were confident that all there was was what their light illumined. We men of the second half of the twentieth century found to our horror that there are abysses that the light from our little candle does not reach, and that evil seems at times to erupt from their depths. It behooves us, therefore, to learn from one of the boldest, one of the most unfettered, courageous, profound, and darkest products of the human imagination. Peering beyond the reaches of normal human sight, tearing the veil and pointing to what lies beyond, the poet discovered that our faith, our complacent human faith, cannot take the measure of the forces at the depths. Is there any cause in nature that makes these hard hearts? There must be. But not in the nature of

> . . .the shadowy forest. . .with champains rich'd,
> With plenteous rivers and wide skirted meads. . . .

That is one nature, or one face of it: a benign nature fit for human felicity. But there is another nature or another face of it, and that is the nature of the wanton gods. That too is nature. It is the nature that the writers of theodicies, whether presented as literary criticism or as philosophical treatises, would prettify. They can only do it by denying the depths that tragedy presents.

Jaspers is right. Tragedy is not enough. No one can live sanely from day to day while facing the dread portent of un-mitigated tragedy. But without its help we are not likely to see, unless we are endowed with the poetic powers of a Shakespeare, into the depths of the abyss.

NOTE

[1] An interpretation of the play that overlooks the role played by nature or the gods—and by the storm, which is the manifest expression of their anger—is thus not an interpretation of the play Shakespeare wrote but of something thinner and considerably less substantial. (See "The Avoidance of Love: A Reading of King Lear," in Stanley Cavell, *Must We Mean What We Say: A Book of Essays* (New York, 1969), pp. 267-353.)